TANDEM

Any Way You Like

Gloria Eisenway, small, blonde and curvaceous in her psychedelically-coloured bikini, gave a throaty chuckle and smiled at Albert. 'You mustn't mind me,' she said. 'We develop very sexual senses of humour out here. It's being so close to nature. I mean, some of those male baboons. . . . You wouldn't believe the notes I've taken for my book.'

Albert smiled back, not sure if she was having him on. 'You're writing a book?'

'Actually it hasn't been published yet. But the publishers are certain it's going to be a best-seller. They want a whole series. The first one's called *Getting It Up*, and sub-titled *The Modern Girl's Guide to Enslaving Men Through Bed*. I'm working on the second right now. It's called *Getting It Up in Africa*, and deals with everything to do with sex on the continent. We'll cover all the major areas of the world and of course if space travel ever leads to the discovery of life on another planet . . .'

'But . . . but how do you research the books?' Albert asked, his eyes on the psychedelic bulging of her breasts.

'I find out whatever I can of what's been written already and then I do my own research. In depth and in breadth. Vertically and horizontally, as it were.'

Albert tried to figure out exactly how such research would be programmed. But the complexities escaped him . . .

Also by Stephen John

I LIKE IT THAT WAY
HOW ABOUT THIS WAY?
THIS WAY, PLEASE!

Tandem editions 35p

Any Way You Like

Stephen John

TANDEM
14 Gloucester Road, London SW7

First published in Great Britain by Universal-Tandem
Publishing Co. Ltd, 1972
Reprinted January 1973

Made and printed in Great Britain by
Hunt Barnard Printing Ltd, Aylesbury, Bucks.

Chapter One

THE PALE winter sunshine filtered through the big windows of the luxury penthouse fourteen storeys above the gray River Thames and gave a reddish sheen to the over-sized penis of the negroid statuette on the desk.

Albert Divine and Cornelia O. Bottom, the affected but none-the-less fetching personal assistant to tycoon Julius Jack Freedman, gazed in mild embarrassment at the huge, near-perpendicular appendage.

'It's an ithyphallic statue,' Cornelia Bottom said rather stiltedly, brushing back a loop of fine, blonde hair from her brow.

'*What* phallic?' Albert demanded.

Cornelia Bottom's blue eyes clouded uncertainly and her lilac-lipsticked mouth – matching the lilac tweed of her short-skirted suit – pursed nervously.

'*Ithy*phallic,' she repeated.

'Sounds rather nasty to me,' Albert said. 'What does it mean?'

Cornelia Bottom looked at him helplessly. She fingered a leather button on her jacket and a slight rosiness suffused her well-powdered cheeks.

'I – I thought you'd know,' she said. 'You're the art expert.'

'You mean to say you're throwing around a word you don't know the meaning of in hopes that other people will understand it? What sort of personal assistant are you?'

The blush deepened in Cornelia Bottom's cheeks. She toyed with the wooden penis in absent-minded confusion, caught herself and jerked her hand away.

'It's a word that Mr Freedman uses,' she said defensively. 'I meant to look it up. I know I've been somewhat remiss.

The fact is that I thought for some time he was referring to it as itchyphallic – and that seemed self-explanatory.'

She uttered an embarrassed giggle, which she suppressed almost immediately.

'I see,' Albert said. 'Maybe what he said was "Is he phallic?" and he has a lisp.'

'Oh but that would be a terribly stupid question,' Cornelia Bottom said.

'I suppose so,' Albert agreed. 'But how about "*Is* he phallic!" Expletive and still with the lisp, of course.'

'Mr Freedman doesn't have a lisp,' Cornelia Bottom said in a superior tone.

'Listen, ' Albert said. 'I'm only trying to help you. Maybe he said ichthyphallic. *Ichthys* is Greek for fish.'

'I don't quite see . . . '

'Well, it could be sort of descriptive. You know the shape of some fish . . . '

'I still don't quite . . . I mean, when you imagine a plaice or a flounder . . . '

'I was thinking more in terms of a swordfish – or a conger eel,' Albert said.

'A swordfish – mmmmm.'

Cornelia Bottom stroked the penis thoughtfully, tracing its tip with a well manicured fingernail. She caught herself again and pulled her finger away with a startled cough.

'I think I'd better look it up,' she said.

She moved to the bookshelves on one side of the room and Albert's eyes strayed to the lithe movement of her buttocks, faintly suggested under the sensible tweed. She was not inaptly named, he reflected. She climbed a short stepladder and reached up for a dictionary, stretching her calf muscles taut so that they bulged a little through the tan nylons, revealing how fluidly her thighs were moulded to her buttocks.

Albert leapt across the room and sank his teeth into her calf. He nibbled his way up the stockinged thigh under the skirt and bit a juicy slice from her pantie-covered rump.

Cornelia Bottom climbed backwards down the steps with the volume and came across the room towards him. She saw the odd look in his eye. She stopped, involuntarily smoothing her skirt.

'Is anything wrong, Mr Divine?'

Albert, the ithyphallic African chief, advanced on the nubile white slave, the only captive from the annihilated safari. On her he would wreak the vengeance of his people for the wrongs done to African womanhood by the wicked colonials. If she screamed as he first explored and then devastated her body, the pitiful sounds would be lost in a thousand miles of untamed bush . . .

'Mr Divine!' Cornelia Bottom's voice was charged with apprehension. 'Are you all right?'

Albert pulled himself together. He put a hand to his forehead.

'It's the height,' he said weakly. 'I have no head for heights.'

Cornelia Bottom gazed around, bewildered.

'But . . . but we are *inside*, Mr Divine. I mean, I know this is a penthouse, but we're not even near the window.'

'It's the claustrophobia,' Albert whispered.

'But that's fear of confined spaces. I thought you said . . .'

'It's a mixture,' Albert murmured, closing his eyes. 'Seventy per cent claustrophobia, thirty per cent acrophobia.'

'How extraordinary – I've never heard of that.'

'Well you hadn't heard of ithyphallic either. Anyway, it's very rare. They don't even have a name for it yet.'

'Can I do anything for you?' Cornelia Bottom asked.

Albert's eyes alighted on the swell of her bosom against the white blouse under the jacket. She could strip off for a start and then . . . He controlled himself with an effort. Too much imagination. Always been his trouble.

'It's all right,' he said. 'It happens very rarely and then only for a moment. I'll just sit down for a second.'

'Can I get you a glass of water?'

'No, really.' Albert blinked and shook his head. 'It's gone already.'

'Well I do hope so,' Cornelia Bottom said. 'It must make

things rather difficult. I mean, it's a good thing you don't live in a tiny house in a tall tree, or something . . . '. She gave a small giggle.

'I suppose it is,' Albert said. 'Mind you I've never been a slave to civic fashion so the danger's limited.'

Cornelia Bottom smiled uncertainly.

'Well, I'll just look up the word,' she said.

She placed the dictionary on the desk beside the statuette. Albert contemplated her neatly curvaceous back view. Julius Freedman certainly had some dolly birds in his penthouse-cum-office. They exuded an air of efficiency and experience – quite apart from their looks. After all, you couldn't call not knowing what ithyphallic meant inefficiency. Probably a word nice girls shouldn't know anyway.

Cornelia Bottom was running a silver-varnished fingernail down a page.

'Here it is,' she said.

There was a long silence.

'I can never resist the rest of the page either,' Albert said. 'In fact I often forget what I was looking up.'

The silence continued.

'Come on,' Albert said. 'What's it mean?'

Cornelia Bottom's face had turned slightly pink again. She sniffed.

'It means an erect penis,' she said, adding after a pause: '*Ithys* – Greek for straight.'

Albert grinned.

'Well fancy that,' he said. 'You could have fooled me.'

Cornelia Bottom plucked up the dictionary and mounted the ladder to the bookshelf.

'I'm afraid I thought it was some sort of style,' she said over her shoulder. 'Some sort of African style.'

'Well it is,' Albert said. 'Though not exclusively African.'

He watched her skirt hitch up in a lateral crease just above her buttocks. Her muscles tightened, thighs extended . . .

A door swung open noisily and a large body, with an even larger voice, surged into the room.

'Sorry to keep you waiting, Mr Divine,' the voice rasped.

'Urgent business. I trust Miss Bottom has been taking care of you.'

Albert reluctantly withdrew his eyes from Cornelia Bottom's bottom and focused them on the interruption.

Julius Jack Freedman came striding towards him, beaming, huge paw extended. A big man in his fifties, who looked as if he still did exercises in front of an open window every morning and still played a good set of ferociously competitive tennis. Still willing to throw a hefty punch, too, if those intense and slightly crazy-looking gray eyes were anything to go by.

Albert tensed his hand, attempting to meet on equal terms the bonecrushing shake which was clearly due. His mismatched hand wilted almost immediately, however, under the tycoon's grip and his unprepared shoulder shrank under the hammer blow of a pulverising slap.

'Sit down, sit down – have a cigar.' Julius Jack Freedman thrust out his pugnacious rock of a jaw and waved Albert to a chair. 'Miss Bottom, quit horsing about on that ladder and get us a drink.'

Cornelia Bottom descended the ladder haughtily and busied herself at a cocktail cabinet.

'What'll it be Mr Divine?'

'Straight vodka,' Albert said.

'Vodka, eh? We got any of that, Miss Bottom? Leave that stuff to the Ruskies myself. Bourbon on the rocks' my poison. Nothing better.'

'Yes, there is,' Albert said.

'There is?' Julius Jack Freedman glared at him and then said with unwitting belligerence: 'I hope you're not being taken in by Commie propaganda, Mr Divine. You just tell me what's better than Bourbon.'

'My grandmother's home-made dandelion wine.'

Julius Jack Freedman's glare dwindled. His mouth opened, eyes lit up.

'Your grandmother's home-made . . .? Ha! Ha, ha, ha! Oh yes, I like that. Give me a man with a sense of humour every time. I can see we're going to get on okay, Mr Divine.

Here – here's your Commie drink. How come we had vodka, Miss Bottom?'

'You never told me not to get it, Mr Freedman.'

'Never told you not to get Nigerian palm wine either, did I? Sometimes I wonder just what you're up to, Miss Bottom.'

Albert stood up. Only one way to deal with a nutcase. He gulped down the vodka, came smartly to attention and hurled the glass over his shoulder. It smashed against a wall and shattered in splinters all over the carpet.

Julius Jack Freedman stiffened on the point of sipping his Bourbon. His crazy eyes fixed on Albert, startled.

'Hey, what . . .?'

'It's a Russian custom,' Albert said. 'There's no other way to drink vodka.'

'That's quite right, Mr Freedman,' Cornelia Bottom blurted in obvious panic.

'What the hell would you know about it, Miss Bottom? Anyway I know what those Ruskies get up to.'

Albert sat down. Julius Jack Freedman glared at him a little more and then retreated cautiously behind his desk and lowered himself carefully into a chair.

'I think we'd better get down to business, Mr Divine,' he said slowly. 'Okay Miss Bottom, you can clear up the glass later.'

They watched her retreating back view. Julius Jack Freedman seemed somewhat mollified at the sight. In fact, he continued to gaze at the door with a glint in his eye for some seconds after it was closed. Then he remembered Albert and surveyed him warily.

'Okay, Mr Divine, okay,' he said. 'I guess you probably know something about me. Plenty of people will tell what a bastard and son-of-a-bitch I am, though you don't want to believe all you hear. I guess I'm not short of a dollar and that always excites envy from the penniless layabouts who think the part of the world that works owes them handouts on account of them being so brilliant and beautiful.'

He smirked.

'Okay, so I'm brilliant and beautiful, too. Difference is I work like a nigger. You give me balloons to sell on the street corner, I'll sell three times as many as the next bastard; you tell me build skyscrapers, I'll build them twice as fast, twice as high as the competition. Okay? Okay.'

He threw back his Bourbon twice as fast as the next man as if to underline his point.

'Okay,' he resumed. 'So this makes me a very busy man. Four months here, four months New York, four months shooting around the world like a blue-assed monkey. Only so much a man can do. So I got to delegate responsibility. That's where you come in.'

'I'm no good for building skyscrapers,' Albert said. 'I was just telling your secretary how I have no head for heights. Balloons are all right – as long as you don't expect me to blow them up.'

'Ha, ha, ha! You're okay, son, you're okay. Here, forget that Commie liquor. Have a Bourbon. Come on! A good American Bourbon on the rocks with me.'

'Protecting your glassware?' Albert said.

'Protecting . . . ? Oh. Ha, ha, ha! Sure – why not, heh, heh! No wonder those Ruskies got no consumer goods. Smashing all those glasses!'

Julius Jack Freedman poured two Bourbons and passed one to Albert. He raised his glass, smiling.

'That's the boy,' he said. 'Here's to the good old United States and its Bourbon – and Britain, of course.'

Albert stood up, knocked back the Bourbon and flung the glass over his shoulder. It crashed against the wall behind him and the pieces showered down, tinkling on to theexisting layer of splinters.

Julius Jack Freedman lowered his own untouched drink to the desk.

'What the hell . . .?' he demanded.

'Sorry,' Albert said. 'Sheer habit.'

'Well you gotta get out of that habit,' Julius Jack Freedman said indignantly. 'Bourbon drinkers just don't do that sort of thing. You get vodka drinkers *and* Bourbon drinkers smashing their glasses, the industry won't be able to keep up. End up drinking from plastic cups. Ruin the taste of the Bourbon.'

'You have a point there,' Albert said.

'Sure I have a point.'

The door opened suddenly and a rather frightened Cornelia Bottom peered in.

'Yes?' Julius Jack Freedman snapped.

'I – I thought I heard you call,' Cornelia Bottom said, flustered.

'Since when have I been calling through doors? And since when has my voice sounded like breaking glass?' Julius Jack Freedman growled.

His secretary glanced wonderingly at the growing pile of debris and withdrew in confusion. Albert figured that breaking glass was not a bad description of the sound of Julius Jack Freedman's voice. Glass being ground, rather. Very tough glass – frosted. Probably reinforced with wire.

The tycoon scowled down at his Bourbon and in turn knocked it back with a single, quick movement. He shook his head.

'By Jesus, I don't know what the hell's going on today!' he snapped. 'Everyone's going crazy around here!'

'It's probably the height above sea level,' Albert said. 'The rarefied air. Makes people erratic.'

Julius Jack Freedman distractedly poured himself another Bourbon on the rocks. He swallowed half of it and stared at Albert.

'Okay, okay,' he said. 'So I know something about you, Mr Divine. I don't delegate responsibility to any Smart Alec who thinks he knows the score. Now you and I have qualities in common. I'm not talking about your Commie drinking habits. I guess every man has a weakness. No, I'm talking about your capitalistic flair and your artistic know-how. You and I both came up from the ground floor, the hard way. Yeah – I've been checking on your record. Correct me if I'm wrong, but I figure you started selling pictures in a market stall not too long ago and now you have one of the smartest galleries, best stocks, richest clientele in this city. I like that. Sort of quality you can count on. Now I'll come to the point. The fact is, Mr Divine, I've been getting sort of interested in art lately – African art, in particular.

Read a few books, had a look at one or two museums, even acquired a few little odds and ends. What I want is to build up a real collection: sculpture, masks, jewellery – you know the sort of thing.'

'So you want me to represent you at the auctions,' Albert said. 'I'm not an African specialist, you know.'

'No, Mr Divine. What I want is for you to go to Africa for me.'

Albert stared at him in amazement.

'Go to Africa!' he said. 'What on earth for? There are more African antiquities in European collections than in Africa.'

Julius Jack Freedman's eyes gleamed.

'Aha!' he said. 'I'm not talking about your Benin bronzes, your Ashanti masks. I'm talking about work being done by present-day wood-carvers and sculptors and certain tribal treasures that might be on the market for a good price.'

'I see,' Albert said without enthusiasm. 'Well I'd say all you're likely to be offered are mass-produced figures of giraffes and elephants. As for tribal treasures, they almost invariably have religious significance. It would be like asking the Catholic Church to sell you the cross from the altar. Frankly you'd stand just about as much chance of acquiring something by getting permission to excavate and then arguing a split with the government concerned.'

Julius Jack Freedman chuckled.

'Yeah, yeah,' he said. 'You British. Underplay it. Everyone a pessimist. For Chrissake, all I want is some good native workmanship and you can be the judge. Someone like you knows the difference between mass production and the genuine article.'

This began to sound to Albert like a really bird-brained scheme.

'Anyway, I wouldn't know where to start,' he said.

Julius Jack Freedman grinned cheerfully.

'I'll tell you where to start,' he said. 'You start in Nairobi. That's the capital of Kenya. I've got a cousin there. A screwball, but he'll help all right if I cross his palm with greenbacks. Matter of fact he's already been rooting out a selection – just to make it easy for you. All you got to do is pick and choose, just give your approval.'

'I can't see why you need me,' Albert said. 'Why go to all the trouble of sending someone out there. Get him to ship the whole lot over.'

Julius Jack Freedman uttered a short, incredulous laugh.

'Jesus, you British!' he cried. 'Here am I offering you a couple of grand and all expenses paid for a trip to Africa during the English winter – and you start holding out on me! It's simple, I tell you. I like to have my experts on the spot. So my cousin shows you something and it's great and you say "where did this come from? – we'll have some more". He shows you something else and you say "that's crap – stick it up your loincloth". I just gotta have a good man there. No louse-ups.'

Albert shook his head. This guy was even nuttier than he'd thought. What sane man would pay that kind of money for a sort of artistic courier?

'I don't know that it's convenient for me to go to Africa right now,' he said.

'Now look, Mr Divine,' Julius Jack Freedman said, 'I know you're a busy man, but you can treat this how you like – a few days, or a few weeks. You know what the temperature is in Nairobi right now?'

'How the hell would I know that?'

The tycoon beamed tolerantly.

'Well I can tell you that it's 24 degrees Centigrade – 75 Fahrenheit. How about that? Right now, according to measurements on the Air Ministry roof, it's three degrees Centigrade, 37 Fahrenheit. You know how much sunshine they had in Nairobi yesterday?'

'Seven hours, thirty-two minutes, forty-five seconds.'

'Just a few minutes under ten hours,' Julius Jack Freedman said, triumphantly.

'I like the English winter,' Albert lied. 'Very bracing.'

'Goddam liar!' Julius Jack Freedman grinned. 'All you British lie about liking your weather. You hate it! *When's it gonna rain? Should I take my umbrella, wear a mackintosh?*

Will it snow? Will it freeze my balls off? Come on, Mr Divine!'

'Well I like a bit of variety,' Albert insisted.

'Oh yeah, sure. But what sort of variety? You want variety – okay. You know what the temperature was in Mombasa yesterday?'

If I had another drink, Albert reflected, I'd throw the glass at his head.

'The temperature in Mombasa yesterday – now remember Mombasa's at sea level and Nairobi's 5,000 feet up – was 30 degrees Centigrade, 86 Fahrenheit. Now that's the sort of variety you want. Not the difference between what turns you blue and what turns you purple.'

'The hell with it,' Albert said. 'I'd be losing money, get out of touch. Besides there's a film I want to see at my local Odeon.'

'*Three* grand and expenses for two – why not take a girl friend?' Julius Jack Freedman said with a hint of desperation. 'Now don't be difficult, Mr Divine. I know you're my man. Forget the Commie drinking. I have a sixth sense about it.'

Albert began to feel a hint of desperation himself. His eyes alighted on the wooden statuette. Maybe insult would work where protestation failed.

'This one of the little odds and ends you were talking about, Mr Freedman?' he asked.

'Yeah. An ithyphallic Kikuyu statuette. What do you think of it?'

'You want my honest opinion, Mr Freedman?'

'Of course I want your goddam honest opinion.'

'I think it's a vulgar, glossy bit of mass production. It may be a copy of an interesting original. As it stands it's a cheap bagatelle you'd probably find in any bazaar.'

Albert took a breath. If that didn't settle the issue then he'd surrender – abjectly.

Julius Jack Freedman looked from the statuette to Albert and his crazy eyes glowed.

'You're absolutely goddam right!' he cried. 'I knew you were my man. It's a cheap copy of the Kikuyu original – had it made by a friend of mine. Who're you trying to kid about not knowing your Africa, eh?'

'Okay, Mr Freedman,' Albert said. 'Two grand is perfectly all right.'

Julius Jack Freedman opened his eyes wide and wild. He came around the desk.

'Jesus, if that isn't what I like about you British,' he said. 'All that crap and then – zoom – the gentlemanly retort. Not for three grand, Mr Freedman. Two grand is quite enough!'

He came to an abrupt halt in front of Albert, who had risen apprehensively. He roared with a laughter that made the place shake. He reached out and crushed Albert's hand to a painful pulp, slapped his shoulder right through his neck.

'No, Mr Divine,' he cried. 'Three grand is the sum – and expenses for two. When I say something, I mean it. Have another Bour . . . ' His eyes caught the glitter of broken glass . . . ' Have a cigar.'

'Well, when do you want me to go, Mr Freedman?'

'Any time to suit you, Mr Divine. The sooner the better. How about the weekend? I'll fix up the flight. You need jabs for smallpox and yellow fever. Everything else I'll have my cousin lay on for you. Don't worry about a thing. Not a goddam thing.'

'I won't,' Albert said.

Now it was all decided, he felt rather pleased. Africa in January, all expenses paid. Bikini beaches, Thomson's gazelle, flamingoes over the lake, a winter tan . . . two winter tans. Angela would be back from her modelling stint in the States in a couple of days, just in time to join him on safari. Question. Would the elephants go rogue at the sight of her famous jiggle? Would the lion stop dead in his tracks and ogle? 'Lion ogles jiggle'. How was that for a headline. On a par with 'man bites dog' any day. The mere thought of Angela jiggling through the jungle was bringing out the ithyphallic in Albert. Words were like people, he reflected. Once known, you never got away from them.

Julius Jack Freedman lit up a cigar and smoke puffed in energetic clouds through the room. He took some photographs from a drawer and handed them to Albert.

'Since we're all set, you'd better have a look at these,' he said.

Albert studied them in turn. They were pictures of a number of statuettes, including what looked like the original of the one on his host's desk. The others included a figurine of a naked negress conspicuously displaying her vagina, the two figures in a series of copulatory positions and, finally, the negress suckling a baby.

'And what do you think of those, Mr Divine?' Julius Jack Freedman demanded.

'I think you're on to a good line,' Albert said. 'Etchings are out. Come up and see my ithyphallic photos.'

Julius Jack Freedman gazed at him intensely. He took back the photographs and held them up in one hand.

'These are *it*, Mr Divine,' he said. 'The whole bundle of Kikuyu fertility figurines. I want you to take these pictures and note them well. My cousin's getting hold of the originals for you.'

'Really?' Albert said dubiously. 'I would have thought that was rather tricky. Why doesn't your friend make copies of them all instead? If he doesn't polish them up so much, leaves them a little rougher . . . '

'Because they don't work,' Julius Jack Freedman interrupted. 'They're copies. They don't work!'

'Don't work . . .?'

Albert was a little out of his depth here.

'That's what . . . ' The tycoon glanced suddenly at his gold wrist watch. 'By Jesus!'

He stubbed out his cigar in some agitation and strode across the room. At the door he glanced back at Albert distractedly.

'Hang on, Mr Divine,' he said. 'Make yourself at home. Have a Bourbon. I've just remembered some urgent business. Say fifteen minutes . . . '.

He was gone before Albert could demur. Albert went to the cocktail cabinet and poured himself a vodka with which to toast his new venture. Cornelia Bottom came in through another door and looked at him apprehensively. She had a dustpan and brush in her hand.

'It's quite all right,' Albert said. 'I'm only a quarter Russian so I've already smashed my quota today.'

'You really should be careful,' she said bending down with the brush and pan. 'Mr Freedman's very – unpredictable.'

'You can say that again,' Albert agreed, contemplating her protruding posterior. 'He just rushed off in mid-sentence.'

Cornelia Bottom straightened with a gasp. She glanced at her watch.

'Oh lord!' she said.

The intercom buzzed – and buzzed again, furiously. She went to the desk and pressed a switch.

'Hello?' she said.

'Miss Bottom,' Julius Jack Freedman's voice rasped. 'I've been looking all over for you. Get in here, will you – it's right on time.'

'I'm just sweeping up the glass, Mr Free . . .'

'To hell with the glass, Miss Bottom!' Julius Jack Freedman's voice rose in exasperation. 'Just get your ass over here double quick.'

Cornelia Bottom glanced at Albert in embarrassment. She placed the dustpan and brush on the floor.

'I'll do that later,' she murmured, trotting past him with averted face.

'To hell with it, Miss Bottom,' Albert mimicked, watching her go with some amusement.

Alone in the room he sipped his vodka and gazed out at the patchily clouded London sky. He chuckled. It would never have occurred to him to go to Africa in a million years. Well, certainly not this year. What a change it would be to see all those animals outside cages; all that sunshine . . . His thoughts were abruptly interrupted by the sound of voices. It took him a few seconds to realise they were coming through the open intercom.

'Julius,' Cornelia Bottom was saying, 'I do wish you wouldn't speak to me like that in front of other people. Just because you're my employer doesn't give you the right to humiliate me.'

'Humiliate you?' Julius Jack Freedman's voice said. 'Aw come on, Bottie, I was just getting anxious – that's all.'

'Well I keep telling you the point of maximum fertility is fairly elastic. I mean, any time today would do.'

'We just don't wanta take any chances, do we Bottie. Come on honey, get those pants off.'

There was a sound of rustling and then Cornelia Bottom said: 'Anyway, we've been trying so long. I really think you should see a doctor, Julius.'

'Come on baby, there's nothing wrong with Julius Jack Freedman's virility. Just haven't hit it right yet. Hey, wassa matter with this catch . . .?'

'All right, Julius, I'll do it . . . It's not just me, after all. Patsy, Emma, Gwendoline and Genevieve can't all be incapable. Careful of those nylons.'

'I told you Bottie, there's nothing wrong with me. I guess those dames don't relax enough. Can't forget I'm their boss – that's why they don't get a bun in the oven.'

'Don't be silly Julius – I'm sure they try just as hard as I do.'

'Well, whatever, I just gotta have an heir, Bottie. It's up to you chicks. Whoever wants to be the next Mrs Freedman just gotta produce the goods. Say, you're putting on a little weight around the boobies. It's okay, feels good. I like it.'

There was an audible intake of breath from Cornelia Bottom. After a moment, she said a little breathlessly: 'Perhaps you should adopt an heir, Julius, and then . . . '

Her voice was cut off suddenly. There was the sound of heavy breathing.

'It's gonna be all right, Bottie,' Julius Jack Freedman said after a short silence. 'Either you or one of the others is gonna get knocked up pretty soon. In the meantime isn't this fun?'

'Oh Julius!' Cornelia Bottom's voice was quite breathless now. 'You're so, so – ithyphallic!'

'All the better to screw you with my dear, heh, heh! Hey just put your hand down here. Yeah. Nice and gentle. I can just feel it's gonna work.'

'But, but – its been a year now, Julius. How . . . how long

can this go on?'

The answer was a series of short sharp grunts from Julius Jack Freedman.

'I mean you can't . . . expect . . . all your secretaries . . . to go on . . . '

'Forget it, Bottie,' Julius Jack Freedman croaked. 'Boy, you got a little plumper around the ass, too. I swear it.'

'Julius . . . I wish . . . you wouldn't use . . . that language . . . '

'Don't be so hoity-toity, Bottie. An ass is an ass and you got one to be proud of. Something really to get hold of. Just squeeze a little harder – Jesus!'

'Anyway, Julius . . . Emma . . . has a . . . boyfriend now . . . Suppose . . . '

'The hell she does! She better be careful. I warned you all about that. I'll have blood tests made. You ready, honey? Just slip this cushion under and open a little wider – uh.'

Further rustlings.

'But Julius . . . we could go on . . . like this . . . for years . . . '

'You complaining? Just stroke down there a bit, okay?'

'Of course not, Julius . . . it's just the continuation . . . of your line . . . that we have at . . . '

'Don't worry, Bottie. Once we get these fertility statues everything's gonna be all right . . . Jesus . . . Even if you dames are having trouble right now . . . Christ! . . . I'm coming in . . .'

'But Julius, you don't really think . . . Oooooh!'

'Jesus, Bottie, Jesus!'

'Oh Julius, Julius!'

A riot of soft creakings and choked breathing began to batter Albert's ears. He sat transfixed, gazing at the impersonal plastic structure of the intercom with its array of switches as if it were Helen of Troy. Pulsating images of Cornelia Bottom giving her all whirled through his head. Disembodied sounds of passion filled the room.

'Oh Julius! Oh, oh, oh!'

'Yeah, baby . . . Yeah . . . Jesus!'

'So big Julius! Oh yes! Hold me there! Yes, yes!'

'Baby that's good! Wider Yow!'

'Oh I want it all, Julius! All!'

'You got it baby! You're beautiful! Christ!'

'Give it to me, Julius! Oh yes! Give it!'

Albert leapt at the desk and slammed off the intercom. He took out a handkerchief and mopped his sweating brow. Only so much a man could take. He poured himself a very large vodka. Imagine having him wait while they . . . The least Julius Freedman could have done was to offer him another of his secretaries. Ah, but of course, the blood tests. Very time-wasting.

He sat down, somewhat weak at the knees. There was now no doubt the guy was crazy. Did the sterile bastard really think those statues were going to provide him with offspring! Maybe it was just a subtle scheme to keep his harem in tow.

Albert stood up and paced around the room. He looked at the intercom. Smug piece of equipment. Squatting there feigning innocence. He moved towards it, hesitated, reached out suddenly and pushed a switch. The innocence shattered with the explosion of lust rushing to its ultimate . . . Friction of flesh against flesh, mouthings, moanings, gruntings . . . 'Julius, I'm ready – oh! . . . '. 'Yeah baby . . . oof!' Screamings, slappings, obscenities. . . . 'An heir! An heir!' . . . Albert leapt over and flicked it off again. His throat was dry, heart pounding. He resumed pacing around the room. Two days before Angela's return! How could anyone expect him to be faithful when he was exposed to things like intercourse by intercom. Maybe he could date Cornelia Bottom on the quiet. Perhaps she had a neglected diaphragm she could bring out from cold storage. He sat down. He stood up again. He poured himself a tonic water for his dry throat. He took a piece of ice from a bucket and held it to his heated brow. Such enthusiasm she showed, too! Who would have thought . . . ? He glanced at the fertility statuette with irrational hostility. Another smug bloody piece of equipment. Parading its permanent erection with impossible phlegm . . .

Five minutes later Julius Jack Freedman burst noisily back into the room. His eyes gleamed satisfaction.

'Sorry to keep you Mr Divine. Something I'd overlooked. Just couldn't put it off. You managed to entertain yourself I trust?'

'Unfortunately I had nobody else to entertain me,' Albert said with the bitter weariness of a nervous wreck.

Julius Jack Freedman was aware of little but his own sense of wellbeing.

'That's great,' he said.

He moved around the desk and his eyes alighted curiously on the melting ice cube which Albert had distractedly placed there.

'My apologies,' Albert said.

Julius Jack Freedman picked up the ice and placed it on a piece of blotting paper.

'That another Russkie custom?' he demanded with a grin.

'No,' Albert said. 'I'm always leaving ice around.'

Julius Jack Freedman glanced at him with interest.

'You don't say,' he murmured. 'You know, Mr Divine, I reckon you're a pretty eccentric guy. Not that I mind that. Oh no. Guy's eccentric, he's gonna use his own mind, own individuality. Won't let himself be coerced by any so-called Socialist dictatorship. So where were we? Oh yeah. How about Saturday? Get you on an evening flight, you have dinner on the plane, breakfast in Nairobi. My cousin'll book you into the New Stanley Hotel and you can meet him later. You don't need a visa as you're British, just health clearance which you can do at the Hospital for Tropical Diseases here. I'll have Miss Bottom fix an appointment for you. We'll see you're insured for personal accident, get your travellers' cheques and some ready cash. Miss Bottom'll do all that with you. Anything you want, just let me know.'

Cornelia Bottom for a start – or maybe Patsy, Emma, Gwendoline, Genevieve. The way Albert felt right now all five of them at once wouldn't come amiss.

Julius Jack Freedman towered up like a great bear and came around the desk.

'Okay, Mr Divine, I'm sure you're gonna do a great job. And don't forget, Bourbon's the drink. You wanta impress those African chiefs, you drink Bourbon.'

'I'll wear an emblem on the back of my suit,' Albert said.

'Yeah, ha, ha. Seriously Mr Divine, there's a lot of Commie activity going on in Africa. We gotta help even up the score.'

Julius Jack Freedman's hand came out and Albert reluctantly surrendered his for the crunch.

'Okay, okay. Good safari,' Julius Jack Freedman said.

He accompanied Albert to the door and waved him goodbye. He eyes strayed to a clock on the wall and Albert heard him mutter, 'Jesus!'

As Albert passed through one of the outer offices where a group of very nubile secretaries were typing and filing, an intercom buzzed.

The dark-haired beauty in the tight green sweater and even tighter black satin trousers answered it. Julius Jack Freedman's voice boomed through the office.

'Miss Jennings, will you drop what you're doing and get your ass in here double quick. It's right on time.'

Chapter Two

ALBERT TOOK a sip of the champagne he'd been unable to restrain himself from opening and surveyed the main room of his Battersea flat with satisfaction.

The cosy aroma of roast duck wafted in from the kitchen, the mixed salad hors d'oeuvre was all prepared, the cheese-board was fully stocked and the maple walnut ice cream was ready in the refrigerator. Allied with the unaccustomed sensation connected with eating at home, was the unexpected pleasure the new look of his flat was giving him. Angela, due to arrive very shortly, should be pleased. For as long as he could remember, she had been trying to persuade him to re-decorate, but his inertia concerning the appearance of his surroundings had proved an adequate defence against all her blandishments. His Jermyn Street gallery was a different matter. He had to impress people with that. But in Battersea, just across the river from the vibrant excesses of Chelsea, he was not trying to impress anyone and his natural ability to live in homely, not to say rugged, inelegance was everywhere apparent.

But suddenly, during Angela's latest modelling absence, he had suffered a brainstorm. Not only had he thoroughly redecorated, but he had thrown out various monstrosities of furniture and drapings and replaced them with elegant modern items. He had also acquired an opulent new record-player and a colour television.

Albert had endured a number of qualms while this bout of insanity had him in its grip, but now he was quite pleased with the result. It had, in fact, induced him to invite Angela to the flat for dinner rather than go out on the town. They would have a quiet, elegant reunion. The sort of thing you saw in advertisements, with crystal chandeliers glistening in the candlelight. Yes, his madness had extended to the purchase of a black, wrought-iron candelabra and a chandelier. The chandelier, admittedly, was not crystal. Plastic in fact, from Woolworth's. He had considered this for a long time and finally decided he was quite unable to tell the difference. This was the one stand his spirit made against Angela's influence.

The room glowed warmly in the candlelight: shades of rich varnish from the furniture, rich green from the fitted carpet and the curtains covering the French windows to the balcony overlooking the park. The chandelier glistened exactly like the advertisements.

Albert placed a disc on the recordplayer and in a moment the music of Ravi Shankar's sitar rippled through the room. He took a satisfying draught of the cold champagne and poured himself another, noting that the new ice bucket also glistened as in the advertisements. He couldn't wait to have Angela's pink and whiteness glistening – perhaps not exactly as in the advertisements. The magazine supplements hadn't yet got around to nude full frontals in the romantic ads.

The doorbell buzzed and Albert went into the small hall, a light tingling in his stomach, and opened the front door.

Angela's cheekily beautiful face smiled at him from the top of a long black fur and suede coat against which her long, auburn hair was dazzling. He smiled back. She moved towards him, opened the coat wide and enclosed him in it, pressing against him. Albert kissed her hair and slipped his arms around her. Yes, the famous buttocks were intact, their shapely projection as exciting to the touch as ever. She turned her head and looked up at him, still smiling, hazel eyes shining.

'Hello Albert,' she said.

Albert opened his mouth, but no words issued before her tongue slipped into it. Her delicate perfume enveloped him like a fragrant mist; the warm, vital reality of her curvaceous body was a startling reminder of how empty the world was in her absence – except, of course when it was filled with the warm, vital reality of other bodies.

Angela drew her face back from his, looking at him with

the saucily promising expression that never failed to stir his ardour.

'Darling Albert,' she said.

'Jambo,' Albert murmured.

'*What*.'

'It's a Swahili greeting.'

She slipped out of his arms and gazed at him reproachfully.

'I knew it, Albert Divine. As soon as I'm out of your sight you forget me completely. You don't even know which continent I'm in.'

'Angela, I have a surprise for you.'

'You have a Swahili girl friend.'

'Don't be silly. Swahili is just the name of a language. You can't have a Swahili girl friend.'

'What do you mean? English is the name of a language, isn't it – not to mention French, German, Spanish, Chinese . . .'

'No, no, it's not the same,' Albert said, aware that the news he wanted to get across was being gratuitously sidetracked. 'There is no Swahili nation or person. It's the same as . . . ' He searched in vain for a simple parallel.

'Well, anyway, you have a new girl friend who speaks Swahili. I know there's something going on or you'd have had my clothes off by now.'

Albert made a lustful movement towards her and she sprang away from him.

'Oh no, Albert. You can't expect to confuse me with your Swahili girl friend and have me fall into your wayward embrace just like that.'

'You don't fool me with that ploy,' Albert retorted. 'If you hadn't been satiated by all those snazzy New York executives, you'd have had your own clothes off by now.' He paused and added haughtily: 'Anyway, if you'll excuse me I have to go and baste the duck. Kindly help yourself to champagne.'

'Champagne! How heavenly!' Angela enthused.

'There's no need to exaggerate,' Albert said. 'You know you never drink anything else these days.'

'Oh I do, Albert. I drank Bourbon in New York, tequila in New Mexico and Chinese rice wine in San Francisco.'

'My god!' Albert cried, turning towards the kitchen. 'It was just one long debauch, wasn't it?'

'It was lovely.'

'And you have the cheek to complain about my Swahili girl friend!'

'So you admit everything!'

Albert went into the redecorated kitchen with its brand new kitchen unit and Portuguese tiles. He basted the duck and thought about Angela being back and the champagne and the redecorated bedroom and Africa looming sunnily up.

'Albert!' Angela's voice floated through the flat. 'Albert, darling, what have you done to everything?'

'Do you like it?'

'It's marvellous, darling. Just like the magazine ads. What happened to you?'

Albert carried the salad and accessories up the corridor from the kitchen, through the small hall and into the main room. Angela had removed her coat and gloves and was studying the chandelier, a glass of champagne cupped in her hands. She was dressed in a black sweater and white gaucho pants which clasped her hips, showing to full advantage those luscious convexities which had won her the international nickname, 'The Jiggle', on account of their provocative thrusting motion. Albert stopped short and gazed.

'I had a brainstorm,' he murmured.

He placed the salad tray on a coffee table and switched on the colour television.

'I went the whole hog,' he said. 'It's terrible.'

'It's not, Albert. It just shows you can be adaptable.'

'No, I mean the television.'

The picture flashed on the screen. A Cabinet Minister was talking about pollution. His face was an unnatural shade of pink with a bluish tinge. In fact, everything in the picture was an unnatural shade of pink with a bluish tinge – even the greens and yellows. Albert hurriedly turned down the sound.

'Everything has teething troubles,' he said. 'It's not too

bad for football matches.'

'It's quite attractive,' Angela said, 'if you forget it's television and think of it as a sort of kaleidoscope with a blue and pink theme. Anyway, the candles are gorgeous, darling – and you got a crystal chandelier. It must have cost the earth.'

'I knew you'd like it Angela. What does cost matter?'

'Oh Albert!'

She came and pressed herself against him and her tongue began a fresh invasion of his mouth. A great surge of martial spirit rose up in Albert's loins.

Angela pulled away from him suddenly.

'Albert, you didn't do all this redecoration alone – somebody helped you.'

'No they didn't,' Albert said. 'I'm a very fast worker.'

'I'm well aware of that.'

Angela stared around the room with fresh interest.

'There's a woman's touch here, Albert,' she said. 'There's no point in denying it.'

Albert made a slack-wristed gesture.

'We all have our feminine side,' he said.

'You had your Swahili woman in here, didn't you? Who is she, Albert?'

'Do you know any Swahili women?'

'Of course not.'

'Then how could I tell you who she is? It wouldn't mean anything, would it.'

'So you admit she exists?'

'Have some salad – shredded red cabbage, carrots, avocado pear and walnuts. My own creation.'

Albert refilled her glass and Angela stared thoughtfully at the bubbling liquid.

'It's lovely champagne,' she said. 'I do approve of your being a rich man now, Albert.'

'I don't know,' Albert said. 'There was something delightfully basic about that vin ordinaire we used to drink. I'm a peasant at heart, you know.'

'Oh exactly. All peasants like to drive Rolls Royce Silver Clouds, have holidays in luxury yachts off the South of France and make love to Swahili women.'

'Certainly they do in their dreams.'

Angela paused in the act of serving out some salad.

'So you used to dream about making love to a Swahili woman before you actually did it?' She held up her fork. 'No, Albert, don't say anything. I don't want to hear about it.'

Albert munched away at the salad, which was extraordinarily good – even if he did say so himself. Angela also ate and speculated on the room.

'It's a marvellous salad, Albert,' she said after a while. 'You really have been taking a crash course in things while I've been away. And since when have you liked the colour green . . . ' She motioned with a pronged walnut towards the curtains. 'I thought you detested green.'

'Don't be ridiculous,' Albert said. 'Green's one of my favourite colours. Don't you remember that green twin set of yours?'

'The one you were always ripping because you couldn't get it off fast enough? I thought you hated it. The language you used! That was no way to treat a colour you like.'

'That was only because I liked the colours underneath better,' Albert said, leering theatrically. 'The tender pink and the soft, virginal white . . . '

'Are you sure you don't mean coffee, or chocolate?'

'Angela, where would I find a Swahili woman?'

'Since a few minutes ago you were denying their existence, I daresay your ingenuity wouldn't be over-taxed.'

'You seem to have a bee in your bonnet about browns and chocolates,' Albert said. 'No doubt you were posing in the ghettoes.'

Angela speared the last of her salad and directed it demurely into her mouth. She held out her glass for more champagne.

'Those people in the ghettoes are very underprivileged,' she said.

'I bet you gave them a chance to make up on a few privileges.'

Angela sipped the champagne and looked at him over the rim of the glass.

'I made some very interesting visits,' she said. 'I always like to know what everything's about at first hand.'

'The first hand that tries.'

Angela stood up haughtily and began to inspect the room, undulating her hips in the tight gaucho pants. Albert's eyes were mesmerised by the bursting vitality of the buttocks. Surely even the toughest pants the gauchos could provide would surrender and rend apart . . .

'The American under-privileged are very nice,' she said. 'Those Negroes, the Puerto Ricans, Mexicans. They have all those stuffy, well-heeled whites knocked for six.'

'And all those sex-starved, well-heeled white women, no doubt,' Albert said.

'You wouldn't put me in that category, would you, Albert?'

'God no,' Albert said. 'If anybody was surfeited . . . '.

'Then your implication falls down, doesn't it? Anyway, listen to the pot calling the kettle black.'

'Exactly,' Albert said. 'You have black on the brain. Excuse me, I have to carve the duck.'

He returned to the kitchen and did the neccssary with the duck, the roast potatoes and the cauliflower gratiné. Angela drifted in after him.

'Mmmmm,' she murmured. 'Smells lovely. I shouldn't eat potatoes, though.'

'Why worry,' Albert said. 'You do everything else you shouldn't.'

'Who says I shouldn't?'

Albert arranged dishes on a tray and took another bottle of champagne from the refrigerator.

'I hope you don't mind drinking champagne throughout the meal,' he said.

'It's a lovely idea, Albert. And then you won't be able to ask me what wine I think it is and have me get it wrong.'

'You mean like thinking a Chateau Latour 1947 is an Algerian 1969?'

'There's no need to throw it in my face.'

Albert carried the tray from the kitchen with Angela jiggling after him.

'You've done the whole place, haven't you, Albert?'

Albert placed the tray on the coffee table, handed one of the dishes to Angela and refilled their glasses.

'Have you done the bedroom?' she asked.

'You should just see what I've done to the bedroom.'

Angela put down her dish and jiggled towards him. She put her tongue very slightly out over her bottom lip.

'When?'

Albert grabbed her voraciously.

'Whenever you like,' he said. 'I'll even forego the roast duck.'

Angela pressed her hips hard against him for a moment and then jerked away.

'What *have* you done to the bedroom?' she demanded.

'Well I had the worst bit of my brainstorm then,' Albert said. 'I did the ceiling orange and the walls slate blue.'

'I knew it!' Angela snapped. She picked up her plate and began furiously to devour the duck. 'All black people adore bright colours.'

'And pink Cadillacs to you,' Albert said.

Angela brandished a duck bone at him.

'Albert Divine, you'd never have chosen those colours yourself. Orange ceiling! Slate blue walls! I never heard of anything so crazy.'

'Don't be silly,' Albert said. 'It's hot tropical weight overhead with vibrating metal-heat all around.'

'Yes – and a hot, tropical vibrating Swahali woman on the bed. With some parts of her more hot, tropical and vibrating than others.'

'They're just like any other women,' Albert said.

'Don't be ridiculous. What other women would want slate blue walls and orange ceilings. It's because they're so wild.'

'So what's your taste? vermilion ceilings, white hot walls and charcoal friezes?'

'It's no good trying to evade the issue Albert. You've been making passionate love to a Swahili woman in my absence. Doing all sorts of crazy, wild, perverted things to her that only Swahili women go along with.'

'Are you jealous?'

Angela ate her duck furiously. She knocked back her champagne and refilled the glass.

'As a matter of fact,' Angela said, 'I find black people very stimulating lovers, too – and Puerto Ricans and Mexicans.'

Albert finished his champagne and poured himself some more. He began to feel rather flushed.

'So that *is* what you were up to over there. Nothing to do with those smart, executive types.'

'Oh there's nothing wrong with them either,' Angela said. 'It's just they haven't got the same degree of vengeance to take as the underprivileged.'

Albert swigged back his champagne.

'Get your clothes off!' he cried.

The record came to a sudden end and silence fell.

'There's no need to shout,' Angela said. 'Is that the way you talk to your Swahili woman. I always heard they were very subordinate to the man.'

'Just get them off.'

Angela swayed up on to her feet and turned the record over, displaying her buttocks.

'You sound like the underprivileged,' she said.

'Is that how they treated you?'

'Heavens no – they just ripped them off.'

'Rubbish! They wouldn't have to.'

'Albert Divine, you are a pig.'

Angela pulled off her sweater and hurled it at him.

'And you are a bitch.'

Albert tore off his woollen polo and flung it at her. He had reached that pleasant stage of inebriation where the room seemed to have shrunk to the section within his immediate vision.

'Albert, what does your Swahili woman like to do to you her?'

She slipped out of her gaucho pants, confronting him in black tights and a small, half-cup brassiere. Albert eased off his trousers.

'Use your imagination,' he said. 'Blazing orange. Vibrating, sadistic blue.'

Angela unclipped her brassiere and her pretty breasts swung cheekily into view. She pressed one thigh over the other.

'Albert, what do you mean *sadistic* blue?'

'It was you who said they like to subjugate themselves to men. What do you think?'

Angela wriggled her tights over her hips and down her thighs, jiggling her luscious convexities all over the place.

'They may be more emancipated these days,' she panted. 'Perhaps you had to rape her. Perhaps she liked that.'

'Don't judge everyone by yourself,' Albert said. 'I suppose you gave your shirtless ones the pleasure of thinking they'd raped you. Helping them with their vengeance.'

'Once they're shirtless,' Angela said, 'it's too late for a girl to do anything about it.'

Albert tore off his underpants and his masculinity sprang towards the ceiling. Angela's eyes gleamed. She slid her briefs hastily down her legs and stepped out of them. Albert moved towards her and she put out her hands to ward him off.

'Help!' she cried. 'You sadistic brute. I will not be subjugated to your will!'

She turned and danced away around the coffee table, her buttocks jostling each other in dimpling enticement below the slimness of her waist and shoulders.

Albert lunged after her and grabbed her shoulders. She allowed herself to flow back at him, silky flesh agonisingly brushing his and then crushing against his body with force. Albert staggered and they both fell headlong over the coffee table, scattering dishes over the floor. Angela rolled over and sprang away from him again.

'You savage Swahili warrior!' she cried. 'You're trying to enslave my body!'

She swung away around the room, breasts bobbing, bottom twitching. Albert disentangled himself from the dishes, removing a sharp piece of duck bone from his left thigh.

'I suppose this is how you titillated your underprivileged,' he said unevenly. 'Showing them all that flesh, saying come on in, I want to be sacrificed.'

'Why don't you call a fuck a fuck the way they do,' Angela said with mock contempt. 'You're too genteel for a merciless warrior.'

Albert grabbed at her again. She turned and wrestled with him – an excruciating friction. They fell against the soundless television, which turned over with a rending crash, shattering its blues and pinks against a stool. An antenna stabbed Albert in the back and buckled under him.

Angela slithered away across the floor, a superb sexual display and got to her knees.

'We African women are very strong,' she breathed. 'We do all the heavy work, you know.'

She climbed drunkenly to her feet, smoothing her hands over her flat belly. Albert stumbled upright, pulsating.

'They get beaten if they resist,' he said.

'Ooooh!'

He charged at Angela, who whisked around a chair, slipped on a spilled slab of Old English Cheddar and fell against his new bookcase. Albert flung himself on her, crushing her face down across the low cabinet. He would spare her the beating since he couldn't wait. Angela kicked out at his shins and he staggered back, pulling her with him. She grabbed at the glass doors. There was a rending of wooden frame as a hinge gave way and then a shattering of glass as the whole structure toppled forward, smashing against the coffee table. A cascade of books inundated them.

Angela began to laugh deliriously. She pelted Albert with books.

'What an imperious warrior!' she cried. 'I think your Swahili woman had to rape *you*!' They're not like this in America, you know.'

Albert rose up out of a mound of volumes.

'They didn't have to contend with a library of classics,' he cried.

He sprang wildly at Angela, who fled around a chair. Albert lashed out at the flying buttocks, catching them a stinging blow with the palm of his hand. Angela shrieked and sprang at the curtains, clambering up them like a monkey. Her thighs swung at Albert's eye level. He lashed out at the vulnerable bottom again and Angela yelled, swinging her legs up horizontally. Albert seized her around the hips and tugged.

The curtains ripped and came away from the rail. He and Angela tottered back against a table bearing the candelabra. There was an almighty crashing and Albert found himself sitting in the centre of the smashed record player with the last despairing squeak of the sitar singing in his ears. Angela landed on his stomach, winding him. Desperately he held her, a breast in each hand, his masculinity soaring between her splayed thighs.

'Oh Albert!' she gasped.

He tried to roll over and pull her with him. But sharp points of smashed record and the jagged edge of the player's arm forced him to squirm back again. Angela squirmed with him, her buttocks pressed into his abdomen, thighs holding his sex as she finally accepted the warrior victory and waited to be forced into welcome submission.

Albert heaved his body sideways, fighting the debris. He couldn't make love on the equivalent of a bed of nails. Angela heaved sideways, too, with her back towards him. They fitted each other like two spoons. Albert's throat constricted. He drew back his hips a little, ranged himself . . .

He uttered a piercing cry as a sharp burning sensation seared his left buttock. He jerked forward and his manhood rammed, without deliberation, into Angela's submissive parts.

'Oh Albert, Albert!' she moaned.

Albert short-sightedly ignored his blistered backside as he unleashed his fury between her quivering thighs. But the increased brightness in the room and a sudden, strong smell of burning could not be ignored. He twisted his head, uttered a cry of horror and attempted to disengage himself from Angela's clinging body. The place was on fire!

The candelabra had crashed to the floor where it had already scorched a huge patch in his carpet and started the ripped curtains flickering.

Albert jerked like a puppet among the debris, but Angela stretched back her arms and clasped his buttocks with convulsive strength, crushing him against her and repeating his name over and over.

'Fire!' Albert yelled.

'No darling, not yet – hold it!' Angela moaned.

'We're on fire!' Albert cried, struggling to free himself with movements the impaled Angela took for mounting passion.

'Yes darling, oh yes!' she murmured ecstatically.

The combined forces of drink, debris and Angela's clasp were too strong for Albert. His eyes rolled wildly. The fire had caught a chairleg and the charred patch of carpet was rapidly extending like the world war burnt earth policy of Russian lands.

'Angela!' he cried. 'We're going up in fire and smoke! We'll be consumed!'

'Albert, my darling, darling, we shall! I'm so hot I think I'm going to faint!'

'Angela, the room's on fire!' Albert bawled, wrenching his hips backwards.

'I know, Albert,' Angela groaned, thrusting her bottom back with his hips. 'It's been so long – it's so beautiful!'

'Angela, it's burning my behind!'

'And mine, darling. I'm burning all over!'

'Angela – the candelabra! It's on the floor setting the room on fire!'

'Yes, on fire . . .' Angela ground on to him slowly, blissfully. 'On fire!' . . . She twisted her head abruptly, saw the flames leaping and let out a scream.

She and Albert floundered up from the pile of wreckage, falling against each other, stubbing their toes. The flames had now extended to the upholstery of a new sofa and the curtains were burning merrily.

Albert grabbed one of his brand new silk cushions and began to beat vainly at the flames. Smoke and charred embers swirled everywhere. Strange shadows loomed.

Behind Albert a champagne corked popped and a jet of champagne hit him in the back of the neck, bounced off and careened around the walls, before Angela got it under control and directed the last dribble on to the flames.

No doubting the quality of that champagne, Albert thought in a rush to the kitchen. He seized a bowl, filled it with water and rushed back through the flat, spilling it all the way. He arrived in time to see a second champagne jet shooting around the walls out of Angela's drunken control, before he flung the bowl of water at the blaze, accidentally letting the bowl go with it. A section of the fire sizzled and hissed. The bowl crumpled in the heat, its plastic fabric turning black.

'We must call the fire brigade!' Angela cried.

'Not yet, not yet!'

Albert snatched up the cushion again and began to beat at the rejuvenating flames. The cushion suddenly caught fire in his hand and he fled with it to the kitchen to fling it in the sink. He filled a basin and stumbled back to the conflagration.

Angela was beating at the curtains with volume A-K of his Webster's Third New International Dictionary. A corner was already blackened before Albert wrested it from her, replacing it with his Complete Works of Shakespeare, which was less expensive, but also less effective.

The basin of water dampened the flames without extinguishing them. Albert seized the ice buckets and flung their contents around the room. The charred patch of carpet was now a yard square and eaten away to the floorboards. The spilled Cheddar was sizzling and bubbling, together with a left-over morsel of roast duck.

Only one thing for it. Albert grabbed the covers off a divan and turned the entire mattress on to the burning floor. It covered most of the ravaged area and he leapt up and down on it, smothering the flames. Angela joined him, uttering cries that sounded more gleeful than anxious. They both danced and stamped like dervishes, surrounded by tiny floating smuts of unrecognisable material. Their war dance went on until they were both smudged with soot and their legs ached. Albert subsided and watched Angela.

'I'm sorry to spoil your enjoyment,' he said after a couple of minutes, 'but the fire's out.'

Angela slumped into a chair, whose front legs crumpled

and tipped her gently onto the floor.

Albert gingerly turned the mattress over, heaving it back on to the divan. A charred smell like a dead forest fire filled the room. The mattress itself was charred and rotting in several places; the floor was devastated over a considerable area – a black, soggy pulp; the curtains, recordplayer, television, chairs, bookcase, coffee table were ruined; the walls were spattered with smuts and scorch marks and dripping champagne.

'Oh Albert,' Angela whispered soberly. 'It was all my fault.'

'It wasn't really me anyway,' Albert said.

'I bet your Swahili woman never engendered heat like that, Albert. How can I make it up to you?'

Albert looked at her, scratched and dishevelled, yet as beautiful and desirable as if she'd just stepped from the bath.

'We'd better go to the bedroom and just pretend it has plain white walls and ceiling,' he said.

Angela came over and stroked him gently with the tips of her fingers.

'Yes darling – and you can do anything you like with me . . . ' Her voice betrayed a tremor of excitement. ' . . . I deserve to be punished.'

Following the sexual beckoning of her jiggling rump towards the bedroom, Albert marvelled at the ability of sex to spring external to the human breast, reaching up again – despite all adversity – to the near vertical.

The news of Africa and its ithyphallic statuettes could wait until morning.

Tonight belonged to Battersea and its ithyphallic art dealer.

Chapter Three

ANGELA AND Albert sat on the black leather banquette in the Long Bar of the New Stanley Hotel sipping their Tom Collins's from long glasses and savouring the exotic sensation of being in darkest Africa.

The Long Bar, once the traditional white hunters' resort with its air of nostalgia for the Mother Country typified by the turn of the century murals behind the bar – country fair, Piccadilly Circus and hunting scene – was filled with a hearty lunchtime crowd. They were almost exclusively European. The British suburban wives chatted loudly around the tables at the side of the long room opposite the bar. Their farmer husbands boomed gossip and crop news, standing separately in the centre space or leaning on the wooden bar itself. And the bar stools were mostly occupied by itinerant air crews and air hostesses, there for the weekend. They were interspersed with a few incongruous types like the big, paunchy, black-bearded European with dark hair straggling down to his shoulders and his equally burly grey-bearded companion in white hunter's raiment, who were propping up one of the white pillars built into the bar.

'Do you think they're white hunters, Albert?' Angela whispered.

'More likely do a comic turn at one of the night clubs,' Albert said.

'They look very interesting.'

Albert was more interested in the airline hostesses, whose wellcut uniforms swathed their bodies like tissue paper around an arrangement of superb fruit. He had once heard some old pilot's tale that the vibration ten thousand feet up made them randy as rabbits and the air routes were warrens of orgiastic activity.

He sipped his Tom Collins. Angela's colonial idea. Personally, he didn't like having to cope with fruit on the way to the liquor. Preferred his drinks straight. However, it was refreshing and, of course, all at Julius Jack Freedman's expense.

Albert stretched his khaki-clad legs contentedly. In here it was cool. Outside it was pleasantly hot and cosmopolitan crowds were ambling through the sunshine under the palm trees and the blue-flowering jacarandas. Perhaps they should stay a week or two just to get the full feel of this striking city with its magnificent avenues and parks, its bright modern buildings with the circular Hilton towering over all. Albert was impressed, not least by the luxurious air-conditioned suite at the New Stanley which was all theirs for as long as they desired. Not to mention the fantastically pneumatic beds. He glanced at Angela, remembering. Breakfast had come second following their arrival. Definitely something to do with the 'plane's vibrations. Angela now looked a picture of cool, poised beauty in her huge, black Christian Dior chapeau and sleeveless white gabardine dress with its black buttons, high collar and wrap-over skirt. Her hair, piled on top for a change, revealed her long, elegant neck. And the slit in the skirt showed so much of her long, elegant legs in their white tights that Albert feared for her safety in such a passionately hot climate.

She glanced at him and smiled, as if reading his thoughts.

'Isn't it exciting, Albert. I can't wait to see the bush and all those wild animals.'

'Not to mention those wild Masai warriors.'

'Well actually you're quite wild enough,' Angela said. 'I think this African air has a stimulating effect.'

She rested her fingers on his thigh.

'In fact . . .' she added. 'How long before we're due to meet this friend of yours.'

'Fifteen minutes,' Albert said. He caught her look and added: 'We haven't time.'

'We could be late.'

Albert undid a button at his shirtneck.

'That would be very bad form,' he said.

'Oh Albert, don't be so orthodox. Anyway, we might not need more than fifteen minutes – in all this heat.'

'You're forgetting the superb quality of the air conditioning,' Albert said. 'Besides you know perfectly well we took forty-five minutes this morning.'

'No I don't, darling. I practically passed out. Time meant nothing.'

Albert wiped perspiration from his upper lip.

'It's out of the question,' he said, with a hint of desperation. 'I can't guarantee fifteen minutes.'

'I'm sure you could if you concentrated,' Angela said. 'I could guarantee *five* right now.'

'No!' Albert said loudly. He stood up and sat down again immediately on account of his frustration showing.

'For god's sake stop it,' he said. 'I can't even go and get a fresh drink.'

'Well that proves my point, darling.'

'No!'

He stood up again, grabbing their glasses with one hand and a beer-mat with the other. He advanced to the bar, inadequately attempting to cover himself with the beer-mat. A couple of curvaceous air hostesses eyed him with interest. The beer-mat was a total mistake. Far from concealment, it drew attention to his discomposure. He saw their knowing glances hover around the mat and slowly rise to confront him. Albert's face grew hot. It was true then – about the vibrations. He'd have to travel by air alone some time on the strength of this new knowledge. Or perhaps it would be enough just to wait at London Airport. Catch them as they came off the plane. Maybe even one of the air terminals would do.

He ordered fresh drinks.

'Sorry sah,' the barman said. 'You got to put the mat down.'

Albert stared at him. He was a fat, elderly African with a very lined face. He was wearing the bright red jacket and red fez which constituted the hotel's bar uniform. He looked ridiculous. Albert kept a firm hold on the mat.

'Please sah – the mat. No souvenirs permitted.'

'I don't want a souvenir,' Albert said. 'Will you change it for an old newspaper, then?'

The barman frowned.

'What you mean sah? Please not to make trouble.'

'I need this beer-mat,' Albert insisted.

'Then it's two shillings, sah.'

'That's perfectly all right,' Albert said.

The barman moved off muttering. He watched Albert darkly as he mixed the drinks. Albert stared straight ahead, forcing himself to think of garbage piles, concrete mixers, coal barges . . . By the time the barman returned with the drinks, Albert's proportions had deflated to normal. He placed the beer-mat on the counter.

'I don't want it after all,' he said.

'Ah'm only doing my job, sah,' the barman said. He took the money and ambled off muttering.

Albert had a hand around each glass when a rather high-pitched male voice beside him said: 'That's a classic example of covert racial prejudice, you know.'

Albert turned. The big, black-beared European stood beside him, his bland face rather lost behind the hair and big, black-rimmed spectacles. Beyond him the grey-bearded white hunter eyed Albert over a glass of Scotch and water.

'Don't be ridiculous,' Albert said. 'What's it got to do with you anyway?'

'Don't get tough, son,' the white hunter said.

Blackbeard studied Albert with absolute composure.

'I wouldn't suggest it was malicious prejudice,' he said mildly. 'More likely some inbuilt reaction you can't escape. Don't even realise it's there.'

'You're nuts,' Albert said.

Blackbeard regarded him clinically.

'Yes,' he said. 'The stock reaction to criticism of unconscious motivation.'

'I don't need my motivation criticised,' Albert said. 'I am not racially prejudiced. Some of my best friends are badgers.'

They both stared at him, but Blackbeard was not thrown.

'Clearly the subject reduces you to a completely irrational frame of mind,' he said. 'There is a syndrome, you know.'

'I also have quite amicable relations with a number of cybernauts,' Albert said.

Blackbeard studied him with interest. The white hunter suddenly grinned, his heavy, lined face crinkling above the grizzled beard.

'Permit me to analyse this situation,' Blackbeard said. 'You wanted the beer-mat, presumably for a collection. You were quietly incensed that the African barman should baulk you in your intention. At first you tried to humiliate him with contemptuous levity concerning an old newspaper. Determined to get your way you then agreed to pay for the mat, but then, unable to overcome your fury at being opposed by the inferior being, you rejected the mat – thus rejecting the barman and his race. On the basis of the facts there is no other possible explanation. Can you bring yourself to admit that?'

Albert released the glasses.

'Your analysis is entirely misconceived,' he said. 'You have absolutely no idea why I needed the beer-mat to begin with and why I didn't need it to end with.'

'It might be therapeutic for you to state your own view of your behaviour,' Blackbeard said.

'Well it was partly the air hostesses, but mainly Angela ...'

Albert suddenly remembered Angela. He glanced over to where she was sitting. She was watching, tapping her foot impatiently. As she caught his eye, she placed her hands on her hips.

'You'll have to excuse . . .' Albert began.

'Your answer is inevitably incomprehensible,' Blackbeard cut in. 'Such a degree of unrecognised and deeply-rooted prejudice gives very little hope for inter-personal cooperation. In fact it could be very dangerous.'

The white hunter swigged down his Scotch and smacked the glass on the bar.

'He's right anyway, Elmer,' he said gruffly. 'These Africans are too cocky. Give 'em an inch and they take a yard. Once knew a gun bearer was allowed a shot at a hyena. Thought he was world champion marksman after that. Shot somebody's toe off. What's your drink, son?'

'Well I've just ordered,' Albert said. 'Besides . . . '

One of the glasses was suddenly removed from his hand He swung round to Angela.

'Excuse me,' she said loftily. 'I only have two weeks' holiday and I can't afford to wait.'

Blackbeard and white hunter looked at her with interest.

'My apologies,' Blackbeard said in his high-pitched voice. 'I'm afraid I kept him. I can never allow an example of racial prejudice to pass unchallenged. It's only by bringing every germ under the spotlight that we may eventually eradicate the disease.'

'Trouble with you, Elmer,' the white hunter said, 'you never will understand the difference between them and us. What's the memsahib drinking?'

Albert indicated the freshly filled glasses.

'Thanks all the same, but we already . . . '

'I'll have another Tom Collins,' Angela said. She smiled at Albert – an 'it's-your-own-fault' smile.

'I'm afraid we're expecting to meet someone here at any moment,' Albert said. 'A business meeting.'

There was no telling where involvement with these two weirdos might end.

The white hunter ignored him, however, and ordered two more Scotches and two Tom Collins's.

'Lose a lot of liquid in this heat,' he said. 'Have to replace it.'

'Are you a hunter?' Angela asked, taking the fresh drink from him. She held one in each hand and sipped from each alternately. The white hunter looked at her with satisfaction.

'I like a woman who can take her liquor,' he said. 'Sure, I do some hunting.'

Blackbeard smiled and glanced at his wrist watch.

'Have to go in a minute, George,' he said. 'Your visitors should be here pretty soon.'

'They'll be late,' the white hunter said. 'Arty types. Mess you around. Never on time.'

Albert had a sudden, sinking recognition.

'Are you by any chance George Eisenway?' he asked.

The white hunter's bushy grey eyebrows arched.

'How come you know my name, son?'

Albert knocked back one of his Tom Collinses.

'Because I'm Albert Divine and this is Angela Carter,' he said. I'm afraid we were early.'

They all looked at one another. The white hunter gave a throaty chuckle. He thrust out his hand.

'That's how it goes,' he said. 'No offence intended. I guess there are arty types and arty types. Welcome to Africa.'

They shook hands and George Eisenway introduced Blackbeard.

'This is Dr Elmer Krapstein. You have to be careful what you say to him: he's a psychiatrist. Knows what you mean before you do yourself – or even if you don't.'

'That's not often difficult,' Dr Krapstein said.

'It's action that counts,' Eisenway said. 'Worth all your talk.'

'I don't disagree,' Dr Krapstein said. 'But what is to be the basis for action? George, I do hope you'll attend my project. Perhaps you can persuade your guests also to come. It may help Mr Divine overcome his prejudice.'

'You won't get me fooling about with that crazy stuff,' Eisenway said.

The doctor tapped him solicitously on the shoulder.

'Give yourself a chance, George, give yourself a chance,' he said.

He picked up a shabby shoulder bag.

'Goodbye my friends,' he said. 'I expect to see you again while you are here.'

They watched him elbow his way with genial blandness through the crowded bar.

'Elmer's all right if you don't take him too seriously,' Eisenway said. 'He's a nut.'

'What *is* his project?' Angela asked.

'Some baloney to do with improving race relations,' Eisenway said. 'Runs an institute here, backed by America. Government here'll tolerate anything if someone else pays. Elmer has some crazy idea for what he calls . . . no, what the hell is that? Oh yeah – a non-verbal meditation encounter, between blacks and whites. Sometimes I think he should be in an institution.'

'Sounds a nice idea,' Angela said.

'I thought you'd already had your fill of that,' Albert said.

'You're right, son,' Eisenway said. 'The only encounter worth having with a black is when he knows his place. I've had some good houseboys in my time – but you've got to watch they don't get cocky.'

'I didn't say that,' Albert objected.

'I know how you feel,' Eisenway persisted. 'I'm not saying there aren't good Africans. Fine, loyal people, many of them – and brave. Follow you anywhere, never leave your side. It's when they get uppity . . . ' He made a hissing sound with curled lip and Albert thought for a moment he was going to spit on the bar. 'Anyway, you'll get to know more about that. Did you have a good trip? Hotel comfortable? Sorry I couldn't meet you earlier, but I just got back from a shooting safari.'

'A safari!' Angela exclaimed. 'How marvellous!'

Eisenway scrutinised her.

'You want to see some bush country while you're here? Well, I guess we can fix that.'

'I'd be a little afraid of the wild animals,' Angela said. 'I once saw a film where a rhinocerous chased a truck. He actually speared it with his horn. I thought he was going to turn it right over. It was terrifying.'

'Don't worry,' Eisenway said. 'I know how to deal with this country.'

'I'm sure you're very tough, Mr Eisenway,' Angela said.

George Eisenway gave a crooked smile and flexed his hairy fingers.

'I know how to take care of myself,' he said. 'Had some hard times, rough times.'

'Did you ever get mauled by a lion?'

Albert glanced at Angela. Where did she get this bloodthirsty curiosity?'

'Daughter, I've been mauled by everything.'

Angela's eyes were all admiration. She finished both drinks and placed them on the bar where Albert eyed them cautiously. He didn't want them getting stoned out of their minds. He was supposed to be a responsible art dealer, after all and he was being paid a lot of money to do some sort of job other than drink himself under the table. You had to watch it with hard-bitten, hard-drinking types like Eisenway He'd have no respect for a man who couldn't take his liquor. Probably contact Julius Jack Freedman and have him cancel the whole deal

But Angela's two glasses were resoundingly empty on the bar and Eisenway now raised his and drained his Scotch.

Albert placed some money on the bar and motioned to the empty glasses The barman said – Albert could have sworn with malicious intent: 'How about you, sah?'

'I'm all right,' Albert said

Indeed he was. One-and-a-half glasses full to be precise.

'Come on, son,' Eisenway said. 'This is Africa. We do things in a big way here. Can't have you dropping out.'

'I'm not dropping out,' Albert said. 'Just slowing down.'

'You can always tell a man by the way he takes his liquor,' Eisenway said, predictably. 'No man's worth his salt in my view if he can't or won't keep up. Can't keep up – he's got no guts; won't keep up – what low-down trick's he trying to pull.'

A new hazard! Albert emptied one glass, held his breath and poured the second down his throat. Better to be sacked for drinking too much than for not drinking at all.

'Good going, son. First thing a man learns in this country is to take his liquor. You wake up at dawn out there in the bush under canvas, first thing you want is a mug of whisky, wake you up.'

On the contrary, Albert thought – the very last thing. At least, next to last. Last would be getting up at dawn in the first place.

'True, I had special training,' Eisenway continued. 'The war years in Europe, drinking and fighting, going through hell on a hangover. The years in Paris, Spain. The cheap liquor, the binges, fist fights. Had to learn to take it all.'

'What were you doing in Paris, Mr Eisenway?' Albert asked.

'Bit of this and that, like everyone else, son.'

This son and daughter business was beginning to make Albert feel incestuous.

'Why don't you call me Albert, Mr Eisenway,' he suggested.

'And I'm Angela.'

'Okay daughter. Most people call me Papa.'

'Oh I couldn't do that,' Angela said. 'It makes you sound like an old man.'

'Well I know I'm not that old,' Eisenway said. 'I guess people like to call me Papa on account of the sense of security I give them. If you like, just call me George.'

The fresh drinks arrived. To Albert's dismay the waiter had continued the pattern of supplying them with two apiece.

'Like people who do things in a large way,' Eisenway said, cheerfully surveying the array of glasses. 'A man's gotta have a generous spirit. Too many mean, cramped sons-a-bitches around. No guts.'

'If we're not careful we won't have any guts either,' Albert said.

A new voice cut in on them suddenly, an upper-class English voice with sharp, clipped articulation and a quiver of anger.

'If you're referring to me Eisenway, you'd better take those words back before they get rammed down your throat!'

They turned, all three of them, to see a bristling, stocky little man in immaculate sports shirt and slacks. He had a military haircut, bready brown eyes, a bushy moustache and a pugnacious cleft jaw. His small, square face was slightly flushed from drink.

Eisenway stared down at him.

'Why, hello Everett-Smithers,' he said. 'What'll you have?'

Everett-Smithers, who was more like a snappy, wire-haired terrier than anyone Albert had ever met, glared up at him.

'Don't give me that soft soap, Eisenway!' he snapped. 'If

you're man enough to admit you were calling me a mean cramped son-of-a-bitch, I'll take you outside and give you a thrashing.'

'Take it easy,' Eisenway said. 'Of course I wasn't referring to you.'

'You're a damned liar!'

Albert and Angela looked at Eisenway. Albert moved back a little. There was going to be hell to pay in a minute and he didn't want to get in the way of the American's punch.

'Calm down, calm down,' Eisenway said. 'Have a drink.'

'Not only a damned liar, but a coward!'

Angela, customarily more intrepid, or perhaps rash, than Albert, also moved back a step.

'Aw, you don't really mean that, Smithy,' Eisenway said.

Albert was amazed at his tolerance. Of course – discipline as well as toughness.

'You know bloody well I mean it, you layabout! And if you call me Smithy again, you'll find yourself in hospital.'

Eisenway glanced around the bar.

'Keep it down,' he said. 'You'll get us thrown out.'

'I'll throw you out myself, you poltroon.'

People nearby were throwing glances. Albert began to wish Eisenway would throw the punch and finish it.

'Look, fellah, I'm sorry you misinterpreted my remarks,' Eisenway said. 'I assure you I have nothing but the highest regard for you.' He downed one Scotch and fingered the second glass.

Everrett-Smithers' flush deepened. He raised a fist and poked his knuckles into the American's belly.

'Shut up you blasted hypocrite,' he swore. 'It's got back to me how you've been boasting that you took me in for fifty pounds and calling me a mean son-of-a-bitch for expecting you to keep your word on the repayment.'

Eisenway flinched and drew back from the poking knuckles.

'Steady on,' he said. 'Somebody's been spreading false tales. Besides, I'm going to pay you back.'

'You were due to pay me back a month ago.'

'Just haven't been able to get it together. Give me another week.'

'You're a wretched specimen,' Everett-Smithers snapped contemptuously. 'Small wonder you don't go back to America; they've no place for degenerates.'

Albert blanched and Angela moved so close to him so suddenly that the brim of her hat nearly took his eye out.

Eisenway picked up his second drink and gulped it down.

'You're wrong fellah,' he said. 'You're not being fair.'

'Fair!' Everett-Smithers raised his fist and waved it in the American's face. 'I'll teach you what's fair, you scum!'

Eisenway drew back quickly.

'Now don't lose your cool,' he said. 'I apologise.'

'You lousy cad!'

Everett-Smithers moved after him fist raised. Eisenway retreated along the bar, hands extended in front of him in an attempt to shoo off the attack.

'Harry!' he called. 'Harry!'

The elderly African barman came unhurriedly around the bar and got between them. Two more elderly African waiters in their red jackets and fezzes somewhat diffidently hovered nearby. The whole bar was now watching the scene.

'He was gonna hit me, Harry,' Eisenway complained. 'I didn't do anything.'

'I'll break his bloody jaw,' Everett-Smithers snarled over Harry's shoulder. 'The blackguard. All those bad debts; spends a fortune swilling alcohol into his guts. Don't touch me, barman. You tell that swine to come outside and take what he deserves.'

Between them the three barmen, looking like something from an oriental opera, managed to usher Everett-Smithers away to a corner, where he stood voicing his displeasure to an apparently sympathetic section of the crowd.

Albert took a bracing draught of his Tom Collins. He glanced at Eisenway in astonishment. The American was visibly trembling. And while Albert tried desperately to think of something suitable to say, Eisenway reached out blindly, picked up one of Angela's Tom Collins's and drained it. The barmen returned to their business. The hum of conversation resumed.

'This *is* an exciting country,' Angela said, demurely, in the silence around them.

Eisenway looked at her as if he'd forgotten who she was. He dropped his eyes, grabbed Albert's second drink and swigged it down.

'Excitable type,' he murmured. 'He's almost certifiable, you know. Can't take advantage of a man like that. Like hitting a drunk. I'd most likely have killed him. Crazy, you see – wouldn't have been able to defend himself.'

'You were very good,' Angela said. 'Most people would have lost control and belted him.'

Albert was thankful for the cue.

'You really showed admirable restraint,' he said. 'He's a very lucky chap.'

He coughed in embarrassment, not sure that he wasn't overdoing it. He needed a drink, now, but Eisenway had scoffed the lot.

The American looked around the bar. His grizzled beard and moustache were moist around his lips. His voice, when he spoke, had thickened a little.

'If he'd been a whole man I'da let him have it,' he said. 'Maybe I was too soft with the son-of-a-bitch.'

'You were very noble to spare him,' Angela said.

'A weaker spirit would have flattened him,' Albert said.

'Wouldna been a fair fight,' Eisenway said. 'I gotta see fair play.'

'He owes everything to your being so honourable,' Angela said.

'I take my hat off to you,' Albert declared.

Eisenway cast bloodshot eyes on the empty glasses. He gave a quick sidelong glance to the far end of the bar where a group of people appeared to be gently restraining Everett-Smithers.

'The hell with this joint,' he said. 'Let's go find another bar. Otherwise I might just not be able to hold myself back. Take a slug at that punk.'

Before either of them could respond, he turned and rapidly disappeared through the entrance to the street. Albert and

Angela were taken aback. They looked at each other in wonderment.

'He was running!' Angela said.

Chapter Four

ALBERT AND Angela stepped from the bar into the spacious animation of multi-lane Kenyatta Avenue. The sun hit them hard. For a moment they were slightly confused by the sudden display of bustling traffic, palm trees, shop windows, crowds in a colourful array of shirts, shorts, lightweight suits, cotton dresses, saris . . . And then they caught sight of George Eisenway in the deep shade of an awning. He had removed his hat and was mopping his brow with a huge khaki handkerchief.

'What happened to you?' he drawled as they approached.

'We lost track,' Albert said.

Eisenway slowly replaced his hat and belched into the handkerchief.

'One thing you gotta learn in this country, son,' he said. 'You gotta move fast. Can be the difference between life and death. If you're slow when the lion starts his run, crocodile opens his jaws, you've had it, son. Kaput.'

'It's the same in England really,' Albert said. 'Those buses, cars. Hyde Park Corner's really lethal.'

'And skinheads and hell's angels,' Angela added.

Eisenway moved off fast, though unsteadily. Albert and Angela followed, almost at a trot.

They reached the top of Kenyatta Avenue and turned into the square where taxis waited outside the foyer of the New Stanley. The pavement – Thorn Tree – cafe was packed with people and tourists with cameras and binoculars passed to and from the hotel, hailed by the vendors of African carvings.

'What we need is a drink,' Eisenway said, shading his eyes. He lurched forward, beckoning them into the shaded foyer of the hotel where more tourists were buying maps and postcards. He led them up a short, broad stairway to the first floor coffee lounge and bar – a quiet, deep-carpeted haven, insulated from the outside by wall-high windows giving clear views of the city. A few elderly Europeans were sipping coffee at the widely-spaced tables and some Africans in dark suits were sedately drinking at the bar.

'This'll have to do for the time being,' Eisenway grunted, slumping into a huge armchair.

A waiter appeared and the American ordered three double Scotches.

'We were drinking Tom Collinses,' Angela said.

'Yeah,' Eisenway agreed absently, making no attempt to change the order.

'And Tom Collinses for us,' Albert said, quickly and discreetly to the departing waiter, who gave him a dubious look and nodded.

'I shoulda slugged that son-of-a-bitch,' Eisenway muttered. 'You show pity, people take advantage, think they c'n get away with murder. Bombastic little bastard. Little men – inferiority complex. But I shouldna been so sensitive about him being round the bend. I was afraid I might do him some permanent damage. You gotta heavy punch and you hit a guy with a thin skull, you can kill him. Woulda served the punk right.'

'You shouldn't reproach yourself for being a gentleman,' Angela said.

'That's right,' Eisenway agreed. 'I was waiting for him to hit first. That's why I was so anxious. I knew if he hit me I'd hit him back and the poor bastard woulda had it.'

'Who is he anyway?' Albert asked in an attempt to move the subject a fraction.

'He's a son-of-a-bitch.'

'But what's he do?'

'Goes around risking sudden death picking fights with bigger, tougher guys.'

The waiter appeared with a tray of drinks. Albert gazed at them aghast. The three double Scotches were there – and so were six Tom Collinses.

'We didn't order six of those!' Albert protested.

'The gentleman asked for three double Scotches and you asked for Tom Collins,' the waiter said patiently.

'I meant . . . '

'That's lovely, Albert,' Angela interrupted. 'Now we don't have to keep ordering.'

'But we don't want all those drinks!'

Albert no longer felt the necessity to impress George Eisenway.

'Since when did you get all self-denying and abstemious, darling,' Angela said. 'This is Africa. We have to do things in a big way.'

Eisenway leaned forward precariously in his chair, eyes narrowing as if he had some difficulty in seeing.

'Right – you got the idea, daughter,' he said. 'You're a fine girl. A lovely girl.'

'You see,' Angela said.

'Okay,' Albert said begrudgingly to the waiter.

He pulled some notes from his wallet. If he remembered correctly it was Eisenway's round, but the American was making no move to cough up. Small fortune for this lot, too. Maybe he should threaten to punch him. That way he'd probably buy them lunch as well.

'Fine girl you got there,' Eisenway said, turning his bloodshot eyes on Albert. 'Another reason I didn't wanta hurt that son-of-a-bitch. He spills out all his teeth in a poola blood, it's not a pretty sight for a lovely girl to see.'

'You're wrong there,' Albert said rather belligerently as he tried to work out the tip. 'Nothing she likes better than the sight of blood. You should see her wetting her drawers at bull fights, all-in wrestling, cockfights and public executions.'

Angela smiled at him indulgently.

Eisenway fixed his eyes on her intensely. He stared for some seconds as if he wanted to say something but couldn't get it out.

'Yeah,' he said finally. 'Yeah. You like that, you'd like hunting lion. Can be dangerous as hell – and bloody.'

He knocked back one of the whiskies, smacking the glass down heavily on the table. He glared at the glass as if it had offended him.

'Remember one safari,' he resumed. 'Took this Englishman out looking for kudu. Knew I had a punk on my hands. Bastard didn't drink. Lion kept us awake roaring all night in the bush. The Englishman wants him and we track him down next day . . . ' He raised a finger at Angela. 'First point you gotta remember shooting lion – it's the first bullet that counts. You don't shoot unless it's close enough to be sure. And you gotta have a steady hand . . . '

He paused, took up the second Scotch with lightly trembling fingers, swigged down a draught, belched and looked momentarily around the lounge as if trying to figure out where he was.

'What's kudu?' Angela whispered to Albert.

'It's a sort of song doves make when they're on the job,' Albert said. 'Coo-doo . . . coo-doo . . . '

Angela gave him a withering glance and Eisenway, who had lowered his chin on his chest, glanced up at the noise, searched to regain his subject and continued: 'Found the lion on the rise of a bank among trees. Wind against us, no smell – he didn't see us. Broadside on eighty yards off. Magnificent specimen, easy target.' He thrust his bearded chin forward. 'This Englishman is so shit-scared, first he forgets to take the safety off and then he hits the lion in the flank. Beast runs off trailing blood. Guy sprays bullets in the dust, gets him once more in the guts before he disappears in a clumpa high grass and holes up there.'

Eisenway took a couple of long pulls at his Scotch. Albert took a reflective sip of his Tom Collins. There was something strangely familiar about this story.

'We wait so's he'll get sick from losin' the blood,' Eisenway went on. 'An' you know that funky bastard wants to send in beaters to bring the lion out. I told him, none of our boys is going in there with a wounded lion waiting to charge. Somebody's gonna get hurt . . . '

He looked away around the lounge again, seeming to lose interest in his story for a moment, but then he jerked his attention back to Albert and Angela.

'A lion'll make himself flat in cover you wouldn't think'd hide a rabbit,' he said. 'Somebody'd sure get hurt. And then the son-of-a-bitch says, why don't we leave him there. I nearly told him what a bastard he was. Lion's suffering, I say, besides someone else might fall on him. Guy just looks at me. Shit-scared. So I say, I'll finish him off. You don't have to get involved. Course, the guy can't take that. Has his woman along. He asks for a drink of water and I think, you lousy chicken, what you need is a coupla stiff whiskies . . .'

As if that reminded him, Eisenway finished off his second Scotch and placed his hand reassuringly around the third glass.

'So we move into the grass and almost immediately we hear this sort of coughing grunt and the grass is swishing where the lion's rushing us.'

Eisenway's head sagged forward, loosely, and his chin rested on his chest again. He stayed that way for a few seconds and Albert thought he'd gone to sleep, when suddenly he jolted up again.

'You know what that bastard does?' he demanded.

'He starts running,' Albert said.

Eisenway blinked slowly at Albert. He slipped forward on the edge of his chair, righted himself.

'You got it,' he said. 'You got it.'

'And you shot the lion,' Albert said.

'I sure did, son. I sure did. Daughter here woulda liked the bloodshed. Two quick shots, *carawong!* . . . *carawong* Bastard with half his head shot away comes crawling at me. Hell of a lion. I shoot again and he stiffens almost at my feet . . .'

Eisenway's body seemed to be stiffening as he spoke. He slipped backwards in the chair, peered through closing lids, opened his mouth as if he wanted to add a postscript and then slumped against the backrest.

Albert and Angela watched him struggling to stay conscious. They both sipped their Tom Collinses, watching.

Eisenway abruptly opened his eyes, staring intently.

'Bastard . . . shoulda slugged him . . . *carawong!*'

His eyes closed again, head slumped, righted itself, eyes opened looking around glazed, hand reached out for the Scotch, didn't make it, trembling fingers slipped away, head fell back then slumped forward and his mouth fell open to emit thick, guttural snuffling sounds.

Albert and Angela continued to sit in silence, sipping their drinks, waiting for any sign of sudden revival.

'You know,' Albert said at last, 'you can always tell a man by the way he takes his liquor.

Angela giggled.

'That's not very kind, Albert. He must have had an awful lot.'

'That's the trouble with these tough sons-a-bitches. Never know when to throw in the towel. Well, what are we going to do with him. We don't know where he lives, but we can't just leave him here.'

'We could,' Angela said. She finished her second Tom Collins and smiled woozily at Albert. 'We could go upstairs for a while and by the time we come back he'd have recovered.'

'Aren't you over-estimating? On current form we'd be back in about forty-five minutes – and he's obviously out for hours.'

'We could take a little longer, darling – or a few encores.'

'They might just throw him out into the street.'

'Not in a discreet place like this.'

'If they want to keep it discreet they might. We'd better take him up to our suite.'

'That's a bit kinky, Albert. Would you like to invite a few more people up?'

'I don't see anybody else I fancy right now.'

'He looks too heavy, anyway.'

'Stop making difficulties,' Albert said.

He stood up, holding on to the arm of the chair. Confronting the considerable bulk of the American and the hazard involved in getting him down the stairs and through the foyer to the lift, Albert suddenly recognised his own degree of inebriation. He moved carefully over to Eisenway's collapsed body and caught his arm. The snuffles accelerated unevenly. Albert heaved him forward on to the edge of the chair and the American's eyes slitted open.

'Come on, Papa,' Albert said.

He dragged the American to his feet.

'Angela, get his other arm around your shoulders,' he said.

'He might think I'm making advances and try to seduce me.'

'Yes, he's obviously on top of his form. Come on, darling, I can't hold him up much longer.'

'But Albert, how about our drinks?'

'Leave them,' Albert said. 'Who knows, maybe one of these days we'll come across some more.'

'Oh Albert, we can't leave those *delicious* drinks.'

Angela stood up and approached him unsteadily, hazel eyes, shining Christian Dior hat slewing over one eye.

'Besides,' she said, 'you might need a pick-me-up for the encores.'

'Anyway, it's not allowed,' Albert said.

'You mean to say this is the sort of hotel that limits sex by consenting adults in private?'

'No, I mean taking drinks out of the bar. Now get his other arm.'

Angela, however, wafted away, leaving Albert tottering precariously with the big American draped over him.

'Yoo-hoo!'

She made an alluring little finger-wave to the waiter, who approached rather warily, his eyes flitting from one to the other of them.

'May we take our drinks to bed with us?' Angela asked. 'I mean, may we take them to our suite?'

'Yes, Ma'am,' the waiter said. He began to gather the drinks on to a tray.

'Oh don't bother,' Angela said. She smiled seductively at him. 'It's very sweet of you, but we can manage.'

So saying, she tipped Eisenway's remaining Scotch half and half into the two remaining Tom Collinses, thrust one into Albert's free hand and slipped her arm around the American. Eisenway's head swung about, eyes opened, closed, opened.

'Wassa . . . gon' on . . . slug . . . punk,' he murmured.

'We're going for a drink,' Angela said. 'A DRINK!'

The American's eyes jerked open, rolled. His legs actually

seemed to gain some vitality and the weight eased off Albert and Angela's shoulders.

'Yeah, yeah!' he murmured. 'Liquor . . . guts.'

Watched by a worried waiter, who kept taking convulsive half steps towards them, they headed erratically across the lounge to the top of the steps, Albert and Angela clutching a drink in their free hands, holding up the semi-conscious Eisenway between them. A couple of Africans at the bar glanced in their direction with curiosity. Down in the foyer, a few tourists looked up in amusement.

The swaying trio tottered for a long moment on the top step, exercised shaky control and began the descent.

'I hope George is a respected character here,' Angela whispered with a giggle.

Albert, breathing heavily from the exertion, glanced at the lolling head and the legs which alternated between sagging steps and puppet-like flopping. His own knee gave out momentarily and he almost dropped his drink.

'Try to act naturally,' he said in an over-loud voice.

'I do hope we're not giving a bad impression,' Angela said in a fresh outburst of giggling.

'Careful,' Albert warned, as they reached the bottom step. 'Keep in close, or he slews me round.'

'We're all slewed, darling,' Angela chortled.

They began a slow, uneven trek across the foyer, staggering against the showcases and the tourists, who drew aside to let them pass. A dark-suited receptionist hurried from the desk.

'Anything wrong, sir?' he asked.

'We have no complaints at all,' Albert said loudly. 'Just going up to our suite for a drink.'

Eisenway's eyes rolled open. He lurched sideways and Angela almost fell.

'Shitscared . . .' he muttered – and his eyes closed again.

The receptionist looked alarmed, but kept his head.

'Carry on to the lift, sir,' he said quickly. 'I'll get your key.'

On the final stretch, Eisenway's legs seemed to lose their last vestige of viability and simply dragged behind him, toes scraping along the floor.

A small crowd gathered to watch them stagger and squeeze themselves into the lift. Eisenway was now completely unconscious and Angela was lost in a fit of uncontrollable giggling. Albert smiled pleasantly and noted that the liftman, clearly having learned English aplomb, acted as if this were an everyday occurrence.

'Thank you,' Albert said, bowing ceremoniously, before stumbling out into their corridor.

In the suite, Angela, giggling wildly, dropped Eisenway completely. Albert grinning, manhandled him into a chair, where he slumped in a dead heap.

'Come into the bedroom, Albert,' Angela said.

She jiggled away from him, caught her foot and thudded to the floor, laughing hysterically.

Albert removed Eisenway's shoes and arranged him a little more comfortably. He finished his drink. God, what a mixture! He grinned, did a little jig and waltzed into the bedroom.

Angela, minus clothes, leapt at him with a roar and bounced away on to the bed.

'This is a lioness, Albert,' she cried. 'Welcome to Africa.'

She rolled on to her back and slithered her bottom on the counterpane, opening her legs and growling at him.

Albert struggled out of his clothes, uttering a roar himself.

'This is a lion,' he said. 'Welcome to . . . '

'Albert, how did you know that George's Englishman ran away and George shot the lion. *I* thought the Englishman was going to overcome his fear at the last minute and fight the lion barehanded.'

'Easy,' Albert explained, climbing on to the bed and squirming in towards Angela's warmth. 'It's Hemingway's *The short happy life of Francis Macomber*. Eisenway pinched the entire incident.

'I must say, I can't wait to hear about his experiences in the Spanish civil war.'

Chapter Five

THE SUN blazed down from a sky stencilled with tiny wisps of cloud and sparkled on the ice in the drinks.

Albert, Angela and Eisenway were at it again. Same drinks, different locale.

The terrace of the Norfolk Hotel overlooked the beds of bougainvillea along Government Road. Across the street the elegant stone masses of the University buildings stood out, clean and bright and colourful ornamental gardens bloomed. Beyond them, was the tree-clad rise of the land leading out of Nairobi and further still, the hazy mass of the Ngong Hills. Occasionally a car passed along the road and people came and went among the University departments, but the atmosphere was one of tranquillity and relaxation.

The Norfolk with its old colonial-style leisureliness had been singled out by Eisenway for this morning's hairs of the dog because he wanted to avoid the bars in the very centre of the city in case he met Everett-Smithers again.

'I'm just not sure I could restrain myself a second time,' he explained. 'I might kill the son-of-a-bitch.'

Whether Eisenway had regained consciousness any time before this morning, Albert was unaware. He and Angela had missed lunch, dinner and breakfast as a cumulative result of too much drink and other excesses. When they had emerged mid-morning from the bedroom, the American was exactly as Albert had placed him the day before, except that his eyes were open and he was clearly trying to figure out where he was and why.

They had snacks in the room and it soon became apparent that Eisenway retained only a censored version of the previous day's events.

'Meant to show you the city,' he said, sipping coffee.

'Shouldn't have come back here for that nap. Dozed off longer than I meant. Pretty tired from the safari, you know.'

'That's perfectly all right,' Angela said. 'We managed to fill in the time.'

'Okay,' Eisenway said. 'Today we'll go back to my place. You can meet the Memsahib, see something of the bits and pieces I've got together for Julius Jack.'

But when they were ready to leave, Eisenway seemed in no hurry to take them anywhere except to the nearest place they could get a drink. They had tumbled into his Land Rover under the impression they were to be given a tour of the city. Instead, the American had driven about a quarter of a mile through the bustling streets to the Norfolk on the Western outskirts.

'I like this place,' Eisenway said. 'Old colonial style.' He waved his hand to the distantly dominating height of the Nairobi Hilton. 'None of that boxed-in skyscraper business.'

It was true the hotel was very charming with its white-washed walls, roofshades over the tables, bougainvillaea, old-fashioned service. There was even an aviary in its grounds. But Albert and Angela had imbibed enough liquor the day before to last them a couple of weeks.

'Why don't we go for a spin?' Angela suggested. 'We could look for lions in the Game Park.'

'Bad day for lions,' Eisenway said. 'Too humid. Don't worry, we got plenty of time to see the lions – and all the rest. Leopard, water-buck, hartebeest, impala, gazelle, giraffe, kudu, zebra, hippo, cheetah, buffalo, rhino, wild dog, jackal, hyena – no end to it. Great country. Gets you. Wouldn't live anywhere else.'

He finished his first Scotch of the day and took a deep breath.

'Yeah, it's a man's country all right,' he said. 'Man had to mould it with his strength, stand on his own against it. Still does.'

'Won't your wife wonder what happened to you?' Angela asked.

Eisenway looked at her.

'What happened to me? Why, my face missing?'

'No, I mean the fact she hasn't seen you since yesterday morning.'

'Daughter – hey waiter, same again – you got a lot to learn. This is a man's country and the woman doesn't question that. She does what she's told. I don't mean he tells her go jump in that crocodile pool and she does it, just she knows it's her man's toughness counts in the end against all the odds she's gonna find here.'

'I don't see how that would stop her wondering why he was missing all night,' Angela said.

The waiter brought new drinks. Albert forked up for them, resolving that this was his last before the next meal. If Eisenway wanted to make a fool of himself in every hotel in Nairobi, that was his affair. Albert was an itinerant alien, after all. He didn't want to be deported.

'Aw – night's just a period of time like a day,' Eisenway said. 'Moon instead of sun. Time doesn't mean that much in a country like this. You've been here a while you get to understand that.'

He started to guzzle through his second Scotch.

'Same in any country, really,' he went on. 'Real woman accepts her man. Question doesn't arise. Woman's good, she knows she'll keep her man. Keep his respect, the way she respects him. Spanish women very wise that way. I remember this girl in Saragossa. During the civil war . . . '.

'Oh!' Angela exclaimed. 'I can't bear it!'

'Yeah,' Eisenway said. 'Pretty tough time, I'll admit. Franco's men did terrible things to the people. Sometimes we were fighting one to five. Guns, knives. Fists.'

Angela began to laugh. She dropped her face in her hands, helplessly. Albert regarded her seriously. She needed to be helped out of this.

'Her father was in the civil war,' he said. 'You must have known him: Colonel Andrew Carter, known as "Carthorse" on account of his great size and his fur boots that looked like fetlocks. He lost his life around Saragossa. Any mention of the civil war makes her hysterical. She laughs as an alternative to crying. Sometimes as a prelude.'

'I remember him, of course,' Eisenway said. He shook his

head sadly. 'He was a good guy. Yeah – a great guy.'

Angela appeared to have stopped laughing, but she kept her face in her hands. Eisenway gripped her forearm gently, reassuringly.

'You're a fine girl,' he said. 'A lovely girl. Your father would be as proud of you as you must be of him.'

Angela peeked reproachfully at Albert through her fingers. She was not at all sure her father's name should be used this way, even to save her from embarrassment. But Albert, having begun, was now in full cry.

'You know, apart from his general grasp of strategy, old Carthorse was a great man for rooting out small entrenched pockets of resistance,' he said. 'Boomerang expert, you know. He could throw his boomerang where nobody could shoot a bullet. Send it behind trees, knolls, buildings. Fantastically accurate. The enemy used to think they were being attacked from behind. Completely unnerved them.'

Eisenway listened with wrapt attention.

'A boomerang!' he muttered. 'Yeah – why not?'

'He was actually training a battalion of boomerang throwers when he was killed,' Albert said. 'He figured they would have been invincible in small operations on difficult terrain. Whole thing fell through because nobody else was capable of teaching the art.'

'Yeah – great idea,' Eisenway enthused. 'I guess you could bring down a bushbuck with a boomerang if you knew how to handle it.'

'Bring down a lion – an elephant,' Albert assured him. 'Old Carthorse once brought down a helicopter. Boomerang went straight through the windscreen, practically sliced the pilot's head off. When they lost the Colonel, there was a movement to bring an aboriginal from Australia. But there weren't the men to spare to organise the acquisition. It was aboriginal and boomerangs, or Soviet tanks. The tank lobby won.'

'No imagination,' Eisenway said. 'They could have . . . '

'Will you please drop the subject,' Angela cut in.

'Carthorse deserved a medal,' Albert said.

'Somebody should raise it with the government in exile,' Eisenway said.

'I thought perhaps you might.'

'Well, I wouldn't say I'm quite the right guy . . . I mean, better coming from a Spaniard. I could put a word . . . '

'Drop it!' Angela yelled.

They both stared at her.

Albert said: 'The memory of her father always disturbs her.'

'Oh sure, daughter,' Eisenway said. 'We oughta know better. Let's get you another drink. Hey waiter – three more of the same.'

'Do you always drink this much, George?' Angela asked.

'Well, I grew up in a hard school. Doesn't seem so much to me.'

'Isn't that Everett-Smithers?' Albert said.

'Where?' Eisenway snapped. 'Where's Everett-Smithers?'

'He was coming along this way,' Albert said. 'Popped into that building.'

'That's the University library,' Eisenway said. 'What's he up to. Anyway, don't worry, I promise I won't hurt the son-of-a-bitch. I guess we'd better finish this liquor and go. The memsahib'll be wondering what happened to me.'

Eisenway gulped down his Scotch, glanced at their unfinished drinks and stood up.

'I'll go bring the buggy along,' he said. 'Take your time.'

He strode off towards the Land Rover parked a little way back on the opposite side of the road.

'How was that for rapid alcohol cure?' Albert said.

'Did you really see that man Everett-Smithers?' Angela asked.

'Who knows? It may have been him.'

'Albert, I don't like you referring to my father as if he were dead. It gives me a funny feeling. And I object to you calling him a carthorse.'

'Nothing wrong with carthorses. Very noble breed. A dying one, of course. But you shouldn't be so supersititious.'

'Do you think George was really in the Spanish civil war?'

'Well, he knew about your father, didn't he.'

'But daddy wasn't . . . Albert, you are impossible!'

'I am, therefore I am not impossible,' Albert said.

Angela pulled a face at him.

'You know, sometimes I feel really sorry for women, having to put up with men.'

Albert slipped an arm around her and squeezed her breast.

'Oh don't do that, Albert. God, I don't know what's coming over me. Must be something to do with the heat.'

Eisenway's Land Rover appeared opposite the terrace. He waved and when they were slow to move began to beckon agitatedly.

'I think he must be feeling the same way,' Angela said. 'Can't wait to get home to his little woman.'

'Butch guys like him can never get enough of it,' Albert said.

They finished their drinks and strolled from the terrace. Eisenway, sitting at the wheel of the Land Rover, glanced back along the road.

'Let's get moving,' he said.

He slipped the car into gear and it juddered without moving. He revved a little, but nothing happened.

'What the hell?' Eisenway snapped in exasperation. He stared anxiously at the dashboard, seeking inspiration. He revved again.

'Something wrong somewhere,' he said.

'You've got the handbrake on,' Albert said.

Eisenway eased off the handbrake.

'Musta got stuck,' he said. 'Mechanism's faulty.'

The vehicle jerked forward nearly hurling Albert and Angela from their seats. It steadied, jerked again, steadied again.

'Preparing you for the sort of terrain you'll find in the bush,' Eisenway said. 'Very tricky. Gotta keep your head at all times.'

A car hooted furiously as the Land Rover swerved out to the crown of the road. Eisenway swung the vehicle back on a straight course.

'Goddam Africans,' he growled. 'Used to driving bullock carts.'

Albert and Angela sat in frozen postures while the Land Rover made erratic headway through the streets and began to climb out of the city to the west.

'Do we have very far to go?' Angela inquired nervously.

'Almost there,' Eisenway said. 'We're up on the brow of the hill. Gotta place out in the bush, too, for weekends.'

The vehicle accelerated towards a group of African children crossing the road, braked and swerved as they ran for safety.

'Get the hell off the road!' Eisenway yelled. 'Little bastards. Think it's a playground.'

Angela's fingers dug hard into Albert's bicep; Albert's muscles were tense all over.

Eisenway suddenly pulled off the tree-lined road into a short drive through a screen of dwarf palms and giant Australian rain trees, whose slender branches seemed to drip their leaves down to the ground. Through the foliage the whitewashed walls of a long, two-storey house came into view, its facade mottled with expanses of pink and purple bougainvillaea. The building was partly surrounded by a plantation of developing fir trees and the shaded patio at one corner was fringed by two jacarandas, whose fallen blue flowers sprinkled the paving.

'How delightful,' Angela cried, her enthusiasm reinforced by relief at the end of the journey.

On the patio some people were sitting on cane chairs, with drinks and sandwiches on a marble-topped table. They looked up as Eisenway came to a halt in front of the house and a small, curvaceous blonde woman of indeterminate age, wearing a brief and psychedelically-coloured bikini, rose and came to meet them. She was very brown and healthy-looking and exuded an air of restless and rather overpowering determination.

'Hello Poor Old Mama,' Eisenway said. 'How's everything?'

'Where the hell were you?' she said good-humouredly.

'I'm sorry, Mama, I just . . .'

'So these are our guests,' she cut in, directing a dazzling smile at Albert and Angela. 'Welcome. I'm Gloria Eisenway.

Come and have a drink.'

She led them on to the patio out of the sun, swinging her curves like a hula-hula dancer. Albert registered approval. Eisenway registered uncertainty.

Her two companions rose from their chairs. One was a pear-shaped, middle-aged Englishman with a flabby, red and sweating face partially obscured by a floppy white hat that might have been a terribly poor cousin of Angela's Christian Dior. The other was a young African with a round, but somehow sinister face, whose lower part was contained in a circle of small black beard and moustache and whose upper part was dominated by the smaller circles of dark-tinted sun glasses. He was wearing sandals and a highly-coloured and embroidered traditional robe.

'This is Miss Angela Carter, the model,' Gloria Eisenway said, 'and this is Mr Albert Divine, the art dealer. May I present Mr Joseph Mbula, who is a very fine artist and Mr Aubrey Fanshawe – he's in the art business, too, Mr Divine.'

They sat down around the table and George Eisenway murmured: 'I'm sorry we didn't show earlier, Poor Old Mama. We just . . . '

But Gloria Eisenway, whose dazzling concentration was completely on the newcomers, didn't seem to hear him. In fact, it soon became apparent that she had a slightly disconcerting habit of not always paying full attention to what other people said, preferring to follow her own energetic line of thought.

'I sure hope George has remained sober enough to show you around a little,' she said. 'If not, we can make up for that in the next few days. It's really very nice to have some attractive new visitors.'

Eisenway's voice made itself diffidently heard as a sort of minor accompaniment to his wife's. He was addressing Aubrey Fanshawe and Joseph Mbula.

'I guess the Memsahib's mad at me . . . '

'We heard so much about you from cousin Julius,' Gloria Eisenway said.

'You gotta expect that sort of thing from a woman now and then . . . ' Eisenway muttered.

'And how is dear Julius – still frantically searching for an heir?' Gloria Eisenway asked. 'Oh George – will you do the drinks please.'

Eisenway moved off and Angela said; 'Well, we don't really know Mr Freedman very well . . . '

'He's still searching,' Albert said.

Gloria Eisenway, brushed a blonde curl back from her sharp, blue eyes.

'The poor soul,' she said. 'But then I guess he has some compensation screwing all those girls.'

She gave a throaty little laugh and Joseph Mbula poked his bearded face forward as if awakened from a dream.

'Pardon? What you say?' he demanded in a deep, rather threatening voice.

Gloria Eisenway repeated her throaty laugh.

'If ever Julius needs a stunt man, Joseph's his boy,' she said.

'What girls are screwing?' Joseph Mbula asked, looking straight at Angela. It was clear he thought she had somehow been put on offer.

'Not screwing,' Gloria Eisenway corrected. 'Being screwed.'

Aubrey Fanshawe spoke in a resonant, patrician voice with just a trace of a lisp. He pronounced his 'r's' like 'w's'.

'Lots of girls think *they* do the scwewing nowadays,' he said. 'Vewy agwessive. Women's libewation and all that.' His three chins wobbled and he became a little breathless towards the end of the comment, as if the effort were strenuous.

Eisenway came to the table with fresh glasses and poured drinks for everyone.

'Are you mad at me, Memsahib?' he asked.

'Mad at you?' Gloria Eisenway said. 'Not too much soda, George. He's always trying to dilute my drinks, you know. I think he believes it atones for his own excess.'

'Mama . . . '

'What girls are being screwed?' Joseph Mbula demanded, still staring at Angela, who involuntarily drew the flaps of her wrapover skirt together.

'English girls you don't know,' Gloria Eisenway said, patting his knee. 'When you go to London we'll have Julius introduce you . . . Maybe he'll end up with a black heir.' She gave a throaty chuckle.

'Swinging London!' Joseph Mbula suddenly barked at Angela. The lines around his jaw creased into a smile below the dark glasses, small white teeth came slowly into view.

By Christ, Albert thought, we've copped a right old lot here. He raised his glass quickly.

'Here's to Ould Daddah,' he said.

'If you're referring to George,' Gloria Eisenway said, 'it's actually Papa he likes to be called.'

'I'm toasting President Ould Daddah of Mauritania,' Albert said solemnly.

Gloria Eisenway chuckled and raised her glass.

'And I'm toasting Madame Old Mama, who keeps the brothels in Saigon,' she said.

'No African would like to hear you say that, Mrs Eisenway,' Albert said. 'President Ould Daddah is a respected leader.'

'Ould Daddah,' Joseph Mbula said threateningly, raising his glass.

'Oh dear – do you mean to say he's an actual person?' Gloria Eisenway said. 'I hope I haven't offended you Joseph.'

'Ould Daddah,' Albert said, chinking glasses with Joseph. 'Ould Daddah.'

There was an uncertain silence. Albert surveyed the company with satisfaction. He tried to inject a little normality into the conversation.

'Tell me about your painting, Mr Mbula.'

Joseph Mbula gazed at him, unseen and for all Albert knew, unseeing, behind the dark glasses. The seconds ticked by. Albert, unsure whether Joseph did not consider him a worthy recipient of his ideals or simply hadn't understood the question, opened his mouth to repeat it.

'Cunt . . . I paint cunt,' Joseph Mbula said.

'You paint . . .?' Albert glanced quickly at the rest of the company for confirmation that his ears had deceived him.

'Cunt . . . you know . . . ' Joseph motioned vaguely towards the point where Angela's skirt flaps had fallen apart again, revealing a long length of thigh.

Aubrey Fanshawe interjected.

'It's symbolic,' he said. 'Joseph is the vewy last person to talk about his work. But you know he is the spearpoint of a new, indigenous Negwo-Afwican culture.'

'Really?' Albert looked at Joseph, whose dark lenses stared back at him.

'Yes, he is,' Aubrey Fanshawe continued. 'You know, Mr Divine, that Afwican art thwough the ages has been intimately bound up with Afwican weligion and witual. Colonialism has been the diswuptive force, interfewing with twibal wituals for mowality's sake, widiculing ancestor worship, pwoducing in the Afwican a psychological disintegwation which has wesulted in turn in a decline in the arts . . . ' He paused, breathlessly, put one pudgy hand on his stomach and with the other removed his hat to fan himself. He glanced at Joseph, sitting impassively with his lenses directed at Angela.

'I am taking the vewy words out of Joseph's mouth,' Aubrey Fanshawe continued. 'He has perceived this with a new clawity. He knows that the wesult of this colonial bludgeoning was that Afwicans either faced persecution or embwaced the colonialist's concepts, including his view of art . . . ' He paused again and moved his hand up his bulging stomach to his narrow chest. 'In this colonial pewiod, Afwican art, in its essentially weligious sense, died and Afwican artists began to pwoduce for the Euwopean market just what that market wanted and was accustomed to . . . Now, Joseph will cowect me if I'm wong, but with the pwocess of decolonisation, there has begun an Afwican spiwitual wenaissance which is the essential pwewequisite of its artistic counterpart. It is in part a weturn to the ancient twaditions: the cult of ancestor worship, wevewence for the dead, hospitality and so on . . . '

He replaced his hat, took a gulp of his drink, pulled a large, white handkerchief from his trouser pocket and mopped his face.

'Joseph Mbula declares,' he intoned, 'that it is essential for the Afwican artist to wecweate that vital link with his twaditions and achieve a psychological webirth, asserting himself against the adversities which have injured him in the colonial past . . . '

At the mention of his name, Joseph had raised his gaze from Angela's thighs and fixed his lenses on Aubrey Fanshawe. Albert took advantage of another breathless pause to break in.

'This is all very interesting,' he said, 'but I don't quite see what it has to do with . . . er . . . '

'Cunt,' Joseph said. His facial lines indicated a smile again. He looked back at Angela and his small white teeth slowly appeared.

'Ah well now . . . ' Aubrey Fanshawe's small hot eyes glowed with satisfaction as if the achievement he was about to describe were his own. 'This is where Joseph Mbula's unique vision comes in. This is where his supweme talent, insight and owiginality come into their own . . . I'm sure you are well aware, Mr Divine, that the discovewies of palaeontologists indicate that mankind was pwobably born in East Afwica. We have Zinjanthwopus dating back two million years and, of course, Pwoconsul going back an incwedible twenty-five million. The work of Dr Louis Leakey is well known and further evidence is still being bwought to light.'

Gloria Eisenway at this point motioned to the glasses and George Eisenway dutifully refilled them.

'Now, it is this fact that Joseph Mbula takes as his centwal, even obsessive, theme,' Aubrey Fanshawe said. 'The birth of mankind here in Afwica. One mankind undivided by any factors of which we are aware. A state mankind has not known since and is awaiting in a new golden age.'

Aubrey Fanshawe came to a triumphant halt. He removed his hat once more and fanned himself, breathing heavily. Joseph Mbula, seemingly unimpressed by this eulogy, or, perhaps taking it for granted, continued to gaze at Angela.

'It sounds very interesting,' Albert said. 'I'd like to see

your work some time, Mr Mbula.'

'I'm quite sure this wemarkable talent is going to be wecognised thwoughout the world before vewy long, before vewy long at all,' Aubrey Fanshawe said. 'As a dealer you would do well to consider that, Mr Divine.'

'What's your involvement, Mr Fanshawe?' Albert asked.

'I run a gallewy, here. Just a sideline. I'm in the import-export business.'

'How does your painting go down here, Mr Mbula?' Albert asked.

'Oh you know how it is, Mr Divine,' Aubrey Fanshawe said. 'A pwophet's without honour in his own countwy. Not much judgement here, you know. Vewy, vewy conservative. Couldn't take Joseph's modern themes and pwesentation. We don't twy to sell here.'

'It's a shame,' Gloria Eisenway said. 'Joseph's a very fine painter.'

'A superlative painter,' Aubrey Fanshawe said fervently.

Joseph Mbula looked from one to the other slowly until his lenses were directed back at Angela.

'I want to paint you,' he said gravely.

'Oh, that's very sweet of you,' Angela said. 'But I'm not an artist's model, you know. I model clothes for magazines.'

'Yes. You model for me.'

'Joseph will be very offended if you refuse,' Gloria Eisenway said.

'Oh but I couldn't,' Angela protested. 'I mean, it's not me – and besides, I wouldn't have time.'

'When a gweat artist seeks your help you should make time.' Aubrey Fanshawe said. 'Besides it's a chance for immortality.'

'Really,' Angela said, 'it's just not in my line.'

Joseph Mbula leaned towards her.

'Racist?' he demanded.

'Oh no!' Angela cried. 'How could you think such a thing! It's just that I have other things to do.'

Joseph Mbula stood up.

'Enoch Powell!' he spat. 'Lester Maddox!'

Angela stared helplessly at Albert, looking for support.

'She's really just one of those fair weather white liberals,' Albert said.

'Oh Albert!' Angela exclaimed. 'All right Mr Mbula, I'll model for you – as long as it doesn't take too long. I mean, this is my first visit to Africa and there's so much I want to see.'

'Good, good,' Joseph Mbula said gravely. He sat down and his facial lines indicated a smile, teeth slowly appeared. 'Much to see,' he added.

'You won't wegwet it, Miss Carter,' Aubrey Fanshawe said. 'It means you will go down to postewity.'

'Good thing for a girl to do,' George Eisenway said thickly. 'Good woman'll help a man create.'

He poured himself another Scotch. Albert figured that if his current rate of imbibing was typical he should have died years ago. Maybe the man *was* tough.

'George creates, you know,' Gloria Eisenway said with a throaty chuckle. 'Scenes, problems. George, can you spare us a drop of that liquor before it all goes?'

Eisenway clambered to his feet and topped up their glasses, slopping some of the liquor over the marble top of the table, for which he apologised to his wife.

'Poor Old Mama,' he said to the company. 'She's a good woman, a fine woman. We have good times. We have very good times, don't we P.O.M.'

'Less soda, George,' Gloria Eisenway said.

'Yeah, it's a good life,' Eisenway persisted. 'Good times, not so good times. But it's a good life. Say, P.O.M., can you loan me some spare cash, I think we're running outa liquor.'

There was a moment's silence in which Aubrey Fanshawe got to his feet.

'I think Joseph and I ought to be . . . '

'George, you've already overspent your allowance,' Gloria Eisenway said. 'But you don't have to worry about the liquor, I got in a fresh supply today.'

She directed a dazzling smile on Albert and Angela.

'Do drink up and have another,' she urged. 'I like to see people happy and drinking.'

There was a sudden snuffle from George Eisenway, who

had flopped back in his chair and closed his eyes, but his wife didn't seem to notice.

'Gloria, my dear,' Aubrey Fanshawe repeated, 'Joseph and I must be going. We have some business to work out.'

'Of course you must, Aubrey. It was delightful to see you. And you Joseph. It's so unusual to find an artist who is so articulate.'

Joseph Mbula also rose to his feet, without deigning to reply. He looked at Angela.

'Tomorrow,' he said.

'I'll pick you up at your hotel about eleven a.m., if that's suitable,' Aubrey Fanshawe said.

Angela found she was having to concentrate very hard against the muzziness induced by the cumulative effect of so much drinking. The modelling. Immortality.

'All right,' she said.

Joseph Mbula suddenly pointed a long, thin finger at her.

'You wear see-through dress in London?'

Angela tried to take in the meaning of the unexpected question.

'Why no,' she said. 'Well, as a matter of fact I did once wear a see-through blouse in the King's Road.'

The African's lenses held her. Eisenway suddenly began to snore and Aubrey Fanshawe said: 'Weady, Joseph?'

The African half turned to leave, his lenses still on Angela. The lines around his moustache deepened into the slight smile, teeth showed.

'London is a great city,' he said. 'Swinging London!'

Chapter Six

LEFT ALONE with Albert and Angela, Gloria Eisenway smiled at them dazzlingly.

'I *am* glad to see you,' she said. 'I'm sure you'll love Africa. It's poetry, you know; sheer poetry.'

She clapped her hands and a couple of bare-footed Africans appeared as if by magic.

'Take the Bwana and put him in his room, please, Henry,' she said to one of them. 'And then bring some more drink out here, *pesi sana*.'

'*Diyo, Memsahib*,' the African said.

They gently picked up the unconscious body of George Eisenway and carried him, slung like a hammock between them, into the house.

'I have to show off my little bit of Swahili,' Gloria Eisenway said with her throaty chuckle. 'George's so helpless we'd be lost if I didn't know a few words.'

Angela giggled and Albert glanced curiously at her.

'Albert knows some Swahili,' she said. 'He has a Swahili girl friend on the sly.'

'Does he really?' Gloria Eisenway looked with renewed interest at Albert. 'You must learn some interesting phrases.'

'Angela's not renowned for her accuracy when she's tiddly,' Albert said.

'Ah, George has been getting you into bad habits,' Gloria Eisenway said. 'He drinks and he has no stomach for liquor, you know.'

'Maybe his liver lets him down,' Albert suggested politely. 'He was telling us about his consumption in Paris.'

'Paris?' Gloria Eisenway said. 'He's never been to Paris. Never been out of Vermont before he came here.'

'Wasn't he in Spain ever?'

She looked mystified.

'What would he be doing in Spain? Liquor's just as strong in Vermont, you know.'

'But wasn't he in Europe for the war?'

'George? He's too clever for that. Convinced them his eyesight was so bad he needed a white stick.'

'But he knew my father in the Spanish civil war,' Angela protested. She hiccuped and put her hand to her mouth with a little giggle.

'Oh he knows an awful lot of people,' Gloria Eisenway said, 'I wouldn't be surprised at him knowing anyone.'

'But if he knew my father . . . ' Angela began. She seemed to lose the thread and her attention was in any case distracted by the return of Henry with a whole tray of bottles and a bucket of ice.

'*Mzuri*, Henry – *asante*,' Gloria Eisenway said. She gave a throaty chuckle for no immediately apparent reason and mixed them all fresh drinks.

'They're all a bit funny here, you know,' she said conspiratorially. 'I think it has to do with the sun – and being cut off. The Europeans get sort of incestuous.'

'That was what George was saying,' Angela said, between giggles. 'Hello son . . . hello daughter . . . ' She collapsed with silent mirth.

Albert watched her fast sinking from the weight of the alcohol. He had a flashing image of all those underprivileged shirtless ones taking advantage of her post-liquor helplessness.

'That's not to say the Africans aren't funny, too,' Gloria Eisenway said. 'But one has to make special allowances for them on account of their history. Joseph's ancestors would have boiled us in oil, you know.'

'I dare say Joseph would, too,' Albert said.

'Yes, he's such a nice boy. I do hope his proconsuls do well.'

'I was frightened of his . . . proconsuls . . . ' Angela said slowly and carefully. 'He never took them . . . off me . . . ' She made circles of her thumbs and forefingers and put them over her eyes, gazing at Albert. She moved them to and fro and finally joined them in a telescope. She began to giggle again, uproariously and nearly fell off her chair.

'Angela,' Gloria Eisenway said. 'I may call you Angela, may I? Maybe you'd like to have a siesta. Most people do in the afternoon heat. And then we can all have a drink before dinner around seven.'

Angela shook her head slowly and very fully from side to side.

'No,' she said, very definitely. 'I need a siesta.'

'You sure do, honey. I'll show you to a bedroom.'

'I mean . . . I mean I *don't* need a siesta,' Angela said. 'They have siestas in Spain.'

As if to prove her point, Angela raised her glass and drained it. Her flushed face was suffused with a fresh onrush of colour.

'They sure know what they're doing,' Gloria Eisenway said. 'Come on dear – you don't want to miss your first African night.'

She stood up and Angela automatically followed her example.

'Think I'll lie down a moment,' Angela said. 'Bit hot in here.'

Gloria Eisenway linked arms with her and led her unprotesting into the cool of the house beyond the patio. Albert watched them go: the clothed jiggle versus the bikini cleavage. He reflected that he'd be no good at all as a judge in a Miss Sexy Figure contest.

Some minutes later Gloria Eisenway reappeared. She dazzled him with her smile.

'Dead to the world,' she said. 'Just like George. How long are you going to last?'

'I'm all right for at least another thirty seconds.'

'That makes conversation difficult. I can't begin a sentence sure you'll hear the end of it.'

'It's okay if you don't use 300-word ones,' Albert said. 'Try short, punchy ones.'

'Angela's a very beautiful girl.'

'Right,' Albert said. 'Short, snappy, serviceable – a perfect organ.'

'Really? She didn't seem short and snappy to me. I can see she's probably *very* serviceable and if you say she has a perfect organ . . . '

'I mean the sentence, not Angela.'

Gloria Eisenway gave her throaty chuckle and studied him over her glass.

'I thought you were being rather clinical,' she said. 'What I meant was how fortunate for you. With a girl like that you need never look at another woman.'

'Oh I don't know,' Albert said. 'You don't avoid looking at Kilimanjaro just because Mount Kenya's there, do you?'

Gloria Eisenway chuckled again.

'What a very clever parallel,' she said. 'Of course, she's very fortunate, too. That is, assuming in addition to your looks you're very serviceable and have a perfect organ.'

Her eyes twinkled at him.

'You mustn't mind me,' she said. 'We develop very sexual senses of humour out here. It's being so close to nature. I mean, the way the baboons copulate all around you . . .! Not to mention the buffalo . . .

'It must be rather off-putting,' Albert said.

'As a matter of fact, it can be quite the opposite. I mean, some of those male baboons . . . Phew!' She raised her eyebrows. 'You wouldn't believe the notes I've taken for my book.'

'You're writing a book?'

'Several.'

'What sort of books?'

'Science books.'

'Really!' Albert hadn't expected this.

'They're sort of textbooks.'

'So you're a qualified scientist?'

'Yes – highly qualified in my subject.'

'Is that general science, or something specialised?'

'There are both general and specialised aspects.'

Albert's mind boggled at such qualifications.

'Don't tell me – space travel,' he said.

'No.'

'Of course – animal behaviour.'

'No.'

'Monkey gland and its effect on the nervous system.'

'No.'

'I give up.'

'Sex.'

She gave him a slow, glowing smile, very different from her fast dazzling one. Albert smiled back, not sure if she was having him on.

'Actually I've only written one so far and it hasn't been published yet. But the publishers are certain it's going to be a best-seller. They want a whole series. The first one's called, "Getting It Up" and sub-titled, "The Modern Girl's Guide to Enslaving Men Through Bed". I'm working on the second right now. It's called "Getting It Up in Africa" and it deals with everything to do with sex on the continent. The publisher reckons the market will take at least half a dozen "Getting It Up" books. We'll cover all the major areas of the world. And then there could be one on animals – I suppose you guessed partly right. And of course if space travel ever does lead to discovery of life on another planet . . . '

'But . . . but how do you research these books?' Albert asked.

'I find whatever I can of what's been written already. And then I do my own research. In depth and in breadth. Vertically and horizontally, as it were.'

Albert's eyes rested on the psychedelic bulging of her breasts. He tried to figure out exactly how this research would be programmed. But the complexities escaped him.

'The space programme must hold certain hazards for you,' he suggested. 'I mean, how would you cope with "Getting It Up on Pluto" or "Getting It Up on the Moons of Alpha Centauri"?'

'Well,' Gloria Eisenway said seriously. 'By that time I'd have probably sold the copyright for a huge sum and someone else could carry on where I'd left off.'

'Just as well I should imagine,' Albert said. 'You'd have reached satiation point.'

'Never.'

'You mean you don't think these books would all begin to sound the same?'

'Albert, you don't imagine a Masai warrior makes love just like a bank clerk in Detroit or an Indian fakir, do you?'

'I'd never thought about it,' Albert admitted.

She gave him the glowing smile.

'Well I have,' she said. 'And as for those little green men around Alpha Centauri . . . '

'Well, if you say so,' Albert said.

Gloria Eisenway stood up with her drink.

'How'd you like to see the promotion material?' she said.

'Okay,' Albert said, without moving.

'Well it's in the study. Pour yourself another drink and we'll go look at it.'

Albert did as he was told, vaguely figuring that he always did what managerial women told him.

He followed her from the patio, hypnotised by the psychedelic cavortings of the lower section of her posterior. Not to mention the plain brown cavortings of the upper. You could follow that cleavage right down through the material. Surely an Indian fakir would have the same reaction as a Detroit bank clerk or a little green man. How could they . . . Albert scuffed his foot on a raffia mat and stumbled against a chair. Furniture was out to get him, as usual. Gloria Eisenway turned and gave him a dazzling-glowing smile.

'Careful,' she said. 'It's been a long thirty seconds.'

Albert found he couldn't quite figure out that reference – although it did have a faintly familiar ring.

She led him through rooms full of cane furniture, potted flowers and hunting trophies to a small study whose windows looked out on the fir trees at the back of the house. She closed the door behind them and locked it. She caught Albert's glance and chuckled.

'I always lock the door,' she said. 'The servants are so nosey. They're always disturbing me when I'm working. "Tea Memsahib? Wataka chai, Memsahib? Whisky Memsahib?" They just want to see what's going on.'

Albert sympathised with that. If there was one thing he couldn't take it'd be having strange servants in the house at all. He sat down heavily in a cane chair, which rocked backwards precariously.

'How do you like my den?' Gloria Eisenway asked, pulling papers from a desk drawer. 'I do quite a bit of research here.'

The room was very simply comfortable. Apart from the desk and chairs there were bookshelves all around, a few lamps, raffia matting and several thick leopard skin rugs.

She placed a whole file of material on the desk and began to spread out its contents next to her portable typewriter.

'This is just the small stuff – magazine advertising,' she said. 'They're going to blow up some of it and make posters for the subway stations, Times Square and so on.'

Albert stood up rather unsteadily and focused on the display.

'There'll be a riot,' he murmured.

The full colour layouts showed Gloria Eisenway lying naked in profile on an enormous bed. She was on her back, her arms were outstretched, her legs slightly raised and apart and her lips open. She was clearly welcoming some off-the-page lover into intimate communion. In bold black lettering above were the words: 'GETTING IT UP' and below, a bold black text read: 'Kinsey and all the others pale into insignificance beside this bombshell. GLORIA EISENWAY pictured above in typical pose has produced the definitive sex work. This is research from the inside. After reading this book, no woman need ever be alone in bed, no man would ever want to be.'

Albert read it very slowly because his alcohol-soaked mind couldn't seem to concentrate on more than one word at a time. Then he studied the picture at great length, trying to figure out what Gloria Eisenway did in bed that was so special. She had a great body. And her face was not at all bad either. But this was doubtless true of many millions of women who would not make Kinsey pale into insignificance.

Gloria Eisenway was studying him.

'Like it?' she said. 'Do you think it'll sell the book?'

'This is going up in Times Square?'

'Giant size – and all over America.'

'Just as long as you make sure you're still out of the country when it happens.'

Gloria Eisenway chuckled.

'That's the kind of reaction my publishers would expect,' she said.

'And what does George think about it all?'

'George?' Gloria Eisenway was mystified. 'What's it got to do with George.?'

'Well, I can't very well answer that,' Albert said. 'I thought he might have played a small part. And that he might have some objections.'

She gave her throaty chuckle and rested her hand lightly on Albert's forearm.

'His part's so small he daren't have any objections,' she said.

Albert felt a little out of his depth. He took a long, slow thoughtful draught of his Tom Collins. Words like research, Kinsey, bed, enslaving and getting it up whirled in his head.

'What I don't understand,' he said carefully, 'is how you I mean one – can "enslave" a man in bed more than other women do. I mean, it's an act between two people, isn't it? Well, occasionally more, perhaps. And there are only so many things you – I mean one – can do.'

'Ah yes, Albert. But it's how I do – I mean one does – them that counts. One has to make use of all the resources at one's disposal.'

Albert considered this. He could feel himself getting into the argumentative mood which heralded a certain stage of inebriation.

'It seems to me,' he said pontifically, 'that what one does, one does naturally, without having to learn it from a book.'

Gloria Eisenway's fingers left his forearm and tapped him gently on the back of his hand.

'But Albert,' she said, 'how many people are natural boxers or hair stylists or tennis players – anything you like to think of. Admittedly they might start with the advantage of a natural aggression, a delicate snip, a combative temperament – and not everybody does – but that's nothing to the heights they can scale if they learn techniques and marry them to their natural abilities. Think about that, honey.'

Albert wrestled with this thought. God it was getting hot in the room.

'But when two people have strong feelings for each other,' he said, measuring each word very carefully, 'they don't need other people to tell them how to show it. It just wells out of them.'

Gloria Eisenway lightly, and as if absently, traced a vein on the back of his hand.

'I'm not saying it doesn't, honey,' she said. 'Sure, if you hate someone and you desperately want to kill him the feeling just wells out of you, too. But you won't automatically succeed, will you? Not unless you know how to do it. Why do you think they train spies? Why do assassins learn to shoot straight?'

Albert pulled a handkerchief from the pocket of his drill trousers and wiped his glistening brow. Gloria Eisenway smilingly took it from him and gently wiped his cheekbones.

'I don't see what all that has to do with sex,' Albert said, contentiously.

'Sit down a minute, sugar and let me explain,' she said, soothingly.

Albert allowed himself to be eased down into the chair and Gloria Eisenway drew up another, facing him. His eyes slewed with a rather glassy concentration from one provocative point of her body to another.

'Albert,' she said seriously. 'I don't know what sort of girls you've gotten involved with, but I can tell you that the vast majority strip quickly, mostly in the dark, leap into bed, open their legs and lie there breathing heavily with an occasional gasp until it's all over. They just have no idea how to make themselves more exciting to their man – and, naturally, increase their own excitement by that very process. Oh sure, I know you'll find the exception who bites a piece out of your neck and scratches your behind – maybe even flings her legs around your neck . . . '.

'I count myself most fortunate,' Albert said solemnly.

'But I expect even they could improve,' Gloria Eisenway continued. 'There's no limit to the way one can better oneself. And there's nothing wrong in letting your body flow with your feeling so that you mould the two into an effective whole.'

Albert listened earnestly, trying at the same time to recall the name of the one girl who had flung her legs around his neck. It had taken him completely by surprise, he remembered, as he would normally have considered the position impossible of achievement. She was, he discovered later, an exponent of yoga. The relevant point was that she had not only startled him into near impotence and cramped his style through sheer awkwardness, but she had also, at the moment of orgasm – hers not his – squeezed him with maniacal strength into semi-consciousness and left him with aches which had forced him to walk with his head at an angle of some thirty degrees from the vertical for the best part of a week. The fact that he could not, now, recall her name was doubtless due to a desire to suppress the painful memory.

'Not everyone wants legs around his neck,' he said. 'I was once nearly strangled.'

'Ah, but darling, the stupid girl was obviously only concerned about herself. If she'd entwined with tenderness that would have been a different matter. What I mean is that even in her own excitement the woman must be sensitive to her man, directing her passion along lines that'll stimulate him.'

Albert now remembered a girl who had bitten his neck so thoroughly and painfully he hadn't been able to wash for a week and given him such nasty yellow bruises people thought he had jaundice. There was also the girl who had . . . But these were probably covered by Gloria Eisenway's provisos. Maybe she was a scientist after all.

'It's too theoretical,' he insisted, unwilling to concede defeat. 'I don't see it working out in practice.'

'Well, Albert, honey, I can't give you a copy of the book since it's not out yet. I hate to think you're a potential non-reader. Maybe I could demonstrate some of the salient points and you can see what you think.'

Albert wasn't too certain about this. What did it mean,

exactly? It was terribly interesting though. Maybe he could write a book in opposition. "I Was Not Enslaved".

Gloria Eisenway stood up and moved her chair away. She looked at him very seriously.

'Now the first point, you'll remember, was not to leap into bed in the dark,' she said. 'In the book I explain that women – many women, anyway – have bodies to be proud of and should use them for visual effect.'

Very sedately she removed first the psychedelic brassiere and then peeled off the matching bikini pants. Albert focused on her appreciatively. A good body – a *very* good body. She twirled before him like a model displaying clothes, showing her absence of superfluous flesh on the well-shaped breasts and thighs and dimpled bottom.

'Now, how is that?' she said, holding out her arms and jutting her lightly-downed pelvis towards him.

'Uh-huh. Yes, it does have some effect,' Albert said reluctantly. 'Mind you, I don't think it's all that original. How about people who make love in the afternoon? Or those who do it in the open air – fields, boats, parking lots.'

'Parking lots?'

'I once saw a couple starkers . . . '

'Well that's only the beginning,' Gloria Eisenway said. 'I wouldn't follow getting undressed by covering my body with a sheet or a car rug. No sir, I'd show it. I'd have some gentle rhythm – recordplayer, radio – and I'd dance a little.'

Humming softly, she began to oscillate her hips with almost professional fluidity from her small waist and give her shoulders an occasional shake that made her breasts wobble. Albert watched, pursing his lips critically. A small triangular area of her loins had been shielded from the sun by the bikini and, when she turned her back, the lower portion of her buttocks formed a vulnerable-looking ellipse of white against the tan. Certainly *that* was effective, Albert figured. But then it was accidental and couldn't really count. He undid a couple of buttons at his shirt neck. God it *was* hot in here. Hadn't they heard of air conditioning.

'What's happened to the air conditioning?' he croaked.

Gloria Eisenway snaked down into a kneeling position in front of him.

'It's full on,' she said.

'It is?'

'And how do you feel about the dancing, honey?'

Albert steadied his thought. No mean feat when his eyes were in danger of crossing and seeing double. There were judicial considerations here. The future of the book could depend on his judgement.

'It's good,' he said soberly. 'Yes, it's good. But remember there's nothing new there. It's even done on the stage these days.'

Gloria Eisenway smiled at him. He found her breasts were suddenly resting warmly on his knees. She took his hands in hers.

'And now, honey,' she said, 'no simple heavy breathing. I give my readers a tongue exercise – reaching out with it as far as they possibly can . . . ' Her face came close to Albert's, not quite in focus. He smelt a fragrance of flowers he couldn't place.

'Open your mouth, Albert . . . '

Her hands left his and gently circled his neck, pulling him down to her. He opened his mouth dutifully. Managerial women!

Her tongue entered and began to explore. It was like a length of highly dexterous velvet and it left no morsel of membrane, no tooth, untouched.

Albert gave her maximum points. If these were tongue exercises, he was all for them.

'Good, good,' he said, emitting the words as muffled mouthings against her lips. She drew her mouth off his.

'Am I proving my point, Albert?' she asked softly.

'I admit that *is* effective,' Albert said. 'Of course, you're fortunate in possessing a particularly long, smooth tongue.'

'Practice, darling. It's all practice. I even give my readers diagrams to show them how to improve their flexibility.'

Albert's hand accidentally brushed her left nipple.

'I *beg* your pardon,' he said. He concentrated his splintering thoughts. 'I'm not sure,' he added, 'that this has to be *learned*.'

Gloria Eisenway made no verbal answer to his doubts.

'Next I teach them to use their hands sensitively,' she said. 'Better if you sit on the rug with me, Albert. Positioning is very important.'

'Oh, I see.'

He allowed himself to be drawn down on to one of the leopard skin rugs.

'That's right,' she said. 'I teach my readers to touch all sorts of materials so that they can tell one man's skin from another's.'

She began to touch him, running her fingers over his neck, shoulders, chest, almost as if she were collecting information to draw a map of his anatomy. Albert was impressed. In fact, she was so butterfly light that his buttons were undone and his shirt, trousers and underpants off before he'd made up his mind just how highly to rate the exercises. Not that it mattered since her hands continued to glide silkily over his skin, savouring every hair, every vein, every minute portion of flesh. Shoulders, chest, stomach, back . . . Yes, very thorough, he'd say that for her technique . . . Buttocks, thighs and forward again around. God, she was *really* getting to know him!

He squirmed and uttered a gasp as she used her fingers sensitively along his member. And then her lips were back on his and her tongue and fingers were making twin points of flaming sensation.

Albert began to tremble; his hands twitched. He took advantage of her tongue having a moment's respite to exclaim: 'I . . . I think you'll have to stop your demonstration!'

She looked down at him, pained.

'But you can't do that,' she said. 'It's only just begun.'

'I'm afraid . . . '

'How can you possibly judge my case if you won't even be bothered to test it?'

Her hand continued to learn the difference between his skin and the next man's while they debated.

'I'm prepared to concede . . . '

'That's very unfair, honey.'

'But I'm almost . . . '

'And very unscientific.'

'I do accept . . . '

'It's also very insensitive to suddenly tell me you're not interested any longer.'

'It's not *that* at . . . '

'It makes a mockery of me and my book.'

'I didn't mean to offend . . . '

'Well, it is offensive, Albert. You really should stick with an investigation.'

'But you're making me . . . '

'Imagine what state the world would be in if Isaac Newton had decided to stop, or Galileo couldn't be bothered.'

She was absolutely right. He wasn't even paying her the courtesy of giving her a hearing – or feeling, as it were. He was showing scant respect for all the research she'd done to build up her methods.

'You're . . . you're absolutely right,' he said, twitching his hips to her finger movement. 'I'm . . . sorry.'

But although Albert felt he'd behaved very shabbily, Gloria Eisenway didn't seem to bear a grudge. As witness the fact that her entire body began to sort of flow into him, so that she was not only using her hands sensitively, but also her nipples, her belly and her gently caressing thighs.

Albert's hands abruptly moved of their own volition, using themselves sensitively to get to know her skin, in turn.

'That's right, darling,' she murmured. 'Let your body flow with your feeling. How are you finding it?'

'The . . . the theory . . . is being borne out . . . very well,' Albert muttered.

'I'm so glad, Albert. And now I teach my readers a little lip sensitivity.'

Her mouth began to move over his body, sucking lips and flickering tongue at his chest, his navel and then . . .! Ye gods, research carried some shocks. No doubt all scientists experienced them some time in their careers. He gasped as her fingertips gently complemented her lips. She was playing him like a flute. He reached down and held her face, tracing the outline of her tantalising mouth. On this performance he was prepared to recommend her book to anyone. He'd even buy it for female acquaintances!

And then she was rising up his body again and pulling him over and on to her, guiding him.

With a groan, Albert suddenly found himself warmly and clingingly ensheathed. Arms and thighs enveloped him tenderly and a series of fetchingly agonising sighs broke from Gloria Eisenway's lips, followed by a passionate murmur of words.

'And still no passive . . . lying on my back . . .' she panted. 'I rotate my hips . . . and bottom . . . use my whole body . . .'

So saying, she took his hands and pulled them gently under her rump so that he felt every tension of the exciting circular movements, first clockwise and then anti-clockwise. Taut in his palms and then relaxed to soft overflowing. At the same time she began to do things with her thighs, alternately drawing them right up to her breasts and then lowering them to grip his hips.

'Have . . . have I made my . . . point, Albert?' she murmured.

'It's a breakthrough,' Albert gasped.

Now she was doing things with her face, too. One moment crushing her cheek against his, the next turning it passionately away. Now flushed and fierce, now flushed and helpless.

'Albert?' she muttered, as if not quite sure he was there (although all the evidence, he felt certain, must leave no doubt about it). 'Albert . . . and then I teach them to . . . goad their men on verbally . . . to say what they want . . . how they want . . . without inhibitions!'

Albert was expectant amidst his ardent writhings, but for some moments Gloria Eisenway was lost for words. Her lips moved silently. And then suddenly the language gushed out: 'Fuck me, Albert . . . hard . . . mercilessly with your hard . . . oh yes . . . your huge . . . is filling me . . . beautifully . . . painfully . . . Albert . . . everything is yours . . . opening wide for you . . . harder . . . your prick . . . oh yes . . . oh yes!'

Her words hammered in Albert's head, stimulating him to a tempestuous peak. It was true, all true! She was driving him out of his mind.

'I'm enslaved!' he cried. 'ENSLAVED!'

And now she was sharply slapping his left buttock, urging him on in his ecstatic penetration and she began to utter a sort of wolverine howl, a long, painful undulation of sound.

'Albert . . . I'm ready . . .' She managed to blurt out. 'Give it . . . give me . . .'

I shall, I shall! Albert's mind screamed back. In the name of science! I am!

And to an internal thunder of eurekas, research reached its ultimate fruition . . .

Chapter Seven

'IT'S THE elemental force of his work that's so awesting,' Aubrey Fanshawe said as he drove his Ford north through the teeming streets of Nairobi. 'One can feel that a gwave wesponsibility wests on him.'

Angela wished he'd shut up about Joseph Mbula for a while so that she could concentrate on the passing scene. They had left the spacious luxury of the city's centre and were now passing through a new territory of narrow streets crowded with exotic grocery stores, Asian restaurants and bars full of Africans drinking beer.

'He's such a beautiful man,' Aubrey Fanshawe went on. 'But he's wather moody. Sometimes one has to be careful how one tweats him. Takes offence, you know. Believes white people think he's infewior.'

'I wish to hell they'd get over that,' Angela said, turning her head to catch a glimpse of a colourful street market.

Aubrey Fanshawe leaned towards her slightly, lowering his voice. His chins corrugated against his fat neck.

'Well, let's face it,' he said. 'They are infewior. Beautiful but infewior.'

Angela pulled her attention back to the conversation. She glanced with distaste at her companion. What a low, fat slob!

'If you think Joseph Mbula's so inferior,' she said sharply, 'how can you think his work's so wonderful?'

'Divine gift, my dear. Nothing to do with him at all. He's just an instwument.'

'I can see he doesn't compare with the Europeans I've met here,' Angela said. 'But, of course, they'd be an elite anywhere.'

Fanshawe turned his small, peevish brown eyes on her for

a second. His flabby face was red and sweating as usual.

'The crème de la crème,' she added, smiling.

Fanshawe maintained an uncertain silence after that and Angela was able to take her fill of the surroundings until they pulled into a small square with a few scrubby palms in its centre matched by the shabbiness of the shopfronts with their peeling paint and defective neon signs. Fanshawe squeezed into a parking space between a couple of delivery vans.

'Joseph has a studio above the spice shop,' he said. 'Large, but hardly luxuwious. The world has never tweated its geniuses worthily.'

A few passers-by glanced at them curiously as he led her to a doorway beside the shop. She followed him up a flight of creaking stairs to a small landing from which another door opened into a large room with an enormous skylight through which the sun blazed and a couple of small windows overlooking a dingy courtyard at the back.

The room was devoid of furniture except for an array of folding wooden chairs and a trestle table covered with painting materials and a bric-a-brac of empty coca-cola bottles, torn and faded paperbacks, a dirty cracked cup and a small pile of darkening banana skins. Canvases were colourfully piled around the grey plaster walls and in one corner a pile of animal skin rugs adorned the bare floorboards. Joseph Mbula was standing at an easel attaching a canvas to a frame.

'We're here, Joseph,' Aubrey Fanshawe called. 'Stwipped and weady for action.'

The African turned towards them, his eyes instantly on Angela. He nodded a greeting and then shook his head from side to side.

'Not stripped,' he said.

Angela laughed to cover her unease.

'It's just an expression,' she said. 'What a big studio.'

'Very good,' Joseph said. 'Much room, much light.'

'Marvellous,' Angela falsely enthused. 'All you could possibly need.'

'No,' Joseph said. 'Million pounds, million dollars, many

concubines, palaces, yachts, automobiles, helicopters – for the people.'

Angela stared at him blankly.

'Joseph means that the world's wealth is unfairly spwead over a vewy small percentage of the population,' Aubrey Fanshawe said, 'and that the world is the hewitage of evewyone and the wiches should be shared by all alike.'

'Did he mean all that?' Angela said.

'He put it poetically; that's the artist in him.'

'You wanna drink?' Joseph asked.

'That would be lovely,' Angela said. 'We'll share your riches with you.'

The African rummaged among the debris on the trestle table and produced a bottle of rather warm beer which he passed to Angela.

'You'll have to dwink fwom the bottle,' Aubrey Fanshawe said. 'It's Joseph's way of dwawing us closer.'

'No glasses,' Joseph said.

Angela took a couple of half-hearted sips. Warm beer was not her idea of perfect refreshment for a hot day. Joseph took the bottle from her gulped down a half pint or so, sucking the top of the bottle where her lips had been, looking at her rather menacingly. He passed the beer to Fanshawe.

'Bottle party,' he said. The slight smile wrinkled around his moustache and beard, teeth gleamed.

Angela smiled nervously. She was not convinced of Joseph Mbula's brotherly love. She glanced anxiously away around the studio and her eyes lit on a large canvas leaning against the wall nearby.

'Your work?' she asked.

'One of his best,' Fanshawe said.

Angela strolled across the floor with a pleasant smile precariously fixed on her face. She wished to hell she hadn't let herself in for this: squalor, warm beer, Joseph Mbula giving her the creeps – and Fanshawe for that matter.

She stopped in front of the painting and knelt down to examine it. The canvas was almost completely filled with an oval pattern of shades of pink, deepening towards the centre in a series of folds. The pink oval was crowned by a dark, bristly growth and surrounded by a brown wash. Angela was puzzled for a moment before the solution came to her. It was some sort of sea anemone. Probably an exotic tropical variety. And the brown border must be some sort of rock background. Very smooth sort of rock, with a lot of shading. Below the anemone the brown rock made a curved pattern and was shaded into rough spheres joined by a small, dark cleft. It reminded her of one of those picture puzzles containing two different images according to the way you saw it. Except that she couldn't completely figure out the image. She leaned closer, inspecting the brown surround wherein she felt lay the clue. The brown lines slanted away from the anemone just below its flowery top. They actually gave a slight overall impression of legs rising up.

Angela felt herself slowly and inexorably blushing crimson. They *were* legs! And that was no anemone. It was a full frontal view of a vagina. Displayed between widespread thighs. The brown border was one huge crotch with the beginning of thighs and buttocks and the anus between.

Angela went on gazing at the canvas without really seeing it while she pulled herself together and tried to overcome her embarrassment. She was not so much shocked by the subject matter – after all this was the age of John Lennon – as by her unwitting concentration on it. They might think she was a homosexual maniac.

Joseph Mbula came and stood beside her. They stared at the vagina together. He removed his dark glasses and studied it with brooding eyes.

'Cunt,' he said, finally.

'Yes, I see,' Angela said helplessly. 'It's very nice.'

'Not nice,' Joseph said angrily. 'Brilliant!'

'Oh yes,' Angela agreed quickly. 'I've never seen such a . . . such a . . . Do you have any more work I can see?'

Joseph waved his hand around the studio.

'All mine,' he said. He took her arm, strong fingers on her bare skin just above the elbow and led her along the wall. 'Look,' he ordered. 'Much cunt.'

There was no escape. With outward calm, Angela set about viewing the most comprehensive array of female genitalia she'd ever imagined.

'What do you think?' Aubrey Fanshawe said in a tone which invited only admiration. 'Such line, such mass!'

Angela raked her mind desperately for acceptable comments, grabbing thankfully at any inspiration.

'Such sensuality,' she said.

'Good, good,' Joseph approved.

'And the orifice there. So alive. Almost as if it wants to speak.'

'It speaks – yes,' Joseph said.

'And you have the clitoris in that one,' Angela said. 'Such an interesting point of focus.'

'Nothing like it's been done before,' Aubrey Fanshawe interjected.

'And I love the pubic hair on this one,' Angela said. 'So expressive.'

'Right, right,' Joseph agreed.

'And this particular anus gives such a balance to the composition.'

'Anus – yes,' Joseph echoed.

'And the splendid proportions of this one,' Angela said. 'Such glorious labia. A regular Amazon. Oh, yes – and this one must be a pygmy. Eeeeeek!'

The cause of her alarm was a wide open vagina – from which was emerging a pre-Neanderthal head.

Aubrey Fanshawe moved alongside, mopping his face, smiling with satisfaction.

'Stwiking, isn't it?' he declared. 'This is the basic philosophy brilliantly interpweted. We see the hominid emerging fwom the eternal women, the archetypal mother. It's this stark dwama that gives Joseph's work its universal power.' He shook his head and his chins wobbled. 'Moving,' he said. 'Unbelievable.'

'May I have some more of that beer?' Angela said faintly. Limp, warm, whatever . . . She needed a drink.

Joseph passed her the bottle and she took a long draught, involuntarily grimacing. The African repeated his indecent sucking of the bottleneck. Aubrey Fanshawe watched them, thrumming his podgy fingers on his bulging, pear-shaped belly.

'You pose now.' Joseph appeared to be commanding rather than questioning.

'Okay.'

Get it over with and get out and have a beautiful iced Tom Collins with the marvellously uncreepy Albert.

'Where do you want me?'

'The rugs,' Joseph said pointing. 'Lying down.'

Angela went over to the rugs. They were rather dusty and she couldn't identify the animal. She lay down on her side facing Joseph and Aubrey Fanshawe. The rugs were very soft and comfortable. She wished she'd brought a book to read, but, then, maybe it wouldn't take too long. An awful thought struck her. Suppose he wanted her to come again! Well, she'd just have to put her foot down. Anyway, he could surely get her on canvas in one session. She was not a prime minister, after all. It didn't have to be a perfect likeness.

Joseph and Aubrey Fanshawe continued to stand silently staring at her. Joseph stroked his beard morosely. She began to feel uneasy.

'Are you turned to stone by my beauty?' she said with false perkiness. 'Or shall we start?'

'Well – you're not quite wight,' Aubrey Fanshawe said. He took off his ridiculous hat and fanned himself.

'How does he want me then? He'd better arrange me.'

'Stripped,' Joseph said arrogantly.

Angela was startled. For some inexplicable reason she had not foreseen this. Of course, artists' models usually posed in the nude, didn't they?

'Naked,' Joseph repeated, with authority. 'No clothes.'

He turned away to his easel and palette and Aubrey Fanshawe, interpreting her hesitation, said quietly: 'You mustn't offend him, you know. Nudity means nothing to an artist. In any case, I'm here as chapewone.'

Angela was very unenthusiastic about this. On the other hand, she had to admit that Benjamin Hailey had often photographed her with very little protecting her modesty.

What was the difference? A small voice began to warn her that Joseph Mbula would take any reluctance on her part as a sign of racial prejudice. Perish the thought!

'Well . . . all right,' she said. 'Just for this one session.'

Joseph began dragging his easel over the floor towards her and Angela removed her Christian Dior chapeau and patted her hair into place. Aubrey Fanshawe wandered to the trestle table and leafed through the paperbacks with an air of disdain.

Angela took off her black belt and started to undo the black buttons on her gabardine dress. She slipped out of it. Neither man paid any attention to her and she kicked off her Charles Jourdan shoes and slipped out of her white tights.

Joseph arranged his easel and began mixing pigment on his palette. Fanshawe appeared engrossed in a novel.

Okay, okay. Angela unclipped her little black bra and wriggled out of her matching briefs. She stood like a guilty schoolgirl before the admonishing headmistress. She felt somehow ultra-naked.

After a few seconds, Joseph Mbula raised his head from his palette and looked at her. Every part of her seemed to twitch as his eyes roved over her. The lines around the lower part of his face deepened in a smile, teeth slowly showed. Angela decided he was more sinister without his dark glasses than with them. At the same time, Aubrey Fanshawe put down his book and looked at her, too, with a curiosity which seemed motivated by distaste.

After several more seconds, during which nobody moved or spoke, Angela asked: 'How do you want me?'

Her words rang loud in her ears and sounded terribly ambiguous.

'I mean, what position do you want me in?'

The attempt at correction sounded deafening and even more suggestive. Joseph continued to smile in a sinister way and Fanshawe shifted his gaze to the African.

'Turn,' Joseph commanded.

Angela half turned so that she was in profile to him. His eyes brooded on her. And then he made a circular movement with his index finger.

'Turn,' he said again. 'Keep turning.'

'What do you mean?' Angela demanded. 'This isn't a cattle market, you know. Just tell me how you want to paint me.'

She saw Aubrey Fanshawe, behind the African, making strange gestures to her with his hands. He was running them over his face and pointing to Joseph. Angela stared at him. No wonder these two gave her the creeps. And then Fanshawe began pinching up the skin of his forearm and motioning to Joseph. Joseph's forearm? Angela began to lose patience.

'Turn,' Joseph repeated menacingly. 'The artist decides.'

'That's all very well . . . '

Now Fanshawe was sketching signs – letters – in the air. He was trying to communicate a message. Or had his reason snapped? In any case, if they were letters they were back to front, from right to left as she looked at them. Fanshawe suddenly seemed to realise this error. He turned his back towards her and began to trace the signs from left to right, glancing anxiously back over his shoulder.

'Model obeys; artist commands,' Joseph said.

The letters were coming across to Angela: B-L-A-C-K . . . Fanshawe pointed again at Joseph. Well of course he was black! Did that stupid, fat man think she thought he was an Albino?

'What the hell . . .?'

But Fanshawe cut her short, urgently placing his finger on his lips. He clenched his fist and made an ineffectual punching movement in Joseph's direction.

'Turn around,' Joseph insisted.

Fanshawe was going to punch Joseph? Black Joseph? In spite of the circumstances, Angela felt a sudden giggling fit welling up dangerously inside her. He was going to take Joseph unawares? Bash him on the head and knock him out?

Aubrey Fanshawe was now shaking his head from side to side in a negative sign, however. He was not going to hit Joseph? The laughter reached Angela's eyes, her lips twitched. Fanshawe pointed to *her* and followed with the punching, head-shaking sequence. He wasn't going to punch Joseph because she was there? He didn't want her to punch Joseph? Did that fat nut think she was crazy? Fanshawe repeated the gesture, gazing at her pleadingly. And suddenly she understood. He was gesturing figuratively. *Racial discrimination.* If she didn't do what Joseph wanted, he'd put it down to his being black. *That* was it. And that was probably just what he *would* think, ridiculous as it was.

Angela turned abruptly and presented them with her back. She felt terribly vulnerable around her famous bottom, as if pots of paint were likely to be hurled over it at any moment.

Joseph left her like that for over a minute.

She glanced back over her shoulder. Joseph was brooding over her. Aubrey Fanshawe was watching him with a funny look in his eyes.

'Is this all right – or not?' Angela demanded, shortly.

Joseph pulled his eyes off her buttocks to her face.

'Profile,' he said.

Angela dutifully turned.

'Now front,' Joseph ordered.

She faced him.

'Now profile.'

Angela pursed her lips in impatience, but did as she was told.

'Now back.'

Angela turned with a tiny 'tut' of annoyance.

Joseph left her in this clearly favoured position for a further minute.

'Profile again,' he commanded.

Angela spun round. Racial discrimination or not, she was fed up with this.

'This is not a Miss World competition,' she said. 'Will you please decide how you want – I mean which posture you want me to adopt.'

'Essential I get to know my subject,' Joseph said grimly. 'Lie down, facing front.'

Well, that was better. At least a comfortable position. She lay down on her side, slightly curled.

'Good,' he said. 'But legs toward me.'

Angela curled herself a little more.

'No. Legs toward me. On your back. Feet point this way.'

Angela lay back, pointing her legs toward him. Odd. The perspective would be difficult from this angle.

'Open legs. Pull up thighs.'

Open legs! Pull up thighs!

Angela sat bolt upright. Indignation shot through her. He wasn't going to do a portrait at all! He intended painting her . . . using her as a vaginal model! The charlatan! That was the only part of her that interested him!

'You must be out of your mind!' she stormed. 'If you think I'm going to lie here with you two staring at my . . .!

'Cunt,' Joseph said imperiously. 'I paint cunt.'

'Not mine, you don't!'

'Vicious. Because I am black.'

'Don't be ridiculous. Black's got nothing to do with it!'

Aubrey Fanshawe waddled forward.

'You must understand,' he said to Angela, 'that to the painter the human body is simply a beautiful object to be imparted to canvas – just like a twee, or a snow-capped mountain. He has as little personal intewest as a doctor.'

'Right,' Joseph said. The smile lines flitted on his face, teeth gleamed.

'When Joseph looks at you, he sees only the weflection of the vision he's attempting to twansmute to canvas,' Aubrey Fanshawe continued. 'You are no longer the particular, the specific, but the genewal, the universal. The painter is his own god, his own law and you are one of the elements in his act of cweation.'

Angela regarded them dubiously. Easy to make a speech like that while Joseph Mbula stared lasciviously at her pubic hair, but not altogether convincing.

'Black,' Joseph said with authority. 'That is the reason. Racialist.'

'But I tell you I'm not a racialist,' Angela insisted. 'I'm just not an artist's model.'

'You think I am inferior – because I'm black.'

'It's not true. You *mustn't* think that.'

'You think I am fit to sweep roads and clean automobiles?'

'Yes, of course I do.'

'Vicious!' Joseph Mbula snarled. 'You think I have no brain. You think I am an animal.'

'I mean of course I think you're fit to do anything,' Angela cried, 'whether it's sweep roads, clean automobiles, build palaces, paint pictures – anything.'

'You think I am fit for anything! A white man is fit only for the best things, superior things. But I am fit for anything!'

Angela put her hand to her cheek.

'Oh god,' she said. 'You're getting it all wrong!'

'Because I am black you won't pose!'

'But I would pose . . . It's just that . . . '

'That I am black!'

'Believe me,' Angela pleaded, 'you're so wrong.'

'Not wrong. Sharpeville. Immigration Law. South African Arms. Bobby Seale. Racist!'

Angela appealed to Fanshawe.

'How can I convince him?' she cried. 'It's absolutely ridiculous that I should be called a racist. Ask anyone who knows me. I can't bear it!'

'Then perhaps you'd better bare it,' Fanshawe said. 'Words count for nothing; deeds are all.'

Angela gazed from one to the other. This was awful.

'All right,' she said with sudden determination. 'I'll prove it.'

She took a deep breath, closed her eyes, lay down, opened her legs wide and drew back her thighs. It was done before she could think about it.

In the silence that followed, her mind began working again, filling her with images of the view she was presenting. Just like his paintings, except the surround was pink and white instead of brown. They'd all been black women before. She was the first white woman. Good heavens! That was discriminatory thinking, wasn't it? Maybe Joseph was right about her.

She opened her eyes. Joseph Mbula was studying her vagina. Fanshawe was looking at it with disdain. She closed her eyes again. Another difficulty was that there was something slightly stimulating about all this exhibitionism.

The door at the far end of the studio suddenly opened. Angela heard it squeak. She opened her eyes again.

She sat up abruptly, clamping her thighs together, covering her breasts with her arms. She uttered a shriek.

Three Africans had entered the studio and were advancing towards Joseph Mbula, carrying all sorts of artist's materials.

Joseph and Fanshawe, who had been too engrossed to notice the entrance, now turned toward the newcomers. Greetings passed to and fro: 'Jambo? Habari? Mzuri.'

Joseph turned back to Angela, his look sardonic.

'More painters,' he said. 'School of Mbula.'

Angela had turned crimson. She tried to cover herself with a rug.

'Tell them to get out,' she screeched. 'What *is* this!'

'Modelling session,' Joseph said. His eyes turned angry. 'My school. All very good painters.'

'But you didn't tell me . . . '.

'They wander in and out, you know,' Fanshawe interrupted. 'Never know when they'll be here. It's perfectly all wight. They're just like Joseph. Minor Joseph's, of course. It's vewy hard on them to have you weact like this.'

Angela was speechless.

'Pose,' Joseph ordered.

The newcomers settled themselves on folding chairs, sketchbooks and pencils poised.

Angela found her voice.

'You can't expect me to . . . '

'Because they are black!' Joseph spat at her. 'Because we are black!'

'No, no! I told you . . . oh God!'

'Your attitude's not logical, you see,' Aubrey Fanshawe said. 'Models pose just as weadily before an art class as before a single painter.'

Angela felt trapped. Caught in a web of logic not of her own species. She lowered the rug slowly. Was she a liberal, or not? The proof of the liberalism must, after all, be in the liberation.

Reluctantly she lay back on the rugs with her eyes closed. She opened her thighs and drew them up. The images flooded back. All those eyes gazing at her exposure. She began to experience a nervous spasm in her vagina as a reaction to the group concentration on it.

Angela became aware of the door opening yet again and more greetings. She dare not open her eyes. Her legs quivered from nervous tension. It was like being on the rack.

More greetings, scraping of chairs, whispers, vague movements.

Her vagina seemed to have developed a consciousness of its own, ogling the men, winking at them, throwing them kisses, dancing out towards them, withdrawing . . .

Joseph's voice sounded nearby, penetrating her disordered fantasy.

'It is for the creation, the beginning. It must be open.'

And suddenly fingers entered her vagina, pushing the labia apart.

Angela jerked away and opened her eyes to gaze wildly around.

The studio was *packed* with Africans! There must have been forty of them, seated in a semi-circle on their folding chairs with their sketchbooks and pencils. Joseph was close by, gazing into her pelvic cavity, from which he had just withdrawn his index and middle fingers.

'What . . . what?' Angela cried. She felt slightly dazed.

'Open,' Joseph commanded. 'For the world's birth.'

'What are all these men!' Angela gasped.

'Painters. All painters.'

Joseph ignored her distress. His fingers moved back to her vagina. An agonising tremor ran through her from head to toe as he opened it. She seemed unable to close her legs. She slithered away from him.

'How dare you!' she cried weakly. 'Get rid of those people!'

'Because I am black!' Joseph snarled. 'Because they are black!'

'No, no!' Angela groaned. 'It's just too much. Too much for me to be all alone with no clothes on . . . '

Joseph raised his hand.

'Don't worry,' he said. 'No trouble.'

He spoke rapidly and authoritatively to the Africans. They lay down their materials and began to strip off.

Angela was aghast. This was developing into a nightmare.

'Stop them!' she cried. 'What are they doing?'

'Unclothing, so you will not be alone,' Joseph said.

He pulled his colourful robe over his head. Aubrey Fanshawe gazed around the studio with wildly excited eyes. His lips quivered.

'Oh God, this is crazy!' Angela moaned. 'It's not what I meant!'

'Better,' Joseph stated. 'Much better.'

An array of naked men of all shapes and sizes confronted Angela. So much for their impersonal interest. Erections towered everywhere. Aubrey Fanshawe looked a little faint. He suddenly began to tear off his clothes, too.

Joseph bent over her, staring closely at her vagina.

'Not right,' he said.

'Don't you touch me!' Angela gasped.

'I arrange the model,' Joseph said, fixing her with his menacing eyes. 'For the creation.'

Angela's stomach heaved. She must not discriminate, she told herself. Must not lay herself open to charges of . . .

Joseph's fingers insinuated themselves into her. He touched her clitoris and her loins fluttered.

'Good?' he demanded, turning his head towards the class.

There was a muttered assent from all sides. Angela felt giddy. Surely this wasn't the practice in English art classes. Oh God! Was that prejudice?

Joseph knelt down in front of her, his fingers still touching the moist cavity.

'Now the creation,' he said. 'Black and white. Non-racial.'

Angela's whole being underwent a sudden sort of freezing heat, like being rolled in snow. He couldn't possibly imagine . . .!

But Joseph had lowered himself so that his body was very close to hers, was moving his hips between her thighs and guiding his sex at her exposed part. For two seconds Angela hesitated while her mind boggled at the labyrinthine problem of whether this was discrimination. She actually felt the stiff beginning of entry and that settled matters. If it *was* prejudice, then it *was*.

She jerked away, writhed across the rugs and stumbled to her feet.

'Are you crazy!' she yelled. 'Do you really think you can . . .'

Joseph Mbula leapt to his feet and advanced on her, eyes fierce, member threatening.

'Because I am black,' he hissed.

'No!' Angela shouted. 'You could be red, white and blue. It wouldn't make any difference. I am not a whore!'

Joseph turned to his fellow painters.

'You hear!' he shouted scornfully. 'She thinks she must be a whore to create with black men!'

A rumble of disapprobation swelled through the studio. She caught a glimpse of Aubrey Fanshawe, fat body, skinny legs, eyes glinting in mad excitement, and then Joseph was advancing on her again.

'You come from swinging London,' he growled. 'See-throughs. Microskirts. Free love. Orgies. Here you will not create because we are black.'

'I tell you that's nonsense!' Angela screamed.

'Racist! You should be put in slave chains! Raped!'

'Raped! Raped! Raped! . . .' A murmur of agreement gathered strength. Men stood up – only too clearly equipped to carry out the injunction.

In desperation, Angela appealed to Aubrey Fanshawe, whose white erection gleamed like a crusader's sword amidst the dark hosts.

'Get me out of here!' she cried. 'Do something!'

Joseph waved an arm in contemptuous triumph.

'You see, she speaks only to the white man,' he cried. 'We are the inferior race.'

Aubrey Fanshawe waddled flabbily forward. A spot of saliva moistened his fat lower lip.

'They're so beautiful,' he said softly, 'I don't see why you want to wesist.'

'Oh!' Angela's hazel eyes sparked at him – at all of them. She bent and grabbed up her clothes and as she did, Joseph Mbula caught her a stinging slap across the buttocks. Angela jack-knifed upwards, flushing.

'How dare . . . '

She caught one glimpse of the look in his eyes and marched quickly past him without waiting to put on her clothes.

'Permissive society – white!' he shouted catching her another smack across the bottom as she passed.

The forty painters were grouped between Angela and the door, glowering at her, a frightening array of aroused virility. She sailed resolutely toward them.

'Lady Chatterley's Lover!' Joseph roared.

Angela walked straight at the wall of masculinity.

'Lolita!' Joseph yelled. 'Fanny Hill!'

The nearest student glared at Angela but gave way before her determined approach. Angela's heart was pounding. She kept her chin up and pointing firmly towards the door, trying not to show her terror. A student slapped her backside hard as she marched through the ranks.

'Frank Harris!' he snarled.

The wall gave and Angela pushed her way through, brushing a forest of erections, having her buttocks slapped at every step.

'Strick's "Ulysses"!' Joseph bellowed.

Angela's behind was scarlet and stinging from the slaps that continued to fall on it like rain. Someone barred her way and grasped a breast in each hand.

'Candy!' he spat into her face.

Angela jerked clear and another pair of hands grabbed her hips.

'Hair!' another voice screamed.

Angela dragged herself free. A fresh tattoo of slaps smattered her buttocks, forcing cries of pain from her. She swished her hips violently in an effort to avoid the blows.

'Andy Warhol – Flesh!' Joseph cried.

'Last Exit to Bwooklyn!'

The renegade, Angela fumed.

'Lennon's lithographs!'

'Portnoy's Complaint!'

'I Like It That Way!'

'Oh Calcutta!'

'Swinging London!'

And the catchphrase for white, permissive, corrupt society was echoed over and over again throughout the studio, the forty-one black voices and the renegade white joining in an ear-shattering chorus as Angela battered her naked way the last few feet to the door.

At the door she turned to face the chanting crowd, confronting them with such fury that the chanting died away. She slipped into her dress with a deft movement. Her heart felt on the point of seizure; she wouldn't be able to sit down for a week. And she had come here to do them a favour. She was overwhelmed by the injustice of it. She filled her lungs with air.

'You stupid black bastards!' she yelled.

And holding her shoes and underclothes, she ran for her life.

Chapter Eight

'WHAT A marvellous penis,' Gloria Eisenway said. 'It's far and away his best attribute, isn't it? He'd be in great demand at any orgy.'

'It's crap,' George Eisenway retorted. 'You just figure it in proportion to his size, Mama. Long as an arm, thick as a thigh. They just have to be kidding.'

'You're just jealous, George.'

'Jealous – what have I got to be jealous about?' Eisenway glanced anxiously at his wife.

'The point is,' Albert said, 'that it's not supposed to be realistic. It's a fertility totem. The artist's accentuated the genital power as the fount of fertility.'

'I don't see what size has to do with it,' Angela said. 'I always thought fertility had to do with sperm strength. I remember being told at school that millions of them die on the way to the uterine tube, but some of those tough little sperms never give up. Against all odds they swim on and on, lashing their tails, and even though they might be at their last gasp . . . '

'You can't expect an African tribe to concern itself with the finer biological points,' Albert interrupted. 'All it wants is a symbol. Anyway, George, where is this statuette – and the others?'

George Eisenway replaced the set of photographs in an envelope.

'Haven't got them yet,' he said. 'But I'm working on it. Maybe pick them up on our safari.'

Albert cast another lukewarm glance over the Kamba carvings laid out on a table. Wild animals, warriors with spears, masks – they were beautifully produced. But they were in virtually the same category as Julius Jack Freedman's ithyphallic statue, whose photograph Gloria had just been drooling over – strictly tourist material. Albert had made a somewhat arbitrary selection from among them without any conviction.

'That would be a good idea,' he said. 'Maybe we can tour around the villages, too, and find some more pieces – something a bit more individual than these.'

'Not necessary,' Eisenway said. 'Waste of time.'

'Listen,' Albert said. 'I don't know about you, but I've been paid quite a bit of money to take back some decent items to your cousin. I wouldn't figure I'd remotely earned it if I went back with this lot.'

Eisenway took a draught of his ever-present Scotch.

'Albert,' he said, 'you're a good guy. A fine guy. Salt of the earth. Fact that you feel the way you do shows it. But son, it's not necessary. The only thing old Julius Jack's interested in is getting these fertility figures so's he can have an heir. He doesn't give a bush pig's balls for the rest.'

'Then why . . .'

'George,' Gloria Eisenway cut in, 'you've been practising your prose.'

'Yeah,' Eisenway said vaguely. 'I'm getting to the truth. Paring it down so only the truth's there. All the slop's out.'

'I didn't know you wrote as well, George,' Angela said.

'Sure I write. As well as what?'

'As well as all those other things – like fighting and drinking and hunting and . . .'

'And being unconscious,' Gloria Eisenway said.

'What do you write?' Angela pursued.

'The truth as I see it – near as I can get.'

'Have you had anything published?'

'I'm not concerned about that, daughter. Anyway people don't wanna hear the truth.'

'Look,' Albert broke in. 'If Julius Jack Freedman is only interested in this set of kikuyu fertility statues, then why the hell did he need to send me out here? It doesn't make sense.'

'It makes perfect sense,' Gloria Eisenway said. 'It means he's a little funny in the head. Family disease.'

'Mama,' George Eisenway said, 'I guess you're still mad at me.'

'Don't worry about it, Albert,' Gloria said. 'Enjoy yourself.'

'Albert gets these attacks of guilt,' Angela explained.

'Not too often, I hope,' Gloria Eisenway said. 'That *would* be inconvenient.'

Angela glanced at her suspiciously.

Albert decided on a rapid change of subject.

'What do you write about, George?' he asked. 'I mean, the truth about what?'

George Eisenway looked a little disconcerted. He took another draught of Scotch.

'Life,' he said. 'Death. The stench of life; the beauty of death. The stench of death; the beauty of life.'

'It sounds very interesting,' Albert said.

'It sounds very smelly,' Gloria Eisenway said.

'And beautiful,' Angela said.

'I try to write about what I know without tricks and without cheating,' Eisenway said. 'I try to write well and truly of something I know about.'

'That reminds me, George,' Gloria Eisenway said. 'You forgot to put Campari on the last liquor list.'

Somewhere in the distance a car horn sounded.

'That'll be the others arriving,' Gloria said. 'Let's take our drinks out front.'

She led the way through the large, cool rooms of the huge, sprawling bush bungalow. Outside, on the long, pillared terrace, surrounded by the ubiquitous bougainvillaea in masses of blue and magenta, they gazed across the sloping lawns to the vast bush with its flat-topped acacias and scrubby thorn trees with hills and forest rising in the background. To a city lad, Albert figured, it was awe inspiring. Nairobi was hours away along miles and miles of red dirt roads through a land of waving grass and gazelles and giraffes and hills with monkeys and mongooses. The only other civilisation within reach was the village hidden by a group of hills, from which supplies came to the Eisenway's weekend residence.

'My grandfather had it built for us,' Gloria Eisenway had explained. 'He didn't feel that mud huts were our style.'

Certainly the long, platinum shirtdress she was wearing was hardly mud hut style, Albert reflected. It glittered and sparkled silvery-blue in the sunlight. It was more like something he'd expect Angela to be wearing at a fashion parade. It was also the way she'd be wearing it – tied at the waist with buttons undone all the way down except for three over the stomach zone. He found it extremely difficult to keep his mind off the glories of scientific research. Angela, on the other hand, seemed to be afflicted with a desire to keep herself covered, to the extent of an olive green bush jacket and shorts.

A cloud of dust rose from the dirt road and a small procession of sturdy vehicles emerged, branched off to the bungalow across rough country and disappeared around the back of the building to park under the bamboo roof of an enormous lean-to. A few minutes later a whole army of people, led by Dr Elmer Krapstein, surged on to the terrace. Greetings, introductions and the chinking provision of refreshment filled the air for some minutes.

Gloria Eisenway moved amongst the guests with her dazzling smile, throwing energetic comments in all directions, listening to nobody's answers. After some minutes she climbed on to a chair and addressed them.

'I'm so glad you could all come,' she said. 'I think it shows a fine spirit that you're all interested in Dr Krapstein's project. I guess we all agree that we privileged folks should be able to relate more directly to our African friends. We don't want a split between the races; we want happy coexistence. And we're going to join with Elmer in doing our best to ensure this.'

'They're the ones who can't relate,' somebody shouted. 'Bloody ex-houseboys think they know as much about farming as we do!'

'Hear, hear! Hear, hear!'

'They've got centuries of backwardness to catch up on!' somebody else cried.

'I worked for my position – nobody handed it to me on a

plate!' another voice yelled.

Gloria Eisenway, slightly put out by this disaffection, raised her shimmering arms for silence. It was less her gesture that achieved immediate quiet than the amount of breast it revealed.

'Now if we weren't interested I'm sure we wouldn't all be here,' she said.

'I'm only here for the beer!' someone shouted.

Gloria Eisenway decided to take a tolerant view. She smiled with the hoots of laughter that greeted the remark.

'Plenty of that,' she said. 'I'm sure it'll help to smooth out any problems. Now, when the others get here Elmer will have a little talk about the project. Okay – enjoy yourselves.'

She climbed down from the chair, producing another moment's reverent silence while she showed a length of brown leg right up to hip level.

In the hubbub of conversation that gathered and the constant clatter of glasses being refilled, Albert had a look at the current candidates for Dr Krapstein's body-touch encounter exercises – or the Eisenway's hospitality if one wanted to be cynical.

Foremost, Gloria Eisenway, emerging as the arch-liberal hostess, getting a kick out of bringing the haves and have-nots together for a cosy cocktail communion; George Eisenway, the reluctant host, who didn't really have anything against Africans, some of his best servants having been black; Mr and Mrs Gerald Duxworthy, two superficially bright ginger people in their thirties, who, having earlier failed at cigarette salesmanship and junior librarianship respectively in London's suburban wastes, were now about to manage a small hotel in the Highlands for a London package tour operator. They had equally brittle, artificial voices, equally insincere beaming smiles and an equally brazen ability to lie about their status and achievement back 'in the old country'. They should have been a perfect match except that she looked like his elder sister and tended to treat him like that in the intervals between flirting with other men. Then there were Mr and Mrs Francis Fordyce-Williams, who had lived and farmed in Kenya for years and could no more rid themselves of their lordly colonial manners than they could the great clusters of freckles which covered their fair skins on all the exposed patches of flesh. He had a face something like a camel's and kept a pet cheetah, which he housed in a corral and exercised on a leash. He preferred the animal to human beings and was rather resentful that Gloria Eisenway had refused to have it in her house. He had almost decided not to come, in fact, but his wife had talked him into accepting the invitation on the ground that their social life was so limited they couldn't pick and choose the way they might have done in England. She was a tall, thin woman with the face of a cosseted poodle. Her favourite pastime was to wax incredulous over the monstrous injustices the British tax system inflicted on people of means and initiative. Although it did not affect her in the slightest degree, she was an expert on its every detail. Then, surprisingly to Albert, there was the terrier face of Everett-Smithers, who turned out to be a former Battle of Britain pilot, now farming. His presence, Albert decided, could only be explained by the clannishness of the European community, which encompassed both love and hate. With him was his daughter, Millicent, a softer and not unattractive edition of her father. She had long, dark hair, regular features, the same cleft chin as her father and a slightly oriental look, which must have been due to her high-necked, slit skirt Chinese dress of dark green satin. And then there were two rather plain research workers from Dr Krapstein's institute. One, Georgette Musky, had a face like a hyena and an angular body which looked as if any joint would serve as a lethal weapon; the other, Janice Troll, had a shy pudding face and a body so splendid that it was difficult to believe the protuberances were her own. In addition to this central group there were other farming couples of such nondescript uniformity that Albert's scrutiny seized up through sheer indifference.

'Where do you think all these hippies came from?' he whispered to Angela.

'Albert, this is terrible,' she whispered back. 'The only thing we can do is get sloshed or hide in the bush.'

'What's wrong with getting sloshed *and* hiding in the bush?'

'Nothing. I just didn't think of it.'

Gloria Eisenway approached, dazzling them with her smile.

'Come on now you two,' she ordered. 'You're prime attractions; you must circulate.'

'If we circulate,' Albert said, 'we can't keep an eye on that man Everett-Smithers and we're afraid he might attack George. They don't get on too well, you know.'

Gloria Eisenway glanced through the crowd to where Everett-Smithers was fondly chatting with his daughter.

'Don't you worry about him,' she said. 'He knows better than to try to do anything to George in my house, I'd throw him out myself.'

'But he might attack before you noticed.'

'He'd better not. Elmer particularly wanted him along. Figures he's a hard case and the project should get rid of some of his belligerence. Come on now – freshen up those drinks and meet some people.'

'Sloshed first, bush later,' Albert whispered to Angela. 'I'll see you under the acacia tree.'

Gloria Eisenway steered them apart. Albert found himself routed for the Fordyce-Williams area. A hint of desperation crept into his rate of liquor consumption.

'We were just saying, Mr Divine, what a terribly depressing business it must be dealing in pictures in Britain,' Mrs Fordyce-Williams said, as he reached them. 'All those amazing prices – and nearly every penny going to the Government. Of course, being on schedule D, I suppose you can fiddle a bit and claim a lot on expenses. But what a scandal that you should have to go to the expense of an accountant just to get a fraction of the proper rewards of your industry.'

'I don't know, Mrs Fordyce-Williams,' Albert said. 'I have my account in Switzerland and I claim for six non-existent dependent relatives and five similar children.'

'I'm very glad to hear it, Mr Divine,' Mrs Fordyce-Williams said earnestly. 'Very glad. Have you tried claiming housekeeper allowance?'

'I fear that might be a little complicated.'

'Not if you're an unmarried person maintaining a female relative who lives with you to look after a brother or sister for whom child allowance is given. Or a widower.'

'I see,' Albert said. 'I'll have my accountant look into it.'

'You must, Mr Divine, you must. Don't let anything go by default. They'll rob you of every penny they can. They want to force you to emigrate, you know. Britain's over-populated and they're trying to tax people into leaving.'

'They don't need to tax 'em into doing that, my deah,' Francis Fordyce-Williams cut in. 'Whole country's going to the dogs: shoplifting, strikes, comprehensive education, psychiatric treatment for common criminals, the blacks taking over. God knows where it'll all end! Do you know they're even thinking of preventing people from privately owning certain types of animals. All because some nasty little urchin interfered with a jaguar on a housing estate and the poor animal bit off his fingers. Serve the little hooligan right. *I'd* bite off his fingers if he interfered with *me*. How do they expect a jaguar to react, dammit!'

'Funny,' Albert said. 'The English are usually so fond of animals.'

'Not on housing estates, sir! Not on housing estates!'

'That's all a myth about the English being fond of animals,' Mrs Fordyce-Williams said. 'You can't even claim against income tax for them, you know. No allowance at all. Yet they have to be fed and clothed just like children – and paid for on trains and provided with toys. Don't tell me the English like animals!'

'Clothed?' Albert queried.

He seemed to recall some crazy society that had gone around dressing the hind quarters and udders of cows in pants and brassieres and putting jock straps on bulls, claiming they were indecent without them. But surely that had been in America, not England.

'Oh they need their little coats for the cold weather,' Mrs Fordyce-Williams explained. 'And collars – and bows. They all wear out and have to be replaced, you know.'

'Of course,' Albert agreed.

He glanced around rather helplessly for a fresh injection of alcohol into his empty glass and caught the eye of Mrs Gerald Duxworthy, who'd clearly been watching him. She smiled brightly and sailed over, radiating brittle, ginger presence.

'Hello,' she said vibrantly. 'So you're Albert Divine.'

Albert looked warily at the sparkling eyes and the sharp, white face. He was invariably irritated by people telling him who he was. He had to stifle retorts like: 'So what?' and 'What of it?'

'I am,' he agreed. 'And you're . . . you're . . . ' His attempt to retaliate foundered on his inability to remember her name.

'Jennifer Duxworthy,' she said. 'I run a hotel here – with my husband.'

'It's not open yet, though, is it my dear?' Mrs Fordyce-Williams said. 'I do wish you'd tell me when it is. Some of my aunt's household staff have been talking about holidaying in Africa this year and I'm sure they'd have to find somewhere cheap.'

Jennifer Duxworthy, through her unwaveringly bright smile, could clearly have drowned Mrs Fordyce-Williams in acid.

'They'll have to book through our London representative,' she said, with an icy edge to her smile.

'And who might he be, dear?'

Jennifer Duxworthy's eyes were like gimlets.

'Johnson's Safari Sun Tours, 125 Pentonville Road,' she said.

'Forgive me for asking, dear, but there are so many package tour companies jumping on the bandwagon these days, I can never remember addresses.'

Albert reluctantly decided his sympathies were marginally with Jennifer Duxworthy.

'I go everywhere by package tour,' he said. 'It's the only way to have a jolly time without having to worry about anything.'

Francis Fordyce-Williams sparked into life at this.

'As I see it,' he barked, 'they're constantly putting people in the wrong hotels and messing up their holidays.'

'That's what's so marvellous,' Albert enthused. 'Hate everything to be cut and dried. Life's much more interesting with shocks and surprises.'

Jennifer Duxworthy turned her bright smile delightedly on him.

'I do agree, Mr Divine. You're welcome to stay at our hotel as our guest whenever you like.'

Albert raised his glass in acknowledgement. Clearly he was overdoing it.

At that moment a fresh hubbub of car horns penetrated the growing alcoholic haze. They all turned to gaze across the lawns to the dusty road through the bush.

'That'll be the other half arriving,' Gloria cried. 'Now don't forget, we're all brothers and sisters under the skin.'

'You can count me out of that,' Francis Fordyce-Williams snapped.

'Hear, hear!' his wife said.

'Yeah, I guess this is a real nutty idea,' George Eisenway growled.

'Well we do have to get on with the black population,' Jennifer Duxworthy said brightly.

'So long as they don't expect to marry my daughter,' Everett-Smithers scowled.

'You and they don't have to expect anything,' Dr Krapstein cried suddenly in a very loud voice. 'You just let everything happen.'

'Not everything, I hope,' Jennifer Duxworthy quipped. 'At least – not all at once.'

Gerald Duxworthy, smiling brightly, muttered something savagely to his wife and she, smiling even more brightly, muttered something equally savagely back.

The hubbub of conversation resumed and a few minutes later, Gloria Eisenway was ushering on to the terrace a new influx of candidates for Dr Krapstein's project.

Aubrey Fanshawe, looking hot and dishevelled and Joseph Mbula, looking cool and sinister, led a number of Africans into the party.

Angela took one look at them and announced to Albert:

'I am not taking part in this project. Not with Joseph Mbula and all those painters of his!'

'But what are they going to think?' Albert protested.

'It's not for them to think anything after the way they treated me.'

'First of all you refuse to model for them and they put it down to racial prejudice and now you refuse to participate in a project designed to overcome that prejudice. They have every right to think the worst.'

'I don't care. I did not know what part of me they wanted as a model.'

'But he distinctly told you what he painted.'

'Albert, I am not going to argue. I am not taking part.'

Albert shrugged. Irrational female. Or was she keeping something from him? He glanced at her with quick interest, but at that point Dr Krapstein called for order in his unexpectedly high-pitched voice.

'Okay everybody,' he cried, the voice thinly escaping from the mass of black beard and hair. 'Doesn't matter if you haven't been introduced to one another because it's not necessary with a project like this. I guess you have some idea what it's all about and you're interested or you wouldn't be here in the first place.'

'Elmer,' Gloria Eisenway cried expansively, 'you know we're interested. We're all liberals here.'

'I am a Communist!' Joseph Mbula roared.

There was a clamour of supporting dissent.

'I am a Trotskyist!'

'Maoist!'

'Viva Cuba!'

Dr Krapstein raised his rather short arms, confronting them like Canute trying to turn back the waves. His black-rimmed spectacles were huge, all-seeing eyes.

'Right, right!' he cried. 'We are many things. But we are also all one. Humankind. After all the political slogans have been voiced we are *one*. And we have to find the key to that unity. *Work* for it . . .'

'Not one,' Joseph Mbula cried. 'Haves and have-nots!'

There was a rumble of support and Elmer Krapstein gazed

at them challengingly while he figured out how to get off the political and on to the psychological. George Eisenway noisily refilled his glass.

'Maybe, maybe,' Dr Krapstein said. 'But first we've got to recognise our oneness and then the wealth will be for everyone. We can *do* it! I tell you we can do it!'

'I can do it,' Joseph said solemnly. He undulated his loins. The Africans roared with irrepressible laughter.

Dr Krapstein refused to be put off. He waved his hands gently from side to side in a gesture which Albert, for one, found incomprehensible.

'What we're going to do,' he said, 'is break through the barriers that keep people apart. In our non-verbal encounter meditations, we crash through the barrier of conversation, small talk, word blinds that keep us from seeing one another, knowing one another. We *use* the body instead of being frightened of it. We touch. We caress. And maybe we use sounds, pure sounds, instead of words. We follow rules that make us approach one another and make contact rather than withdraw. We find out an awful lot about ourselves as well as discovering new possibilities with other people . . . '

Dr Krapstein paused and gave them a bland, encouraging smile.

'These body-touch exercises form a method which has been highly successful in small groups in many parts of the world,' he explained. 'From the experiences they have had in such gatherings, people have gone on to find new developments in their own personal growth. I know this is a means by which men can come to forget the colour of their skin, whether they're rich or poor, Jew or Gentile. They discover what it is to be one human facing himself and facing another human.'

'You think the white racist is human?' Joseph Mbula called. There was another burst of laughter from the Africans.

'Okay,' Dr Krapstein said, unruffled. 'You just made a statement about Joseph Mbula. Good.'

He paused and inclined his head. His long, black hair fell forward on to his chest.

'That comment from Mr Mbula illustrates the fact that it doesn't really matter too much how you react. If you don't want to join in . . . well, that already tells you something about yourself on which you can reflect. If you only want to go so far, then that's a valid piece of self-learning, too.

'Now we don't follow any rigid rules. I shall lead, but nobody's to feel bound by anything I say. I'll simply be giving you a framework for action. Your reactions, whatever they may be, will teach you a great deal about your own desires and capacities in a situation in which the senses rather than words are the dominant factor.'

Everett-Smithers, bristling in every fibre, suddenly barked: 'Better watch it Krapstein! There are ladies present.'

'Another excellent illustration,' Dr Krapstein said. 'Mr Everett-Smithers begins in his mind by setting the men apart from the ladies, as if the ladies are incapable of, or unwilling to discover anything about themselves. It is from that position, which is obviously a rather restrictive one, that Mr Everett-Smithers must move on – if he is to develop and create new possibilities.'

'I won't take any insults, Krapstein . . .!' Everett-Smithers cried.

'Cuthbert, Cuthbert,' Gloria Eisenway cooed. 'Elmer's not insulting you. He's simply asking you to think about yourself.'

'It sounds very interesting, daddy,' Millicent said in a soft, soothing tone. 'I'm sure the ladies will like it.'

Everett-Smithers did not answer, but appeared slightly mollified.

'You know, animals do it, this body-touching business,' Francis Fordyce-Williams said. 'Might not be a bad thing.'

'You know how the leopard touches the zebra?' Joseph Mbula said to him menacingly.

'Load of crap!' George Eisenway intervened, noisily. 'It's all a load of goddam crap.'

'George,' Gloria Eisenway said reproachfully. 'Is that really your contribution?'

'Mama, you and your sense of humour. I'm referring to . . . to body . . . about . . . about . . . non-verbal bodies

. . . whatever the hell it's called.'

'But George, it's not crap. It's a way of finding out who you really are. Do you know who you are?'

'*Sure* I know who I am. You *still* mad at me Mama?'

'Well, I already said I'm not taking part,' Angela said, glancing meaningfully at Joseph Mbula. 'I'll be touched by whom I want to touch me and not by anyone else.'

'Angela,' Albert demanded. 'Is there something . . .?'

'Nobody has to take part who doesn't want to!' Krapstein cried. 'Miss Carter is the third person to make a clear statement about herself. If at any point you *do* feel you'd like to join in Miss Carter, please feel free to do so.'

'Ha,ha,ha,ha,ha,ha,ha!'

Everyone stared at the source of the merriment. One Dr Daniel Thuka, a jolly, sexy rotund man with quick shrewd eyes, who had been invited along in his capacity of Joseph Mbula's physician.

'Anything wrong, Dr Thuka?' Gloria Eisenway asked.

'Oh no, oh no,' Dr Thuka chortled. 'It is very funny.'

'What's very funny?'

Dr Thuka made a vague gesture all around.

'Another valid personal statement,' Dr Krapstein said. 'We learn from everything. Okay, I think we'd better get started. Will those who are ready please form a circle here. That's right. Not too far apart. And now, whom shall we have? You, perhaps, Dr Thuka and . . . Gloria, will you help to start things going? Yes? Fine. You two in the middle then, please. Now hold each other. No, not there, Dr Thuka. Oh well, it doesn't really matter as long as Gloria doesn't mind. Now I want you both to sway as one, back and forth, back and forth. And we in the surrounding circle will prevent you from falling, with our hands. That's right. That's right! Sway like saplings, blades of grass. Can you trust us? Will you trust us? Marvellous. Two very warm, trusting people . . . '

Albert gently caught the interlocked bodies as they swayed toward him and heaved them back to the vertical so that they fell forward to be puffily caught by Aubrey Fanshawe and returned at a slight angle which threw them toward

Gerald Duxworthy – and back – and so on. This was really quite fun. Gloria Eisenway had her eyes closed, which must make the experience more hair-raising. Of course, it showed a depth of trust on her part, didn't it. Probably was something in all this. And how funny Dr Thuka looked with one hand on her shoulders, the other on her bottom. He was clearly enjoying himself in his rolypoly way: grinning with a flash of gold-filled teeth, gripping her buttock, hand slipping on the platinum shirt dress.

Next time they came to Albert he was going to step aside and let them drop. That should prove something to them. He was filled with fiendish delight at the thought, became anxious in case someone else thought of it first. But then he had a sudden thought. That would be a statement he was making about himself, wouldn't it? Letting them drop? Albert Divine – not to be trusted. A dropper of swaying, non-verbal encounter meditation protagonists. George Eisenway might still decide he was unsuitable for the fulfilment of his commission. Worse. He might not be able to live with himself . . .

'Very good,' Krapstein cried. 'Very good. Two more to take their place, please.'

One of two slim, laughing African girls who had arrived with Joseph went into the middle. Nobody else volunteered.

'How come there are only two African girls?' Albert asked Gloria Eisenway.

'African men won't let them come,' Gloria Eisenway whispered. 'They're very conservative, you know. We just don't know enough emancipated African women.'

'The men are really dictators,' Jennifer Duxworthy whispered in turn. 'They're not gentlemen, you know.' She looked deeply and significantly at Albert, with her bright smile.

Gentleman Albert suddenly bent his arms so that his hands were under his armpits. He made a sort of Frankenstein's monster face and shuffled toward Jennifer Duxworthy. She retreated a step, the radiant smile on her face. Albert mouthed a string of threatening moans, advancing on her. She gave a trillingly selfconscious laugh. Albert slewed his mouth into a grotesque leer, half closed one eye, pinched in his nostrils with a painful effort of breathing technique and raised one hand like a claw toward her. Jennifer Duxworthy backed away, frozenly smiling, fell over a wickerwork stool and ended on her behind, with her summer dress around her hips.

There was a spontaneous burst of applause from the Africans, accompanied by much laughter and slapping of backs. Albert bowed and gallantly offered his hand to the prostrate Jennifer Duxworthy, whose husband was regarding her revealing disarray with outrage.

She accepted the proffered hand with some uncertainty and allowed herself to be pulled to her feet. The smile rearranged itself on her face. Gerald Duxworthy sidled close and hissed: 'What a disgusting exhibition!'

Jennifer Duxworthy turned her unchanging smile on her husband and then looked back at Albert.

'You really sweep me off my feet, Mr Divine,' she said.

'You hurt yourself?' Joseph Mbula demanded, pushing through to her with mock concern. He stooped and brushed her buttocks gently.

Jennifer Duxworthy shied away from him, colliding with Dr Thuka, who steadied her by placing his hands on her sides, smiling jovially.

'No, I'm perfectly all right,' she said. 'Thank you.'

Gerald Duxworthy's lips compressed furiously.

'Please be serious, Mr Divine,' Dr Krapstein said. 'We're waiting for another volunteer for the middle.'

Albert made no response to this hint and Dr Krapstein said: 'How about you, Everett-Smithers?'

'You think I'm . . .

'No, nobody's fallen so far, have they? Why are you so afraid?'

'Afraid! What the hell are you . . .?'

'Go on, daddy,' Millicent murmured. 'It can't be anywhere near as bad as baling out.'

'Of course it's nothing like baling out! You can't compare this idiot game with the exigencies of war. In any case, that's not the . . . '

'Go on, daddy. I'll catch you.'

Everett-Smithers reluctantly allowed himself to be pushed into the centre of the circle. He stared awkwardly at the African girl, sniffed in embarrassment.

'You have to hold each other,' Dr Krapstein prompted.

Everett-Smithers hung back. The African girl looked at him expectantly but rather shyly.

'For God's sake, Cuthbert, you must have held a woman before,' Gloria Eisenway goaded. 'We have Millicent to show for it.'

'Gloria,' Everett-Smithers said, on his dignity. 'I don't think . . .'

'Racist!' Joseph Mbula suddenly snarled. 'Ku Klux Klan!'

'Don't be ridiculous!' Everett-Smithers snapped. He was clearly torn between thumping Joseph and grabbing the girl – and at that moment she settled matters by moving in close and putting her arms around his waist.

'Bravo Cuthbert!' Albert cried audaciously.

'You keep out of this, Divine!' Everett-Smithers snorted. 'Or . . .'

'You have to put your arms around her, too, daddy,' Millicent said.

Everett-Smithers gingerly placed his arms around the girl's shoulders. She smiled at him and he returned the smile brusquely.

'Good!' Dr Krapstein cried. 'Trust us – sway!'

The girl followed his command, but Everett-Smithers could not commit himself. As she swayed backwards, he tottered stiff-legged after her, rising on tip-toe. As she swayed forward, he resisted, bending back only from the hips with her limp in his arms.

'That's no good, Cuthbert,' Gloria Eisenway objected. 'Take a chance. Let yourself go.'

'Let him do it his own way,' Dr Krapstein admonished.

Everett-Smithers leaned back a little farther from the waist, peering over his shoulder. Joseph Mbula stood behind him, waiting. There was a statuesque impasse.

'He will not trust because I am black,' Joseph sneered.

He lashed out suddenly with his foot, catching Everett-

Smithers at the back of the knee. The knee buckled and both Everett-Smithers and the girl toppled back into Joseph's arms, to be immediately ejected by a furious heave that hurtled them both across the circle.

Everett-Smithers released the girl and tried to regain his balance. But he was caught and hurled and hurled and caught, thrown from one to another so fast that he was quite unable to right himself. Gales of laughter accompanied his flailing motion. A chorus of shouts and instruction in English and Swahili rang through the bungalow.

'Hold it, hold it,' Dr Krapstein called. 'That's not right. Hold everything. Stop. STOP!'

Everett-Smithers was abruptly released, staggered and sat down precipitously, gazing around with dazed eyes.

'Who was the bastard responsible for that?' he gasped. 'I'll settle . . .!'

'Everett-Smithers, that was fine,' Dr Krapstein said hurriedly. 'Absolutely fine. You just have to figure out what it is that makes you unwilling to trust other people. Work on the blockage.'

'Blockage!' Everett-Smithers bellowed. 'This is just a stupid party game! Used to play one like it when I was a boy. Blockage my buttocks!'

'I'm sure your reaction was very similar when you were a boy,' Dr Krapstein said blandly. 'It's probable you've learned nothing since then.'

Everett-Smithers hauled himself belligerently to his feet.

'I told you I won't take any insults, Krapstein,' he snorted. If you're suggesting . . . '

'I think it's rather a nice game,' Millicent interrupted. 'I can see that if you let yourself go, you can just sort of waft around like a feather, without a care in the world.'

'Bullshit!' George Eisenway growled from the depths of the room.

'Don't you dare address my daughter in that way!' Everett-Smithers shouted. 'I'll break your bloody nose for you, Eisenway.'

'Not in my house, Cuthbert,' Gloria Eisenway warned. 'You just mind your manners.'

'*My* manners! You tell that cowardly oaf of a husband . . .'

'Okay, okay,' Dr Krapstein broke in, raising his arms. 'We'll leave that one for a bit. Two more in the circle, please.'

As if somehow it were a challenge to Everett-Smithers, Joseph Mbula stepped into the ring.

'Mrs Duxworthy?' Dr Krapstein suggested.

'All right,' she said gamely.

She moved into the centre with her scintillating artificial smile. Gerald Duxworthy's brittle smile covered nervous disapproval.

'Now I want all the rest of you to caress them,' Dr Krapstein said. 'Very gently. And I want you two really to feel your bodies while they're being caressed. Get a thorough sense of them.'

'Well, I don't know . . .' Jennifer Duxworthy murmured.

'What do you mean, caress them?' Gerald Duxworthy asked with steely brightness.

'What I mean is to stroke their cheeks, their hair, beard, arms, backs . . . Don't be afraid to make physical contact. And while you're doing it, I want you to make sounds. Not words – sounds.'

'What sort of sounds?' Mrs Fordyce-Williams demanded with a hint of hostility.

'What sort of sound would you like to make?'

Mrs Fordyce-Williams's hostility became open.

'I don't know that I'd like to make any sound!'

'Okay,' Dr Krapstein said reasonably. 'Then don't make any. Just caress. Nobody has to make sounds if he doesn't want to.'

'Can we make any sound?' Dr Thuka asked merrily.

'Any sound you like.'

Dr Thuka abruptly began clucking like a hen. He flapped his lips, wrinkled his nose and twitched his ears, lost in furious concentration. Almost immediately Francis Fordyce-Williams responded with a string of throaty growls and sharp, coughing roars like a cheetah. He confronted Dr Thuka with savage big cat's eyes. Cheetah against hen.

'Just a minute. Just a *minute!*' Dr Krapstein shouted.

The snarling and clucking sputtered to a reluctant halt.

'Okay, okay,' Dr Krapstein said with endless patience. 'In the first place, the sounds have to accompany the touching. In the second, I don't want animal sounds, no matter how good. When I say sounds, I mean gentle sounds like breathing aloud or "ooooohing" and "aaaaahing". The point is to hear the sound of your own voice. It has to be a release not a vaudeville show. Lots of people can't stand the sound of their own voice, you know; they're afraid of it. It inhibits them. Okay, let's go.'

Joseph Mbula stood in the centre of the circle like a wary panther daring them to try and get him. Jennifer Duxworthy remained a couple of feet away from him, rather tense in her smart cotton dress. Nobody moved.

'You're a lot of very inhibited people,' Dr Krapstein said.

He moved over and began to demonstrate the possibilities. He patted Joseph's cheeks and at the same time pushed out his lips and made strange, guttural noises. Joseph made a grimace and turned his head away.

'Right, right,' Dr Krapstein said. 'React. Good.'

He clutched gently at Joseph's beard, simultaneously changing his sound to an owl-like hooting. Joseph glared at him, opened his mouth and uttered a ferocious 'Uuuuuuugh!' in return.

'Excellent,' Dr Krapstein said. 'Aaaaaaaah!'

'Uuuuuuuugh!'

'Oooooooow!'

Joseph suddenly shoved Dr Krapstein in the chest and the psychiatrist retreated a step, but sprang straight back and patted him on the shoulders. Joseph gave him a harder shove and, at that, Dr Krapstein faltered and waved the rest of the circle in.

'Okay, carry on,' he said.

A group of Joseph's fellow painters began boisterously thumping him on the back, pulling his beard, kicking his behind and making a cacophany like a small zoo. Dr Krapstein regarded them for a moment like a long-suffering referee and finally decided not to intervene, but let the tomfoolery work itself out.

Stirred by this example, Dr Thuka abruptly took hold of Jennifer Duxworthy's left arm and began to stroke it, gazing into her eyes and uttering a new vocalisation much like the cawing of a crow. Jennifer Duxworthy regarded him with a distaste only thinly veiled by her brittle smile. Dr Thuka, completely unconcerned, worked around to her back and insidiously caressed her spinal column. Another African moved in, fondling her long, ginger hair.

Albert, quickly recognising the simple choice between Joseph and Jennifer, also staked his claim. He stood in front of her and ran his fingertips over her features – eyelids, cheekbones, lips, chin . . . Better than it looked, really. Soft skin, good bones. He began to utter a low, prolonged 'Wooooow' and Jennifer Duxworthy favoured him with the most genuine of her artificial smiles.

'Jennifer!' Gerald Duxworthy said sharply. 'Perhaps we'd better sit this one out.'

'Perhaps you had, darling, if you're too inhibited.'

Gerald Duxworthy's pale face went colourless and he withdrew as brightly as he could manage to a corner of the room where George Eisenway was trying to hold a drunken conversation with Angela.

Albert turned his attention back to Jennifer Duxworthy's face. She was now the object of so many hands that they were invading one another's territories. The intrepid Dr Thuka, he noted, had struck out and was pioneering his way to the bulge of Jennifer's rump. In fact, Albert saw her sharply tense her buttocks away from the intrusion.

Dr Krapstein, watching the group around Joseph Mbula, called out: 'Relax, try to trust, open yourself.'

Jennifer Duxworthy relaxed and Dr Thuka plunged on. One of the African girl's began to stroke her breasts and Albert cursed his own lack of initiative. As a small compensation, he moved on to her neck.

The tumult had subsided in Joseph Mbula's sphere where the women had joined the men. In fact . . . Albert could have sworn that hyena-faced Georgette Musky was leading a sly assault on Joseph's loins. Certainly Joseph was no longer showing resistance. Janice Troll had also thrown her weight into Joseph's corner and was making shy, mooing noises as she attempted the difficult task of running her fingers through his tight, crinkly hair. Millicent, too, was standing shoulder to shoulder with a drooling Aubrey Fanshawe, pressing her palms on his latissimus dorsi. Her father, who appeared at rather a loss since his daughter's enthusiastic entry into the project, was wandering from one group to the other, thrusting out his cleft chin pugnaciously and demanding: 'What the devil's it all about? What the devil is it *really* all about?'

Albert concentrated on Jennifer Duxworthy. Her bright smile had lost some of its false glitter. In fact her head was now tilted back, her eyes partly closed and her lips partly open, emitting her own particular sound, rather like an intermittent gas jet. And suddenly her hands swung on to Albert's chest and she began to caress him in turn. She appeared to be getting quite steamed up – and suddenly Albert saw why. Below the rumpine realms of Dr Thuka, the second African girl was kneeling and running her hands up Jennifer's legs. Albert chose to ignore the sad homosexual implications, concentrating instead on the interesting way that Jennifer Duxworthy's bright, brittle insincerity was crumbling away under this provocation.

Dr Krapstein's shrill voice broke in, destroying further reflection on the possibilities.

'All right, everyone,' he cried. 'I think we've achieved a little something. Not so afraid, now. Let's move on.'

The groups broke up, leaving Jennifer Duxworthy and Joseph Mbula in a state of disarray which was rather more difficult for the African to dissemble.

'Right, now I want you to take partners – or threesomes, however you like – and show how your partner makes you feel, in some bodily way. Like I mean you might want to shout at someone, which is perfectly all right, or pull a face at him, or shake hands . . . Let your feelings come out. Don't be afraid. We've simply got to cut through all the generalised, impersonal sparring that goes on and get right down to the elementals.'

There followed a certain amount of jostling for partners. Rather reminiscent of the mad scramble at the opening of the big store sales. Jennifer Duxworthy clung to Albert. But Dr Thuka would not relinquish his claim and stayed with them. Elsewhere, Albert was aware of various odd pairings; Joseph Mbula and Millicent, with Everett-Smithers thrusting fussily in to make a trio; Fordyce-Williams and an African girl; Mrs Fordyce-Williams and one of the painters; Eisenway, who had lurched back into the fray, and another painter; Gloria Eisenway with several of Joseph Mbula's 'school' and Aubrey Fanshawe lurking alongside; Georgette Musky, having lost her claim to Joseph, surrounded by Africans, with Janice Troll shyly on the fringe . . . Only Angela, with the apprehensively bright Gerald Duxworthy, managed to remain aloof, trying to pretend it wasn't happening.

'Honesty, honesty!' Dr Krapstein shouted. 'I do implore you. Remember that is the point of the exercise!'

He joined Gloria and her admirers and gave a sample demonstration in a loud voice: 'You make me feel very protective, Gloria. I feel you need protection, possibly against yourself. And yet, I'm a little afraid of you, too, in a way. A sort of castration fear.'

He put one arm around her shoulders and at the same time held her wrists in one hand as if to prevent an assault on himself.

'Don't be afraid of Poor Old Mama,' Eisenway slurred from a distant point in the room. 'No man has to be afraid of a woman.'

'But I am afraid,' Dr Krapstein said. 'It's a fear that she may show me love, kindness – and then withdraw it at a whim, or for some reason I can't fathom.'

'Don't worry, Elmer,' Gloria Eisenway said. 'I'm not going to castrate you. I mean, I wouldn't want to make anyone ineffectual. I love everyone. I feel I want to give myself to everyone.'

There was an immediate and noisy exodus of Africans from Georgette Musky to Gloria Eisenway. They fell over one another, shoving and pushing, fighting for an advantageous place.

'I feel exactly the same,' Georgette Musky cried desperately. 'I want to take my clothes off.'

There was a clamorous recoil from Gloria Eisenway – a splinter group surging back to Georgette Musky, who ceremoniously doffed her dress and sat smiling in brassiere and pants, with her angular body looking as if it could be taken apart and offered piecemeal to the assembly.

'Put your clothes back on, girl!' Everett-Smithers roared. 'How can you display yourself – in front of these blacks!'

'Racist!' Joseph Mbula roared.

'I'm no racist!' Everett-Smithers shouted back. 'But I do know right from wrong!'

'Daddy!' Millicent cried admiringly. 'You've got the idea. Let it all come out!'

'Just what I'm trying to prevent that unfortunate girl from doing,' Everett-Smithers retorted. 'You can't blame the blacks when she flaunts herself like that!'

This situation was suddenly interrupted by Francis Fordyce-Williams, who began to growl and make coughing roars like a cheetah. His African girl partner drew away from him, startled and the challenge was immediately taken up by Dr Thuka, who launched into his clucking hen imitations, furiously cackling as if he actually believed such a feeble defence might keep a cheetah at bay.

'Good, good!' Dr Krapstein yelled. 'Let it come out! Let's break through to understanding and love!'

Gloria Eisenway, not to be outdone by Georgette Musky, undid the cord of her platinum shirtdress and let it fall open, revealing her naked body. She sat brazenly smiling in the middle of her goggle-eyed entourage.

'Funny, you know I wouldn't mind taking my clothes off either,' Jennifer Duxworthy said, hanging on to her brittle smile by the merest wrinkle. 'Am I being too honest?'

'No baby, you're being right,' the African girl said. 'I'll strip off, too and there won't be no barriers between us.'

Without more ado, she peeled her dress over her head to disclose a body unhindered by underclothing. Albert was mesmerised. No ideal model type, this, but a real child-bearing female. Well, maybe not, to judge from the way she was drooling over Jennifer Duxworthy. Not that Jennifer seemed to notice. Her attention, in fact, was very firmly fixed on Albert as if she held him personally responsible for the hands which stroked her rump and the fingers that were removing her clothes.

Nudity caught on like a forest fire.

'Feel! Trust! Break those barriers!' Dr Krapstein cried.

One by one, two by two, three by three bodies were bared, with one or two exceptions like the reluctant Millicent, the stunned Mrs Fordyce-Williams, the incredulous Everett-Williams and the non-partakers – a little group containing Eisenway, Gerald Duxworthy and Angela, who preferred to take refuge in a haze of alcohol.

Albert, still innocuously and mechanically stroking the quivering neck of Jennifer Duxworthy, observed the interesting release of the unconscious, the unmasked interplay of personality.

The aberrations were perhaps the most interesting, like Francis Fordyce-Williams turning into a cheetah and playfully lashing at his apprehensive partner with a lethal paw.

It hardly needed Gloria Eisenway to carry the project to new levels, but as hostess it was fitting that she set the pace, declaring in a resounding stage whisper: 'I want to give. I want to give!' She lay down abruptly in a manner which Albert recognised as a prelude to research. She began to wriggle her bottom.

Her invitation was a sign for the collapse of all inhibition.

Georgette Musky fractionally won the race to be entered – entirely due to lack of immediate agreement on who should be first partner for Gloria Eisenway. Janice Troll was up-ended by a group of Africans establishing the genuineness of her provocative dimensions. And Mrs Fordyce-Williams, to her horror, was grabbed with lustful intent by two more of the black visitors. At the same time Francis Fordyce-Williams made the final feline lunge on to his prey, who gave a small, thrilled scream and prepared to submit to the inevitable; a couple of white farmers grabbed the lesbian

African away from Jennifer Duxworthy and forced her, shrilly protesting, into an intercourse to which she was entirely unaccustomed; white women all around were being subjected to assault to the accompaniment of vengeful cries of undoubted racial animosity.

Dr Krapstein, overwhelmed by the passions he had set loose, held up his Canute-like arms, crying helplessly: 'Love and understanding, please. Love and understanding, *please*!'

Albert gazed around, dazed. The whole place was going crazy. Joseph Mbula was trying to insert himself through the split in Millicent's dress; Mrs Fordyce-Williams was being raped; Mr Fordyce-Williams was perpetrating on his African girl the intercourse for which he considered her only fit; others were willingly seeking inter-racial orgasm; George Eisenway had passed out; and Dr Thuka had pulled forth his weapon and was attempting to insert it in the still brittly smiling, but very disarranged Jennifer Duxworthy from behind. The smile vanished as he suddenly succeeded. But such an infringement of acceptable manners was too much for the lurking Gerald Duxworthy, who leapt at the doctor, ineffectually pushing, shoving, cuffing. Jennifer held fast to Albert and the four of them, with Dr Thuka refusing to be denied his conquest, staggered around the room.

'Gently, gently!' Dr Krapstein cried.

And Everett-Smithers, who had been virtually paralysed with astonishment, abruptly came to his senses.

'Black swine!' he yelled and lashed out at Joseph, catching him a sharp left hook in the midriff. Joseph uttered a cry for help and Everett-Smithers began to lay about him at the painters who came to Joseph's aid. Fordyce-Williams, putting the call of colour before that of flesh, left his prey and rushed to the farmer's aid. Within minutes there was bedlam. The guests divided themselves automatically into factions of black and white. Feet and fists flew. Bodies rolled and threshed and collapsed in heaps. A minor race war had erupted.

Albert tried to disengage himself from Jennifer Duxworthy, who was still clutching him while Dr Thuka served her from behind and her husband scrambled and staggered around them in an attempt to prise them apart. In the midst of the struggle, Jennifer suddenly lashed out at Gerald and sent him reeling.

'Leave me alone!' she cried. 'I like it!'

Albert took advantage of this division of attention to tear himself away. His hand was grabbed and he turned to defend himself.

It was Angela.

'Quick,' she cried. 'Let's get out of here. Hide in the bush.'

'I'm not sloshed yet,' Albert said.

'We must be flexible.'

'Love and understanding, I beg you!' Dr Krapstein yelled.

They fled through the house and out into the grounds, heading for the trees.

Behind them a window smashed, a door fell off its hinges and the whole bungalow seemed to be heaving as the project for the improvement of race relations got truly under way.

Chapter Nine

'I DON'T see what Elmer's beefing about,' George Eisenway said. 'It must've been a good party. Look at all the damage.'

'If that's the criterion it was the social event of the decade,' Angela said.

The glass had been cleared up and the smashed furniture thrown out, but the bloodstains and the dents in the walls remained as testimony to the previous day's project.

'I guess it might have got a little out of hand,' Eisenway said, scraping some splinters from a door jamb. 'I shoulda stayed awake to control it. Reckon all that driving knocked me out. I don't go for parties so much anyway.'

He took a gulp of Scotch. If ever a man wanted to destroy himself, Angela figured, Eisenway did. She took a sip of Tom Collins. It was contagious.

'What I don't understand is how I got these pains in the back,' Eisenway said. 'Like a herd of elephants ran over me.'

'You must have been sleeping in a draught,' Angela said, diplomatically.

'Trust that weak little bastard Everett-Smithers to start something,' Eisenway said. 'Guy like that involves everyone else just on account of his inferiority.'

He looked at Angela, waiting for her to say something. He wasn't too sure exactly what had gone on the day before, wanted some clues.

'You know,' he said, 'I got a funny idea the women were taking their clothes off. Guess I musta been dreaming.'

'I'm sure you were,' Angela said. 'Actually Albert and I went for a walk and missed the fight.'

'Pity. Albert shoulda been there to help out. White men were outnumbered by those black bastards.'

'Oh I don't know, Albert's not one for violence.'

'You mean he's yellow?'

'Not exactly. Anyway I approve of not fighting. What's it ever achieve?'

'That's a long-haired, half-assed thing to say. You gotta be prepared to fight for your rights or you lose 'em. Can't stand a man who's a coward.'

'It's all right for people like you who don't know the meaning of the word.'

Eisenway looked gratified.

'Well I guess some of us are born with a bit more guts,' he admitted. 'And me being a natural heavyweight . . . '

Angela carried her drink to the doorway and looked out over the terrace and the lawns to the bush beyond with the hills rising misty grey in the distance. It was hot and very pleasant. Now that the African element had gone back to Nairobi, she had borrowed one of Gloria Eisenway's bikinis, feeling safe with the white wreckage of the battle. Not that all the whites had stayed. The Duxworthy's had left in embarrassment and Georgette Musky and Janice Troll had gone off with Joseph and his men. Doubtless the School of Mbula would shortly begin to produce a rash of white studies.

'I dare say Albert's okay in bed,' Eisenway said.

Angela's thoughts came right back to the room. She turned to George Eisenway, who had been staring at her with interest. She was well aware that the borrowed bikini was too small. It revealed roughly a third of each buttock, covered a mere ribbon of her loins and the top was so slight it was hardly worth wearing at all.

'He's okay anywhere,' she retorted. Bed, bush . . . what did it matter?

'Must be to hold a fine girl like you, daughter.'

'That's not the only thing I like about him,' Angela said.

Eisenway finished his Scotch, eyeing her oddly.

'You're a good, loyal girl,' he said. 'A beautiful girl.'

He walked over beside her and leaned on the door looking out at the view.

'This is a great country,' he said. 'Beautiful girl fits in well. As right as the gazelles.'

His arm descended gently and encircled her bare shoulders

'A really great country,' he said. 'Sort of country where anything can happen.'

If you mean what I think you mean, Angela figured, the answer is, no, not anything, Mr Eisenway, George, dear.

'You know, you're just the sort of girl any man would be proud of,' Eisenway went on. 'Beautiful, charming, intelligent, loyal – *sexy.*'

Aha. Exercise in classification: which word does not quite fit the list?

Eisenway's fingers squeezed her shoulder.

'Daughter,' he said. 'We all have to take life's fleeting moments as they come.'

'You're not suggesting incest, are you Papa?' Angela asked with mock innocence.

Eisenway's response was suddenly to gather her in his arms. His hand was on her near naked breast before she knew it.

Angela remained quite passive in his arms. She knew nothing was more designed to dampen unwanted ardour.

'Daughter!' Eisenway breathed. 'Daughter! When a man, a real man speaks to you, you gotta listen. You're a fine girl, a beautiful girl. We gotta make love, beautiful love.'

'But George,' Angela said, putting last things first, 'the others will be back in no time.'

'Another two hours yet. Time they reach the village, have a look around, buy what they want, get back.'

His hand caressed her breast, shoulder, ribs.

'What about Albert,' she said, still trying to be diplomatic. 'And Gloria?'

'They can't get back before the others, can they?' Eisenway said. His hand slid over her back, trembling.

'That's not what I mean,' Angela said. 'I mean what about our loyalty to them.'

'You gotta make exceptions,' Eisenway said. 'Life's full of exceptions.

His hand slid over her bottom, gently brushing the buttocks, first above the flimsy bikini and then under it on her bare flesh. Angela stiffened a little, but he pulled her towards him so that her breasts imprinted themselves on his hairy chest through the open shirt. He lowered his head and kissed her neck.

Angela still tried to play it cool.

'I don't think so,' she said. 'I don't think so. Somebody might arrive.'

Eisenway chuckled and slapped her bottom.

'You don't have to worry about that,' he said. 'Only unexpected visitor we ever had was a White Headed Buffalo Weaver with a broken wing.'

'Oh,' Angela said, trying to steer the conversation into more acceptable channels. 'What happened?'

'We mended it – let him go. You're a lovely girl, daughter. You got a fine, lovely body.'

Her bikini bra suddenly snapped undone and floated to the floor.

'Now George,' Angela said, taking a firmer line at last, 'you're not behaving like a gentleman.'

'No woman wants a man behaves like a gentleman, daughter. Woman wants a red-blooded guy with guts and style.'

He slipped his hand under her bikini and squeezed her posterior. Angela felt an anxious twinge. She suddenly couldn't think why she'd felt so certain she could control him. He might be a phoney, but he was also a big guy. She tried to draw away.

'George,' she said. 'This won't do. You're a very attractive man, but I love Albert.'

'Sure you love Albert. He's a good guy. Albert's for London, swinging, fancy city. Out here in the bush you want a man. Doesn't stop you loving Albert. Right thing at the right time.'

He held her with one arm and pushed down her bikini with the other. Her bottom flopped into view. Angela tried to counteract this undressing by wriggling against it, but managed only to achieve the opposite, actually helping the flimsy garment slip down over her hips. Feeling it slip, she opened her thighs wide, flexing them outwards to prevent the fall. Eisenway mistook the motivation of her movement and deftly – for one who had already that day consumed enough alcohol to put some men on their back–slipped his hand between her legs and stroked the lips of her vagina.

Angela let out a startled breath and jerked away, closing her legs. The bikini fell to the floor and, as she tried to step backwards, she fell, hobbled by the material and finished spreadeagled on the floor.

Eisenway, still misinterpreting her actions, slipped down with her.

'God girl, you're beautiful,' he said.

Angela attempted to slither away, but the bikini restricted her and she kicked it off her ankles.

'It'll be better in the bedroom,' Eisenway murmured, mistaking her writhings for impatience.

But his own impatience appeared to get the better of him and he grabbed her, slithering his hands all over her.

'George – no!' she cried.

'Beautiful girl. Lovely girl.'

He pulled open the front of his drill slacks and half rolled on to her. Angela felt his hairy loins against her thighs, hairy chest on her breasts. What a weight, he was! And with a sudden searing chill she found she couldn't shift him. He was like a huge sack of cement – a sack that held her upper arms and kissed her neck and insinuated itself between her thighs so that she couldn't close them.

She struggled hard, trying to roll him first one way and then the other, waving her legs about vainly. She was helpless.

'You're a fine girl, daughter. So sexy!'

To Eisenway, her struggles for freedom were evidence of mounting passion. Angela was perspiring with her efforts. What a fool, she was. Trying not to hurt his feelings!

'Please, George,' she pleaded. 'Please!'

'I'm trying, daughter, I'm trying!'

Oh Christ! She was wide open to him. He was right there and she couldn't do a thing to stop it. He was going to have her there on the floor!

I'm trying. What did he mean?

And in fact nothing was happening. She was lying with

her thighs wide open and all he had to do was come straight in, yet he was wriggling around ineffectually – and nothing was happening. Absolutely nothing!

Abruptly Eisenway rolled off her and sat up. He put his face in his hands.

Angela lay quite still, astonished. Eisenway didn't stir or say a word. She was moved by curiosity.

'What's the matter, George?'

Slowly, brokenly, he spoke from behind his hands. Angela moved closer to catch the muffled words.

'I – I'm sorry, daughter,' he breathed. 'I – I just can't make it.'

'You can't?'

She supposed that was pretty obvious in retrospect. Any man who got her in that position and didn't . . . well!

'It – it's on account of my organ, daughter.'

'You can't make it *on account of your organ!*'

'It – it's so small. It – it makes me impotent.'

Eisenway took his hands from his face, clenched his fists and gazed at the ceiling. Veins stood out on his forehead.

'It makes me impotent!' he screamed. 'It's so small!'

He lowered his head into his hands again and began to sob.

Angela was moved.

'George, my poor George, don't cry,' she implored.

She put an arm around him.

'It can't be as bad as you make out,' she murmured sympathetically.

'It's minute and it makes me impotent,' Eisenway moaned. 'There's no question about it.'

Angela peered down with curiosity. The maligned member dangled contritely between his thighs. Certainly it looked rather small, but the limp state was not necessarily an accurate criterion. Angela had known cases of midget limpness transforming into spectacularly gigantic rigidity.

'It looks fairly normal to me,' she said.

Eisenway took his hands from his face, produced a handkerchief from his pocket and wiped his eyes. He studied his nether regions with gloomy despair.

'You think that's normal?' he said bitterly.

'Well, once it's up? Once you've got a hard-on? Surely.'

Eisenway shook his head wearily from side to side.

'Harder, but no bigger,' he said.

'I don't believe it.'

'Whether you believe it makes no difference. I tell you it just doesn't get any bigger. Cheroot-prick – that's me.'

He buried his head in his hands again.

Angela looked at him. He was really rather going to seed. Spare tyres, sagging chest, flabby around the neck. Poor man.

'But . . . but even if it is small,' she said, 'surely you can still get some satisfaction. And, after all, not all women are enormous, you know. I have a friend who's had two children and she's still so small that her husband . . . '

'Don't! Don't go on!' Eisenway cried.

'But surely you've had some sex sometime,' Angela said.

'Oh sure.'

'Then if you could make it once . . . well . . . you could make it any time. It's all in the mind, isn't it?'

Eisenway gripped her thigh furiously. He stared straight ahead, face ashen behind the grizzled beard.

'Listen!' he snapped. 'You can't begin to understand what it's like to lie on a woman pumping your guts out and you can't quite feel it and she can't feel it at all. I'd catch them reading posters on the wall, daydreaming, actually going to sleep – bored out of their minds. And finally they'd turn nasty. What the hell do you mean by having a penis like that, they'd scream. That's a matchstick! You can't turn me on with a matchstick! Don't waste my time getting me all worked up and then tickling me with a matchstick! Okay, so they were exaggerating, I admit. But then Gloria put her finger on it. She literally put her finger on it and said: "It's not a matchstick, George. How could anyone be so cruel? It's a cheroot." '

'How awful,' Angela said. 'How could anyone be so insensitive?'

'Oh you can't blame them,' Eisenway said philosophically. He shook his head vigorously. 'You get people all worked up and then frustrate them, you got enemies on your hands. See, every time I think it's gonna work, but then it won't.'

'Well I think it's deplorable,' Angela said. 'You need sympathy, not cruelty and having people poke fun at you.'

Eisenway removed his hand from her thigh. He closed his eyes, gave a deep sigh, hung his head.

'Anyway,' Angela pursued, eyeing the limp flesh. 'I've never heard of a penis that didn't stretch when it went rigid.'

'Oh it maybe fattens up a bit,' Eisenway said disparagingly. 'But it doesn't get any longer.'

Angela rolled over and peered more closely at the unobtrusive object.

'I don't believe it,' she said. 'I think you're just being masochistic.'

Eisenway, who was also staring at his undistinguished masculinity, glanced up at her with sharp resentment.

'Listen,' he said. 'I've put up with this for years. I've suffered. Don't you tell me I'm making it up.'

'I'm not saying you're making it up,' Angela said. 'Just that you might do a little more about getting it up.'

'Four inches and one sixteenth!' Eisenway cried. 'That's the maximum!'

'Maybe it needs exercise,' Angela reflected. 'After all, it's a muscle, isn't it. And if you exercise a muscle you can build it up. I knew a guy who did weight training for a year and . . .'

'Did you ever hear of a weight training programme for a penis?' Eisenway demanded with bitter sarcasm. 'What'll it be now, fellah, lift or curl?'

Angela ran her tongue thoughtfully around her teeth, studying Eisenway's inadequacy, seeking inspiration.

'If you had very light weights,' she said slowly. 'You could get a hard-on and string them on it and try keeping it up against their pressure.'

'Jesus Christ, girl,' Eisenway complained. 'You think I should write Charles Atlas, or whoever the guy is now, and ask him. What course do you recommend for a four and one sixteenth inch penis, Mr Atlas?'

'No,' Angela mused. 'Now I come to think of it, I don't believe you should. You should do it isometrically, without weights at all.'

'Aw, leave me alone, will you!'

Eisenway dropped his head in his hands again. He appeared to be on the verge of a nervous breakdown. Angela knelt in front of him and pulled his hands away from his face.

'Look George,' she said enthusiastically. 'You know what isometrics are?'

'Sure I know what isometrics are.'

'You exercise muscles by tensing them against each other or against an object.'

'It's a crazy idea, a non-idea. Forget it!'

'No George, you've got to let me help you,' Angela insisted. 'Why go on suffering needlessly. Weak men have made themselves into candidates for Mr Universe. Johnny Weissmuller was once a weed.'

'Go ahead – have your fun,' Eisenway choked. A tear rolled down his cheek and got lost in his beard.

'Oh I'm not, I'm not!' Angela cried.

As if to prove her assertion, she caught his penis in her fingers and began a gentle, fluttering massage.

'Look,' she said, 'first of all we'll get you a hard-on and see just what the score is – and then I'll hold it one way while you press or pull in the other.'

Eisenway's member had begun to thicken. He watched Angela's delicate fingers working as if the whole thing had no connection with him, the way a cat might watch someone playing with its tail. Angela stroked and kneaded the expanding flesh, expertly coaxing it up towards the vertical. Eisenway's eyes eventually lifted from her fingers to her arms and her body. He seemed slowly to take in what was happening and his masculinity soared to its pygmy zenith.

'I see what you mean,' Angela said, surveying her handiwork in a detached manner. 'We have to be honest and face the fact that it *is* small. It might well need a rather strenuous programme.'

Eisenway's loins would not keep still.

'It might come up just a fraction more if you stroke my

testicles,' he said slyly.

'Really?' Angela said. She held his scrotum with her free hand and drew her fingertips over the slack hairy flesh.

'Jesus!' Eisenway growled.

'Uh-huh, you're right,' Angela said. 'I felt it distinctly. Just a very tiny bit – but quite distinctly.'

She continued to titillate with both hands. Eisenway's mouth dropped open.

'Okay,' Angela said, 'Now lie back and we'll have the first workout.'

Eisenway lay back cautiously. Angela knelt beside him, very matter-of-fact, like a trainer.

'Right,' she said, 'we'll make it a four-part exercise just to ensure we get most benefit from it. I'll pull it down and you resist – pull it up the way it's pointing now. Then I'll pull it up and you try forcing down. Okay? And then I'll push down as if I'm trying to shove it right through you and you thrust up. And then we reverse – I pull it up and you try to pull it down. Got it?'

Eisenway nodded, gazing at her with haunted eyes.

'Don't worry,' Angela said. 'We'll stop immediately there's any suggestion of strain.'

She rubbed her palms on her thighs and then seized his sex and pulled it down away from his stomach. Eisenway lay with his eyes on the ceiling, tensing his buttocks against the floor.

'Now come on,' Angela said. 'You're not trying. Pull it back with tension. No, no, don't jerk it! A long, smooth pull.'

She reversed the movement, pulling the flesh up so that it lay flat and still along his abdomen.

'Now don't give way,' she urged. 'Push against the pressure of my hand. A little more effort. Good . . . good.'

Eisenway brought his eyes down from the ceiling and raised his neck off the ground for the extra kick of watching her manipulating him.

'No . . .' Angela began. 'Oh well, I guess it's all right if you want to exercise your neck, too. There's nothing against combination exercises. Except I didn't know you had trouble with your neck too.'

She pushed his member down, holding it in the centre of her fist. Eisenway raised his hips.

'You've got it,' Angela said.

She pulled the flesh up and Eisenway pressed his behind into the ground.

'That's right,' Angela enthused. 'Can't you *feel* it working?'

Eisenway made a confirmatory grimace with his mouth. They began to establish a rhythm: forward, back, up, down, forward, back, up, down . . .

'The point about this sort of exercise,' Angela said chattily, as they pushed and pulled, 'is that once you've got the idea, you don't even need a partner. You can do it yourself.'

Eisenway's response was to encircle her hips with his arm and clasp a buttock. He began to squeeze it in time with the genital gymnastics. Angela looked doubtful.

'I don't know about that,' she said. 'Good for the forearm, but you can get an unbalanced development. Did you know that Rod Laver's left forearm is much bigger than his right, because tennis doesn't develop your arms equally?'

Eisenway said nothing. His eyes were closed and he was entering into the exercise with gusto. He began to breathe heavily, his moustache fluttering.

'You're not tiring, are you?' Angela asked. 'I don't know how long we should go on for the first session.'

'No,' Eisenway gasped. 'Not tired.'

He put more and more energy into the exercise and Angela nodded, approvingly.

'If you do it like this every day,' she said, 'you'll have the best developed whatsit in the world within a year.'

Eisenway's fingers dug convulsively into the left cheek of Angela's behind. He was performing the callisthenics like a champion. He opened his eyes and fixed them on her breasts, watching them bob a little as she assisted his development. He began to utter agonised breaths, deep in his throat.

'That's right,' Angela said, pushing and pulling. 'You can do the breathing as well. Very good for the stomach. Out with the thrust, in for the withdrawal.'

Eisenway's lips trembled. His fingertips embedded themselves in Angela's famous buttocks until they were lost to sight.

'George,' she said, 'I think you're going to get your whole body fit if you concentrate like this.'

Eisenway writhed, groaned and jerked upwards as if he was about to levitate.

'It's energy and consistency that . . . '

Angela broke off with a start as a sudden spatter of hot liquid hit her in the eye. She drew back from the area of attack, wiping her face with the back of her hand.

'I'm sorry, I'm sorry,' Eisenway murmured dreamily. 'I lost control. I – I guess the exercise was too advanced for me.'

'That's all right,' Angela said. 'I'm sure it takes time to perfect. In any case, maybe that's a good sign. Have you got a handkerchief?'

Eisenway fumbled in his pocket and apologetically passed her a handkerchief.

'I reckon we should train at least once a day,' he said.

Shadows suddenly filled the doorway to the terrace.

'Well, well, well!' a voice said.

Eisenway sat up abruptly. Angela spun around.

Albert and Gloria Eisenway were framed in the doorway, with the curious faces of the rest of the crowd bobbing behind them. The bodybuilding programme had been so absorbing they'd heard nothing of the early return from the village.

'Well, well, well,' Gloria Eisenway repeated, clearly with more amusement than rancour.

Albert was speechless.

Angela sprang to her feet, realised her total nudity and hastily attempted to struggle into the borrowed bikini.

'Oh please don't jump to conclusions,' she cried. 'We were just doing an exercise.'

'I'll say you were.'

'Albert,' Angela pleaded. 'I know it sounds crazy, but we were starting a programme to develop George's penis.'

'I can see that,' Albert said, staring at the sperm trail across Angela's breast. 'Seems to be coming on quite well.'

Eisenway staggered to his feet, belatedly tucking himself away, buttoning up his slacks.

'It was isometrics,' he said.

'Because Charles Atlas might not have the right weights,' Angela cried.

'She's a very loyal girl,' Eisenway said.

'He's impotent!' Angela shouted.

'And I,' Albert said, fully recovering his voice at last, 'am King Farouk.'

Chapter Ten

ALBERT CLIMBED down from the Land Rover on to the thin grass under the shade of the clump of trees and gazed across the valley.

Copses alternated with bare patches of tall grass and rock. on the far side of the vale a group of large deer were grazing among the sparse trees.

George Eisenway stepped down beside him.

'There they are,' he announced. 'Fine bunch of kudu. Probably find impala and zebra around here, too.'

'They look a long way off,' Albert said. 'How do we get to them?'

Eisenway stuck a finger in his mouth and held it up in the wind like a boy scout.

'Wind's coming from them,' he said. 'We walk – stalk them. Long as we don't show ourselves, make too much noise, we can get pretty close.'

Angela swung down from the vehicle, looking like a film star on location in her neat olive green bush jacket and well creased slacks.

'What I don't understand,' she said, 'is that I always thought you needed lots of porters and gun bearers and people when you went on a hunting safari.'

'Well since we only got one gun to bear, I figure the bearers aren't all that necessary,' Eisenway said.

'He prefers our little ménage à trois,' Albert said.

'Oh Albert,' Angela said. 'I thought you said you'd forget all about that.'

'He's going to carry the gun strapped to his old man – for the exercise.'

'Albert, didn't Gloria vouch for his incapacity. She knew it was a scientific experiment.'

'Oh yes, Gloria knows all about scientific experiments.'

'What do you mean, Albert?'

'Never mind.'

George Eisenway took a bottle of Scotch from a rucksack.

'Here, have a drink, Albert,' he said. 'That was all my fault. We got talking and I got to telling Angela all about myself and then we had this crazy idea. It seemed all right at the time. No harm done, son.'

Albert took a swig of Scotch.

'You can say what you like about the scientific bit,' he said. 'She still hasn't explained to my satisfaction what she was doing with her clothes off.'

'Albert,' Angela repeated. 'What do you mean about Gloria knowing all about scientific experiments?'

'Your girl is okay, believe me,' Eisenway said, taking the Scotch and knocking back a good measure.

'Naturally you would think so.'

'A fine, loyal girl.'

'Albert,' Angela said. 'What's going on?'

'Nothing you'd disapprove of, presumably.'

'What do you mean? Albert have you . . . '

Eisenway interrupted, handing Angela the Scotch.

'Have a drink,' he said.

Angela obediently took a swig, looking attentively at Albert.

'Let's go,' Eisenway said. He walked out from the shade of the trees and began to descend the hillside.

'Can't we take the Land Rover?' Albert called. 'I'm not feeling energetic.'

'No,' Eisenway called back. 'Can't get any nearer. Anyway that's the spot I gotta meet the guy who's bringing the statuettes.'

They watched his burly figure showing above the waist-high grass, bush hat pulled low, rifle slung on his shoulder.

'Come on,' Albert said. 'We'd better keep together.'

'Albert, why aren't you feeling energetic?' Angela demanded, as they followed the slight path Eisenway had made through the grass.

'Has to do with scientific experiments,' Albert said. 'Always find them a little tiring.'

Angela was silent as they moved on through the grass under the hot sun and entered the dappled gloom of forest on the lower slopes of the valley.

'I noticed the way she looked at you when I said you had a Swahili girlfriend,' Angela mused. 'And the way she walks around in those make-believe clothes . . .!'

'Listen to the nude calling the clothes make-believe,' Albert scoffed. 'You don't fool me. Just because the old phoney has a complex and can't make it with his wife, doesn't mean to say he can't make it with anyone.'

'Albert, what did you and Gloria do the afternoon George passed out and I went to bed?'

'We just got talking and telling each other about ourselves,' Albert said. 'No harm done.'

'Hmmmm. Albert I believe you made it with her.'

'At least I wasn't caught in the act like some people I could mention.'

'You screwed that sexy bitch while I was asleep.'

'Just a mad moment. Not like your cunningly contrived staying behind.'

'So you admit it!'

'I said there was no harm done.'

'No harm done! I bet she suffered injury from your dimensions after her husband's four and one sixteenth inches!'

'You actually measured it?'

'I took his word for it.'

'You took it period.'

'Albert, I think I might faint.'

'Is that what you said to George?'

'I told him he should do it every day.'

'I ought to punish you right now.'

'Oh please, Albert, please.'

Eisenway hailed rather plaintively from behind them.

'Hang on you two. I gotta have a rest.'

They turned in surprise. Eisenway was bent double over a tree stump, breathing hard. They'd gone right past him.

They went back and sat on the stump. He passed around the whisky bottle.

'It's on account of I'm carrying all this gear,' he said.

'If we don't have porters, how are we going to carry back the trophies?' Albert asked.

Eisenway wiped his mouth with the sleeve of his bush jacket. His face was bathed in sweat.

'What the hell would we need porters for?' he asked. 'Rucksack's plenty big enough.'

'Good god. That's what I call a pessimist,' Albert said.

'Don't be stupid. We might get a whole bagful. Once you start shooting you can make a hit over and over again.'

Albert gave him a sidelong glance. This guy was definitely crazy. It *did* run in the family.

'But surely,' Angela said, 'even one of those heads . . . I mean, they look so huge, those kudu.'

'Magnificent animals,' Eisenway agreed. 'Some of those bulls have sixty-inch horns. Okay, let's go.'

He began to march forward again, stepping around fallen trunks, brushing low-lying branches with his hat.

'He's nuts,' Albert said softly.

'Perhaps he never manages to shoot anything,' Angela suggested. 'That's why he doesn't need porters. Albert, why didn't Gloria come?'

'How should I know?'

'It's because you've worn her out.'

'More likely she's embarrassed going on safari with her husband and his mistress.'

'Being with her lover would make up for that.'

'Only if she could get lost with him. Very sexy all this heat. She might find it unbearable.'

'Maybe that's why George had to sit down,' Angela said.

'Maybe you two would like to go off and lie down.'

'Well, he hasn't had his exercise today – as far as I know.'

'Better watch that. Start slacking and he might slip back. Four and one thirty-second inches.'

'Albert, you've got a hard-on.'

'At least you can see it. More than one could say for that pinhead prick.'

'Albert, perhaps we could creep off through the trees for a while.'

'He might tell Gloria and I'm not sure she'd like that.'

'Albert, I insist on the truth! Did you make it with her?'

'Ask yourself what you might have done in the circumstances.'

'You think you're very clever, don't you, Albert Divine.'

Her hazel eyes brooded darkly over him and she tripped over a log.

'It's no good lying on the ground,' Albert said. 'You can't entice me.'

Eisenway called back softly.

'Quieten down you two.'

He came to a halt where the forest thinned and the hillside rose above them in bare rocky patches interspersed with clumps of trees and thornbushes. They approached him silently.

The kudu were grazing quietly about seventy yards away, screened by a few trees. The thin white stripes of their flanks and the spiralling convolutions of their fine horns were clearly visible.

'Oh they're beautiful,' Angela whispered. 'I don't think we should shoot any of them.'

'Women,' Eisenway complained. 'Full of contradictions.'

'It doesn't seem fair,' Angela whispered.

'They don't mind,' Eisenway said.

'That's a rather callous thing to say,' Angela said indignantly.

'Don't be stupid. They don't know anything about it.'

'Maybe they don't if it's over quickly, but it still seems terrible.'

'Are you so accurate they don't know anything about it?' Albert asked softly.

'Not always,' Eisenway admitted.

'What happens then?'

'Well, we either try to track them down, or move on to something else.'

Very gently he slipped the rifle from his shoulder and lowered the rucksack from his back.

'Shouldn't we get a bit closer?' Albert suggested.

'Yeah, maybe. I'll take a shot from here and then we can

move in and try again.'

They both stared at him.

'But how can you possibly do that?' Angela asked. 'What's the point in moving in?'

'Whadya think, daughter?' Eisenway muttered, busying himself with the rucksack. 'The point is the second shot'll be closer and better.'

Albert scratched his nose nervously. Definitely nuts. You could get yourself in a funny situation with a guy like this alone in the bush. Perhaps he and Angela should run for it.

'But whichever one you shoot, the others will just run off,' Angela insisted.

'Don't worry,' Eisenway said. 'I'll shoot them all.'

'I don't see that's either necessary or possible,' Angela said rather haughtily.

'Just what I'd expect an amateur to say,' Eisenway chuckled. 'Just about do it if they keep together.'

'Well I don't want any part of it,' Angela said. 'Those poor, beautiful creatures.'

'Well how'd you like that!' Eisenway exclaimed. 'I bring you all the way out here at your own request and then you don't want any part of it.'

'Well, I hadn't really envisaged it until now. If you must go on with it then I'll wait back at the car.'

Eisenway shrugged.

'Okay, have it your way, daughter. But I don't see what you're getting so screwed up about.'

'I don't suppose you do,' Angela said contemptuously.

'I'll see you back to the Land Rover,' Albert said, taking her arm.

'You going back, too!' Eisenway gaped. 'Jesus!'

'I'll be right back,' Albert lied. 'Just see Angela's all right.'

'Okay, okay.'

They edged back through the trees.

'He's nuts,' Albert whispered. 'I'd say he could be dangerous. Best thing we can do is grab that Land Rover and get the hell out of here.'

Angela stopped in her tracks.

'Oh Albert, we couldn't leave him all alone miles from anywhere.'

'Why not? We have to think of our own safety. Anyway, if he gets lonely and bored he can fill in the time doing isometrics.'

'No, Albert. He may be inhuman and callous. He may be nuts. But we can't go off and leave him without food and water.'

'There's some in the vehicle we could dump. Besides, he doesn't really need it; he has his whisky supply.'

'Albert, we'd just be sinking to his barbarous level.'

'How could you make it with a guy who's inhuman, callous, barbarous and nuts?'

'How could you make it with a woman who associates with him?'

'According to you and him and her, he doesn't. Now the truth's slipping out.'

'I didn't mean it that way.'

They stared at each other, desire glowing in their eyes. The silence was vast around them. The silence . . .

Albert became very aware of a message from the silence. Why hadn't Eisenway fired yet? He looked away through the trees to where the American was just visible crouching in the long grass. Angela followed his gaze.

'What the hell's he doing?' Albert whispered.

Eisenway was hunched over, holding something in front of him and peering down at it. As they watched, he looked up, straightening, to where the kudu continued to graze peacefully. He turned and glanced back through the trees.

'Oh god!' Albert muttered. He began to laugh quietly. And then Angela caught his arm and began to laugh, too. They laughed softly, holding on to each other. And then they pulled themselves together and headed back towards the edge of the trees.

Eisenway, camera in hand, saw them coming and watched them dubiously.

'We've had a change of heart,' Albert said, grinning. 'Do you mind if we rejoin you?'

Eisenway looked at Angela.

'I'm terribly sorry for anything unpleasant I said,' she apologised.

Eisenway glanced from one to the other.

'I think you're nuts,' he said. 'A coupla screwballs.'

He began to steal forward through the grass towards the kudu and they followed, still grinning, in his wake. They got to within fifty yards of the animals and Eisenway took another shot. But then, as he tried to get even closer, something disturbed them and they jumped all at once and headed off at speed up the slope, through the trees and rocks, out of sight.

'I guess they musta caught our movement,' Eisenway said. 'No point going after them. We'll have a rest and cut along the edge of the forest. Maybe something else beyond the trees up on that brow.'

A beautiful orange and blue butterfly fluttered out of the grass and perched on a rock some distance off.

'Look at that!' Albert exclaimed.

He moved through the grass towards the gorgeous speck of colour.

'Don't get lost,' Eisenway called. He passed the whisky bottle to Angela.

The butterfly floated away up the rise with Albert following, trying to get close enough for detailed scrutiny. It eluded him constantly, never settling for more than seconds at a time.

He reached the point where the kudu had grazed under the fresh clump of trees, lost the butterfly and glanced back to Eisenway and Angela, squatting with their heads showing above the grass.

He savoured the experience of being in the African bush. The heart of the wild country of Africa, surrounded by wild and exotic flora and fauna and not a soul within miles. He took a deep and rapturous breath. He heard Angela scream and yell his name.

That creep Eisenway – trying to take fresh liberties while she was in the mood. Albert turned back towards them in irritation. But all was not as he had imagined. They were standing up, facing him, making agitated gestures. He saw

Angela's hands go to her face, Eisenway's to his chest.

'What the hell's up,' he shouted.

They seemed somehow unable to respond and Albert moved warily towards them.

He heard the low growl, then, and his scalp crawled.

He spun around and saw the big cat, a darker, more tawny yellow than the grass, crouching on a rock above him, a little way up the rise.

For a long moment Albert was frozen with fear, his mind a complete blank except for the image of the large, surly face of the cheetah, with its ears stretched low and its orange eyes glowing fiercely. It growled again, a long, low concentrated threat.

Albert came back to the land of trembling reality and the former blank of his mind was suddenly jammed with a jumble of hysterical detail. *Run, run! . . . Christ no! A cheetah was the fastest thing on earth, wasn't it? Seventy miles an hour. Maybe half as fast through the trees . . . Hope. No, the human hundred-metre record was only something over twenty! Face it bravely . . . outstare it . . . they had to be joking! To die in Africa! Albert Divine, the city boy, art dealer par excellence . . . Run over by a bus – yes! Torn to pieces by a cheetah – help!*

Thought came to a stop. He stared at it hard, incapable of doing anything else. But its stare was so much more frightening than his. He felt his legs trembling, eyes beginning to water.

And then the great cat came slinking towards him, belly low to the ground, powerful paws gliding noiselessly, terrifying body sinuous as a snake.

Albert turned and ran. He ran straight at the nearest tree. Sprang at a branch well above his head and hauled himself up in a prodigious feat of strength which would have been far beyond him in normal circumstances. He clambered up into the branches, barking his shins, elbows, twisting an ankle, tearing a fingernail, his throat producing a stream of involuntary and exotic sounds.

The cheetah paused under the tree, its long neck slightly to one side, looking up at him. Hysterically, Albert thought of appealing to it. Please, Mr Cheetah, I am a friend . . .

And then it silently and with majestic ease sprang up the trunk after him!

Albert scrambled higher, scratching and clawing, a sheer reflex of terror. Why hadn't anyone ever told him they climbed trees! Lions didn't! What was wrong with education in this world! He floundered amidst leaves and thin branches, losing his footing, regaining it. He would fly if necessary!

The cheetah crawled up the tree behind him. Albert began to shout and yell at it, more from terror than any belief in the discouraging effect of his voice. The great beast crouched along a limb, glaring at him, shoulders powerfully bunched, great claws and teeth showing.

'*Carawong!*'

Albert had totally forgotten Eisenway and Angela. Salvation!

The bullet from Eisenway's rifle slashed the bark just below Albert's feet – much nearer him than the cheetah.

'*Carawong!*'

The next one hit the tree with a thunk somewhere above his head.

'You crazy fool!' Albert screamed. 'You'll kill me!'

In the background he heard Angela shouting furiously and Eisenway yelling something back and then came a number of shots, none of which seemed to hit the tree at all.

The cheetah, upset by the noise, snarled angrily and clawed along the limb. Albert was unable to retreat any farther. He could jump. Fool! Break a leg on the way down. Sitting duck!

With the prospect of a restful old age fading by the second, Albert flung into the African air all the insults that an unnecessary death drew forth, taking in Julius Jack Freedman, whose fault it was and George Eisenway who couldn't shoot straight, not to mention countries that refused to exterminate their wild animals, or at least put them in cages.

A voice called through the trees.

'Bonnington! Bonnington, where are you?'

The cheetah turned its head and a vaguely familiar figure appeared. Francis Fordyce-Williams, with binoculars and shooting stick, came to a halt, gazing up.

'Bonnington! Come down here, sir! This minute!'

The cheetah, growling very softly, slithered backwards, turned, leapt gracefully to the ground, slunk to its master and lay at his feet.

Fordyce-Williams continued to gaze, screwing up his eyes.

'Great Scott, it's Albert Divine!' he cried. 'What the devil are you doing up that tree?'

Albert said nothing. What he needed now was a long, gentle convalescence.

Eisenway and Angela came through the grass, Angela running, shouting tearfully: 'Albert, are you all right?'

Fordyce-Williams gazed at them all in astonishment.

'By Jove,' he said, 'it's a small world, isn't it?'

'You wanta keep that animal under control,' Eisenway said. 'It mighta got killed.'

A slow flush suffused Francis Fordyce-Williams's face.

'Was that you shooting?' he cried. 'Shooting at Bonnington!'

'Think himself lucky I was only firing warning shots.'

'Warning shots!' Angela cried indignantly. 'You just can't shoot straight.'

She held up her arm to Albert. Fordyce-Williams looked from one to the other, aghast.

'My God, you might have killed Bonnington!' he cried. 'I'm reporting this. You ought to be locked up!'

'Don't worry,' Albert called, hoarsely. 'He got nearer to killing me than Bonnington. Much nearer.'

He began gingerly to climb down, wincing at his array of injuries. It was too soon on top of his immense relief to feel any real annoyance.

'It's outrageous!' Fordyce-Williams fumed. 'You conspire to lure a poor dumb animal into a tree so that you can take pot-shots at him. You'll lose your licence over this, George, I promise you!'

Albert perched on the lowest branch examining Bonnington. The cheetah was lying perfectly still, watching them all with roving, moody eyes.

'That isn't the way it was, Mr Fordyce-Williams,' Albert said, angelically reasonable. 'Bonnington chased me up the tree.'

'Don't be ridiculous, Mr Divine. He's much too well-behaved for that.'

'I have two witnesses,' Albert said. 'Besides, you saw us up the tree.'

'Mr Divine, I can assure you that if Bonnington did climb the tree after you it was simply because he was following your example. He thought it was a game and he wanted to play.'

'Mr Fordyce-Williams,' Angela snapped in a gust of exasperation. 'We saw him chase Albert into the tree. He was snarling. He was *ferocious*!'

'Miss Carter,' Fordyce-Williams retorted, 'Bonnington always plays his games realistically.' He turned on Eisenway. 'And you must have badly upset him with that shooting. It's diabolical. Absolutely diabolical!'

'Crap,' Eisenway said.

'Crap is it!' Fordyce-Williams cried indignantly.

Albert took a chance and jumped to the ground, twisting his good ankle in the process. Angela took his arm anxiously. Bonnington raised his head for a second and then lowered it on to his outstretched paws, watching.

'Crap,' Eisenway repeated. 'You oughta keep that animal chained up. No right running around loose frightening people.'

Fordyce-Williams appeared about to throw a fit.

'Chained up!' he exploded. 'No right! Good grief Eisenway, this is his country! I bring him out here precisely so that he can enjoy the free exercise he's denied because human beings have taken over his land. Frightening people! What have you done to him and the other beasts? It's you human beings who are destroying the world – and everything beautiful and free in it!'

The three human beings stared at him and he turned to the cheetah.

'Come on Bonnington,' he said. 'Ignore these creatures. Don't let them bother you.'

He turned on his heel and marched away, with the cheetah gliding at his heels.

'You'll hear more about this, Eisenway,' he called over his shoulder.

They watched him disappear, with Bonnington padding behind, moving gracefully from one side to the other.

'That's the first talking animal I ever met,' Albert said. 'The one with the hat that stood on its hind legs.'

Eisenway gave a chuckle.

'I guess Francis is a bit of a crackpot in his way,' he said. 'Maybe he was right. Did you figure that maybe the animal did just want to play?'

'If you're trying to make me out a spoilsport,' Albert said, 'you should have seen it from my angle.'

'Oh Albert, it was terrifying,' Angela murmured. 'Are you sure you're all right?'

'I'll be all right once I'm on the stretcher. It's just that I have this guilt about letting Bonnington down. Maybe I should have let him have a foot or a couple of fingers to play with.'

Gingerly he tested his ankles. Angela put an arm around him.

'I guess we had enough for one day,' Eisenway said. 'I got this guy to meet, anyway.'

They walked in slow procession through the trees and the long grass and up into the trees again, where the Land Rover was parked in the shade.

An African was already waiting for them, standing motionless beside the vehicle in his simple white garment. His elderly lined face was unhappy, his eyes restless. His spear was leaning against the Land Rover together with a bundle of rags from which various portions of statuary protruded.

The old man looked uncertainly from Angela to Albert, appeared narrowly to decide against flight and harangued Eisenway in a low, frightened voice.

'Looks as if he's been playing with cheetahs, too,' Albert said.

'What's the matter with him?' Angela asked.

'Nothing, nothing,' Eisenway snapped. 'They all get very

excited when they deal with whites.'

'*Mbaya sana, mbaya sana,*' the African kept repeating, pointing through the bush. He held out the bundle to Eisenway, who took it and partly removed the rags. He and Albert studied the series of fertility statuettes.

'Old Ithyphallus himself,' Albert said. 'These look more like the real thing.'

'I guess they are the real thing,' Eisenway agreed.

The African held out his hand to Eisenway.

'*Pesa, pesa, Bwana,*' he urged. He glanced into the bush. '*Pesi sana.*'

'What's he so agitated about?' Albert said, pulling more rags off the figurines.

'Asking for his money.'

Eisenway pulled a bundle of notes from his pocket and counted them into the old man's outstretched hands. With a grunt, the African gave them a rapid nod and glided off through the trees, completely disappearing in a matter of seconds.

'Why is he so frightened?' Angela asked.

'Born that way,' Eisenway said. 'Terrified of their shadows, these blacks. No guts.'

He and Albert examined the statuettes.

'Old Julius Jack is nuts paying good money for this,' Eisenway said.

'Well they're several hundred per cent better than that load of rubbish back at your place,' Albert said. 'They're originals. Not like that mass-produced equivalent of China geese.'

'And they're very affective,' Angela said. 'They make me feel fertile just to look at them.'

'Well I just hope they work after all the trouble I've had,' Eisenway said.

'What trouble?' Albert asked.

The two spears whoosed through the trees simultaneously. One sank into the carriagework of the Land Rover, the other quivered into the ground at their feet.

'What the hell!' Albert cried.

The spears hadn't finished vibrating before Eisenway

moved with unaccustomed decision, yelling: 'Quick! Get in!'

They scrambled madly into the vehicle and Eisenway started it up as a whole shower of spears assailed them. The Land Rover roared into life and shot in a crazy curve through the trees towards the distant red earth roadway.

'Keep your heads down!' Eisenway bawled.

The vehicle surged powerfully through the copse, lashed by low branches, bucking in ruts and hollows. Albert and Angela, crouching low, hung on in horror and astonishment.

There was a sudden burst of gunfire, shatteringly loud. Bullets raked the ground and the trees and smashed into the back of the weaving vehicle.

'My God – a machine gun!' Albert gasped.

They rampaged on to the road and the Land Rover gathered speed, racing away from the scene in a great cloud of red dust. Bursts of gunfire continued intermittently behind them, getting fainter and finally fading out.

Albert and Angela lifted their heads. Eisenway, crouching low over the wheel, was a sickly green.

'What in the name of hell was that about?' Albert demanded, horrified.

Eisenway kept his petrified eyes glued to the road. His hands trembled.

'I guess we musta been trespassing,' he said.

Chapter Eleven

ALBERT EMERGED from the bathroom in his New Stanley luxury suite feeling a new man. With the huge white towel draped around him, he passed through the bedroom where Angela was dozing after the long, hard drive, and into the lounge where Eisenway was sitting toying nervously with a very large Scotch and water.

'That's better,' Albert said. 'I'll have that drink now. Sure you don't want a bath?'

Eisenway shook his head. He poured Albert a drink.

'You oughta . . .' he began.

Albert cut him short.

'Look, George,' he said, 'I don't know what's got into you, but I tell you we're not going until we've seen some more of the country. For Christ's sake, I've never been to Africa before.'

'There might be trouble,' Eisenway said. 'You really oughta . . .'

'Oh for God's sake,' Albert said impatiently. 'What trouble? So we were trespassing – not that I follow that. So some crazy Africans took pot-shots at us. So I'm not catching the next plane out just because the memory terrifies you.'

'For your own safety . . .'

'What is this about *my* safety? How about *your* safety? I don't see you rushing to the airport. I'm beginning to think this is some cheeseparing scheme between you and Julius Jack. Afraid I might buy an elephant on expenses?'

Eisenway looked very uncomfortable.

'I just thought maybe you'd feel homesick,' he said. 'Anyway, you've seen everything.'

Albert gazed at him in amazement.

'Seen everything!' he exploded. 'I can tell you that being

chased by somebody's pet cheetah and taking photographs of kudu at a hundred paces doesn't constitute my idea of a study of wildlife. I want to see the game parks – every single one. I want to go into Tanzania and see Serengeti and Kilimanjaro. I want to see the coast, coral reefs, Mombasa, maybe Zanzibar. I want to go north and see the desert, people on camels. I want to see Lake Victoria. I am Stanley, 1971, and you tell me it's time I went back to smoky old traffic-sodden London because I've seen everything. By God, George, I believe you're on the payroll of the British Tourist Association.'

Eisenway brooded over his drink. Albert found a wet patch on his elbow and dried it vigorously, scowling at the American.

Angela appeared in the doorway in a blue towelling bathrobe.

'Hi,' she said. 'Where's the next stop! I mean, do we have to rush on, or is there time to clean my teeth?'

'Don't you start, daughter,' Eisenway muttered.

'You wouldn't even have time to comb your hair if George had his way,' Albert said.

'I'll have a drink,' Angela said, 'and then you can tell me when the civil war starts.'

Eisenway morosely poured her a large Scotch and added a little water. He jumped as the internal phone buzzed. Albert answered the call.

'Who? Oh, what does she want? Okey, ask her to come up, will you?'

Eisenway moved agitatedly towards him.

'What's that?' he cried. 'Who's coming up here?'

Albert gazed at him, perplexed.

'Lavinia Mungai,' he said.

'Who's she?'

'How should I know?'

'Don't let her in here,' Eisenway barked. 'Call hotel security!'

'Are you sure you're all right, George?' Albert asked, angrily sarcastic. 'Because I think you're finally cracking up.'

Eisenway stepped back nervously, bumping into a chair.

'You can't just invite anyone up here,' he croaked. 'It's asking for trouble.'

'Do you think she's a witch doctor, George?' Angela asked.

'Or a leopard woman?' Albert said.

'She's going to put the evil eye on Albert?'

Eisenway glared at them frantically.

'It's nothing to joke about,' he cried. 'This could be serious. Jesus, I'm getting outa here!'

He seized his hat, watched by a bewildered Albert and Angela and made for the door – as the bell buzzed. Eisenway stood transfixed, quivering like a pointer. Albert walked rather stifly through the small entrance hall. Eisenway was actually making him nervous.

By the time Albert opened the door to the suite, he was half prepared for Dracula, or at the very least Vincent Price. He was *not* prepared for what he found.

Lavinia Mungai was tall and slim, with the lithe body of a limbo dancer. Her unpretentious pink, cotton suit was a tasteful match with her coffee-coloured skin and her darker, curling hair. The whites of her eyes were startlingly bright around the dark, intelligent pupils and her nostrils seemed to flare lazily above the broad lips, which opened equally lazy when she spoke in a quiet voice.

'Mr Divine? I'm sorry to intrude – and you don't even know me.'

'That's quite all right,' Albert said. 'Come in. Any time.'

She followed Albert into the lounge and smiled at Angela and Eisenway.

'You look as if you expected Frankenstein's monster,' she said.

'I was thinking more in terms of Dracula,' Albert said. 'Please sit down.'

'Mr Divine, I represent the Kenya Government and something rather urgent's come up. I hope you don't mind me foregoing the tedious diplomatic approach.'

'Any approach is all right by me,' Albert said.

He made the introductions, vaguely aware that Angela thought this was his Swahili woman. He offered her a drink which she politely refused, while he tried to figure out how they could be held responsible for someone trying to bump *them* off. Even if they had been trespassing . . .

'Mr Divine,' Lavinia Mungai said with soft reticence, having seated herself calmly in a proffered chair, 'I'm afraid you're in a little trouble . . . '

George Eisenway suddenly interrupted in some agitation.

'I paid good money for that stuff! Why the hell can't they just make some more. Jesus Christ, what's all the fuss?'

Lavinia Mungai surveyed him, serenely.

'Mr Eisenway,' she said, 'you've surely been in Africa long enough to know that sacred fertility symbols are irreplaceable in the tribal mind. And apart from that, the money was given to a thief rather than offered to the tribal authorities – for the very good reason, naturally, that they would not have accepted it.'

'Would you mind explaining to me what this is all about?' Albert said, adding savagely: 'What is going *on!*'

'Nothing for you to worry about, Albert,' Eisenway said. 'I can handle this. Miss Mungai, maybe we should go down to the bar and talk it over.'

Lavinia Mungai regarded hims quizzically.

'I would have thought that having a price on his head was definitely something for Mr Divine to worry about,' she said softly. 'Am I to understand from this that he's not aware of the facts?'

'He's an art dealer,' Eisenway said. 'He's come out here on behalf of a client. It's not necessary for him to be concerned with tribal politics.'

Lavinia Mungai shook her head, very disapprovingly.

'You haven't been very fair with Mr Divine, have you?'

'What do you mean, fair?' Albert cried. 'Will somebody please *explain!*'

'Yes, what's that about a price on his head?' Angela asked.

Eisenway was visibly embarrassed and refused to look at either of them.

'Well, it's rather a complicated situation,' Lavinia Mungai said, crossing her slim legs. 'One aspect is that you've removed from a certain Kikuyu sect fertility emblems which are regarded as sacred – the whole future of the sect is considered to depend on them. I'm sorry to say that the penalty for what you've done is death.'

'You mean to say . . .' Albert was flabbergasted.

'Oh it's not as bad as that,' Eisenway muttered. 'They don't know who's got the goddam things.'

Lavinia Mungai gave him a very long, severe look.

'I don't know if you really believe that, Mr Eisenway,' she said, in a tone that indicated she knew very well he didn't, 'but the fact is that the whole operation has been conducted terribly ham-handedly on your part. First of all you approached the tribal authorities to sound them out and then you employ an unstable member of the tribe, who is already regarded with suspicion, to steal them for you. The very fact that he was tracked down almost immediately and that you were attacked, speaks for itself.'

'How the hell do you know all this?' Eisenway demanded with bluster.

'Never mind how she knows it!' Albert exploded. 'Just what the devil have you involved me in, Eisenway?'

'Death sentence for a start!' Angela shrieked.

Albert advanced on Eisenway menacingly.

'By Christ,' he cried, 'you knew exactly what all this was about from the beginning. And Julius Jack! He bloody well employed me on a suicidal mission – and you helped him.'

'Now just a minute, Albert!' Eisenway cried, backing off. 'I had no idea it was going to work out like this. You shoulda been safe back in London without any trouble.'

'The fact is you didn't square with me,' Albert said. 'It was three thousand quid for a marvellous holiday and using my judgement, according to Julius Jack Freedman, not three thousand quid to upset the tribal elders and make me public enemy number one.'

'Now take it easy, Albert,' Eisenway begged, moving behind a chair. 'You leave now and you'll be perfectly safe. You can insist Julius Jack doubles the money. I'm sure you'll find him very reasonable.'

'You're a couple of cheap bastards,' Albert snarled,

crowding threateningly around the chair. 'I should have smelled a rat from the beginning.'

'Calm down, Albert,' Eisenway pleaded. 'Violence won't solve anything.'

'It'll make me feel better,' Albert said.

Lavinia Mungai's voice cut in, quiet but authoritative.

'Mr Eisenway's right in this case,' she said. 'We may not have a lot of time. I think you'd better sit down, Mr Divine, so that we can calmly consider the situation. There are further facts you should know.'

'*Further* facts!'

Albert slumped down weakly in the chair protecting George Eisenway. Lavinia Mungai indicated another chair.

'Would you please sit down, too, Mr Eisenway,' she said.

Eisenway meekly obeyed.

'Right.' Lavinia Mungai said. 'The first thing you need to know is that these statuettes are the sacred property of a sect which is the residue of the Mau Mau of the closing colonial era. This sect had continued in existence, led by men who believe they have not received their due reward in the new Kenya. They are embittered men who want to take over the country and force on it an alien pattern. We nickname them Mao Mao. Now, we have watched these men for some time, noted how they use primitive tribal credulity to their own advantage and how they are increasing in numbers and gaining access to a considerable amount of arms.'

'How can you know all this?' Albert asked.

Very simply. We have infiltrated them on all levels.'

'So why don't you round them up and stick them in a concentration camp?'

Lavinia Mungai smiled tolerantly.

'You know we don't have any, Mr Divine,' she said. 'And we don't arrest them because there are still certain gaps in our information – particularly about their arms sources. When we move, we want to make a clean sweep.'

'Well, if you want to know what I think – the sooner you sweep, the better.'

'I'm coming to you, Mr Divine. The fact is, we have to get you out of the country. For one thing we can't afford the scandal of your death on our soil. Mr Eisenway, you will be afforded protection, but in any case the vengeance will be concentrated on Mr Divine, since he is known to be intending to remove these statuettes from the country.'

'Just a minute,' Albert said. 'It's all very simple as far as I can see. As of now the plans have changed. I give them back the wretched objects. They can keep the money. In fact, I'll see they get a bonus to spend on arms which you can immediately confiscate. If they insist. I'll make a ceremonial apology into the bargain.'

'Of course,' Angela said in great relief. 'Why didn't we think of that straight off.'

'Mr Divine,' Lavinia Mungai said, 'It's not quite as simple as that. You can be of great service to the Kenya Government in return for our overlooking your committing the offence of receiving stolen goods.'

There was an awed silence.

'What?' Albert said. '*What*?'

'You must realise you have committed this offence,' Lavinia Mungai said pleasantly. 'Property is very important in this country and sentences can be quite severe. The idea of foreigners – particularly those of the former imperialist power – coming here to steal sacred emblems purely for their own material gain . . . Well, it really is a throwback to the exploitation of old, isn't it?'

There was a long silence in which Albert clearly didn't trust himself to speak. It was finally Angela who said: 'You *must* be joking. We had no idea what was going on. That's the man you have to deal with!'

Eisenway wilted under the accusing finger.

'One difficulty would be convincing a Kenyan court of this,' Lavinia Mungai said sympathetically. 'I might be perfectly willing to believe you. But, frankly, the facts would seem to indicate otherwise.'

Albert bounced up furiously. He went up to Lavinia Mungai and stared into her face as if he didn't quite believe in her. She looked back at him serenely.

'What the hell do you mean?' he demanded. 'You must know bloody well we haven't wittingly been receiving stolen goods. By Christ, I didn't even want to come to this damned country in the first place, except some nut insisted on throwing a fortune away on me for next to nothing. Anyway, how the hell do I know who *you* are?'

Lavinia Mungai opened a small crocodile skin bag and handed Albert a small stamped card like a miniature passport.

'You may also telephone the Ministry of the Interior if you wish,' she said. 'The Minister will vouch for me personally.'

Albert handed back the card and slumped back in his chair. He felt suddenly exhausted. Perhaps this was some diabolical plan for getting their own back about all those British passport holders that Britain wouldn't let in. Lavinia Mungai remained silent just long enough to let him feel the precariousness of his position.

'Now,' she said, 'in return for us overlooking this alleged offence, all we ask you to do is to take these statuettes out of Kenya and back to London with you.'

Albert shook his head, completely mystified.

'Why can't we just give them back?' Angela begged.

'Because, Miss Carter, one really powerful arm of the sect operates in London. We believe that it's in the British capital that arms deals are made and contacts arranged with countries who support the subversion here. We have many students in London, who manage to remain less suspect then those studying in some Eastern countries.'

'In other words,' Albert said, slowly and distinctly. 'You want to use me as bait.'

'Don't worry, Mr Divine, we'll look after you all the way.'

'You want me to walk out of here carrying these death warrants, drive through the streets, fly in a plane . . . '

'We've worked out a special route,' Lavinia Mungai said. 'Clearly Embakasi will not be safe. We propose to drive you to a small airfield some eighty miles to the West in the Rift Valley. From there, a light aircraft will fly you to the airport of Kisumu on Lake Victoria. There you will join a scheduled airline flight. Once in Britain, you will be carefully protected until they show their hand – as they will most certainly do.'

'Couldn't you round them up here and submit them to horrible tortures so that they give their buddies in England away?' Albert asked.

'Mr Divine, we are a civilised country – besides these fanatics will die a thousand deaths rather than talk.'

Albert turned wearily to George Eisenway, crumpled in his chair in a tense, shamefaced heap.

'If I survive this, George,' he said, with feeling. 'I'll support any complaint Francis Fordyce-Williams makes against you for wantonly shooting at his pet cheetah. I hope you get ten years.'

Eisenway stared at him miserably. Abruptly he stood up.

'Where's my protection, Miss?' he demanded. 'I'm getting outa here.'

The doorbell of the suite buzzed and Eisenway emitted a terrified gasp. Everyone froze and stared at the door to the hall.

Lavinia Mungai sprang to her feet.

'Where are the statuettes?' she whispered.

Albert pointed to the bedroom.

'All right,' she said. 'Just let them in. Do what they say – and don't worry.'

She moved rapidly towards the bedroom. Eisenway withdrew equally rapidly across the room.

'What . . . who . . . they'll kill us . . . !' he cried in a strangled voice.

'If it *is* them, they won't do anything until they've recovered the statuettes,' Lavinia Mungai snapped. 'Trust me. Do as I say!'

'We don't have to let them in,' Albert whispered. 'We can call the police.'

'If you don't answer, they'll shoot the lock in,' Lavinia Mungai said. 'Now – open it!'

She disappeared into the bedroom. Albert and Angela stood quite still staring at the door to the hall. Eisenway, apparently on the point of collapse, got behind a chair. The doorbell buzzed again.

'Maybe it's room service!' Albert cried hopefully.

'We didn't ring for them,' Angela said.

'Perhaps they make routine calls.'

'Don't be ridiculous.'

'I know who it is. It's Gloria, looking for George.'

Fortified by this thought, Albert went through the little hall and opened the door a couple of inches.

It heaved open with a crash, sending him sprawling. Two anonymous-looking Africans in dark glasses and dark, lightweight suits stepped quickly inside, automatic pistols in their hands, and closed the door behind them. Angela uttered a low scream. There was a dull thud as George Eisenway hit the floor in a dead faint.

The Africans, who seemed disinclined to speak, motioned Albert to his feet and drove him into the lounge.

'Where?' one of them demanded simply.

'In the bedroom,' Albert said, adding fatuously. 'What is this?'

One of the men moved quickly to the bedroom and disappeared through the open door. Immediately there was a short grunt. The second African, who had posted himself in the middle of the lounge, covering its occupants, called out something in Swahili. There was no response and he in turn moved cautiously towards the bedroom.

A split second before he reached the door, Lavinia Mungai seemed literally to fly through the doorway, with her left foot shooting out in a lightning kick. The blow caught the African in the solar plexus and doubled him over. Almost in the same moment, his exposed chin was smashed sideways by a sharp, swinging blow from the girl's bent elbow. He fell forward on his face and lay perfectly still.

'Get your things together – hurry!' Lavinia Mungai commanded. 'Come on – move!'

Albert and Angela fled into the bedroom, where the first African was also spreadeagled face down on the floor. Albert began to pack while Angela pulled on some clothes. Every so often they stole sly glances at Lavinia Mungai who was expertly trussing the intruders with strips torn from sheets. Albert hoped the hotel would not add damage to property to their Kenyan crime sheet.

Lavinia Mungai finished securing the bodies and returned

to the lounge. Albert could hear her slapping Eisenway's face. George wouldn't like that – particularly from a black woman. What a woman! Actually he felt pretty safe in the care of a woman who could knock out men like that. Probably fell a rhino. Good thing for Fordyce-Williams she hadn't been around to be chased by Bonnington. Good thing for Bonnington!

'I don't see what there is to grin about!' Angela snapped, pulling on her shoes.

'That's because you've never been chased up a tree by a cheetah.'

'You know, Albert, sometimes I think you have no sense of reality at all. You live . . . '

'Come *on*, you two!' Lavinia Mungai called.

They went into the lounge, where an ashen-faced Eisenway was groggily on his feet. Suppose one made unwanted passes at a woman like that Albert reflected. Ye gods, it wasn't safe being a Don Juan these emancipated days!

'Let's go,' Lavinia Mungai said, taking Eisenway's arm. At the door she paused. 'Okay, I'll go out first,' she said. 'Give Mr Eisenway a hand and don't worry about a thing.'

She glanced curiously at Albert.

'I don't see what's so funny, though,' she said.

Albert's face clouded over anxiously.

'I'm not a Don Juan,' he said. 'Honestly.'

Chapter Twelve

THEY HAD followed the sandy red road through hilly country under fluffy cloud and across an expanse of bush where the tawny grass rippled in the light breeze and herds of hump-backed wildebeest grazed peacefully and giraffes cropped the sparse trees. Now they were travelling through thin forest alongside a small river where logs and crocodiles were indistinguishable and highly coloured birds flitted from branch to branch and swooped across the sluggish waters.

Albert fanned himself with a newspaper as he sadly watched Africa passing away through the windows of the Land Rover.

'You know,' he said, 'I was going to write a little sketch-book – "Albert Divine's travels in Africa" – for free distribution among my clients as a little bonus for their loyal patronage. And now look at it. They can't get us out fast enough.'

'Why don't you change your theme,' Angela suggested. 'How I met the Mau Mau Menace, or Dicing with Death in the Domain of the Dik-Dik.'

'I might do that.'

'The *Daily Express* rather than *The Times*.'

One of the three Kenyan security officers accompanying them turned with a flashing smile.

'I trust you'll be discreet, Mr Divine, and save these revelations for your memoirs.'

'Don't worry,' Albert said. 'If there's one thing I want less to do with than Mau Mau it's newspapers. I can't stand superficiality.'

'Except when it wears a gorgeous figure and throws itself in your arms,' Angela said.

The security officers roared with laughter, slapping their thighs.

'I never heard that definition before,' Albert said.

'Never mind, Mr Divine,' one of the officers said. 'When you come to Kenya again, we will show you all the things you have missed.'

'Well I hope your Government will allow you six months off – nothing less will do.'

'We'll share it between us, Mr Divine – two months each.'

Albert grinned. They were all right, these fellows, even if they were carrying guns under their armpits. He unzipped the travelling bag containing the statuettes, took one out and gave it a reappraisal.

'It's just occurred to me,' he said, 'that if I declare these to British Customs, they'll probably confiscate them as obscene items.'

'That's a sacriligious thought, Mr Divine,' a security officer said good-humouredly. 'They're life's blood to the sect they belong to.'

'Odd isn't it,' Albert said.

'Well, I understand in Britain people make gods of their motor cars, Mr Divine. I find that odder still.'

'There's a tree across the road,' the driver announced.

All three security men drew their guns immediately.

'Reverse!' one of them said. 'On the floor everyone!'

The Land Rover slid to a dusty halt and then began to reverse, rapidly gathering speed. The only sound was the furious revving of the engine and the rasping of the heavy wheels against the earth. They backed right out of sight of the tree and the Land Rover came to a momentary halt, preparing to turn.

'God, my heart!' Angela said.

'Probably nothing, but we can't take chances,' the first security officer said, scanning the trees and the underbrush. 'Turn the vehicle. We'll make a detour.'

The Land Rover began a threequarter turn in the road.

The shots rained down as it was broadside on across the roadway in a burst of unreal thunder. They shattered the windscreen and spattered into the vehicle from all sides. Not random machine gun fire, but a stream of snipers' bullets.

The discharge ended as abruptly as it had begun and the silence was shattering. Angela moved, trembling beneath Albert, who had fallen with his arms around her.

'Are you all right?' she said in a terrified whisper.

Albert moved. He was all right, but . . .

The Land Rover was surrounded by Africans wearing skins and carrying rifles. They had anticipated exactly what the security men would do and the spot at which the vehicle would have to stop and turn. They had fired lethally. The three officers, who had been laughing and joking a few minutes earlier, were now twisted over the upholstery, dripping blood and unmistakably dead.

But Albert and Angela had been left alive. Deliberately.

Albert didn't need a crystal ball to tell him they had been spared for something worse to come.

Chapter Thirteen

THE FLAMES leaping from the fires and the torches filled the clear space in the midst of the village with an uneasy ever-changing light which made grotesque shadows everywhere.

Beyond the huts of thatch and wattle and corrugated iron, bush and forest undulated in an eerie darkness under the huge sky.

Within the rough circle of huts forming the inner ring of the village, the animation was in sharp contrast to the stillness of the vast country all around.

In the central space a crude dais had been erected. Torches burned around it, throwing into relief the series of sacred statuettes. Spreadeagled face down so that her torso was across the top of the dais and her legs hung down its side, was a young black woman. She was naked and her large, pendulous breasts were squashed against the rough structure while her low and very jutting rump bulged out like an artificial embossment. Her face rested on one cheek against the dais and her eyes were rolling in resigned terror. In fact she appeared to be petrified with dread since she remained perfectly still although she was not secured in any way.

Facing the platform at the edge of the circle and piling back into the shadow of the huts, the villagers sat, dressed mainly in simple traditional garments and ornaments, scuffling their feet to the soft, insistent sound of drumming. In the forefront of the mass were a number of men of obvious importance sitting in carved wooden seats. Some wore the rough robes and rat-tailed hair of the traditional Mau Mau; others were dressed in European clothes. Close to them was the small phalanx of drummers in long, leather-thonged skirts with rings of feathers around ankles, wrists and neck.

Angela and Albert were between the crowd and the dais, tethered to heavy stakes embedded in the ground. Albert was still wearing the lightweight suit in which he'd been travelling; Angela was completely naked.

To say that Angela was terrified was not quite accurate. She was, rather, numbed into an almost comforting disbelief about everything that was happening. The sensation of the rough wood against her bare buttocks, the warmth of flame on her naked breasts and belly, the drums, the tribal fury, the vast night . . . the whole situation was so divorced from Benjamin Hailey's photographic studio, from fashion magazines, Albert's West End gallery, the Mirabelle restaurant, that it contained no sense of reality. She had no idea what was going to become of her and she didn't think about it. A lot of the time she kept her eyes closed; the rest she spent staring as if hypnotised at the copulating statuettes and the unclothed girl on the dais. She vaguely remembered once reading a book by Paul Bowles in which a white woman, completely removed from her own background in some exotic Arab land, became virtually anaesthetized to her old habits of feeling. This seemed to be happening to her now. The bloodshed was unreal, Mau Mau was unreal, Africa was unreal . . .

She found herself trying to create titles for Albert's shelved sketchbook: *'Fighting the Fertility Fetish' . . . Rampage in the Realm of the Rat's Tails'. She was gratified at her ingenuity. But perhaps alliteration was unnecessary. 'Albert's Travels in Darkest Africa', explicit, but perhaps a trifle old-fashioned. 'How I did my Thing on Safari' . . .*

She became aware of movement near the tribal leaders and half concentrated on the tall figure advancing towards the dais.

'Investigating the Ithyphallus' – that should intrigue potential readers. The figure wore a simple black garment like a Roman toga and his face was completely covered by a huge mask on which was painted a gargoyle of a face in savage reds, yellows and black.

'Those Kinky Kikuyus' – maybe that sounded a little too

cheap and brassy.

He was carrying a shallow bowl, which he held very carefully so as not to spill the liquid in it. A silence fell on the crowds as they watched, though the drums continued their insidious beat.

How about 'Totem and Taboo in the Tropics'. No, not really. Too derivative.

The masked figure, who may have been some sort of witch doctor, placed the bowl on the dais beside the girl and knelt low before the statuettes, addressing them in a murmured incantation. At the same time the drummers rose to their feet and spread out in a semi-circle thrumming out the beat with flashing hands as their legs and bodies performed an angular, stiff-legged dance.

The masked figure rose with dignity and menace, approached the prostrate girl, dipped his hands in the bowl and began to massage her body with the liquid. He towered over her, his long bony hands rubbing steadily and sensually over her neck and shoulders, down her back and sides, over her upturned buttocks and down the spreadeagled thighs. The girl remained completely limp even when his fingers caressed her crotch.

'Lechery in the Land of Livingstone'. That wasn't bad at all. Possibly a little too resounding – as if promising too much.

The deep-voiced rhythm of the drums filled the air, mingling with the crackling of the fires. And now the masked figure stood directly behind the passive form of the girl. He raised his robe to chest level with both hands and remained still for some seconds. His flesh soared like a witchdoctor's wand above the jutting rump as if casting the girl into further submission.

What about one of those long, laughable titles, like, 'How I Stole the Sacred Statuettes and Mau Mau Ambushed me In Rift Valley Province and . . .' And what?

The masked man moved in close to the spreadeagled girl, flexed his legs and then dropped the robe over her bottom as he thrust into her. The girl opened her mouth and let out a long, breathless cry.

'Ayeeeeee . . .'

Angela's mouth suddenly went dry. A measure of reality flooded back into her with the sound. The girl was being publicly screwed in a fertility ritual!

Angela became freshly aware of her own nudity. She shivered and glanced around at the crowds. They had eyes for nothing but the spectacle. They were, of course, denied sight of the actual union of bodies since only the girls' torso and thighs were visible. But the jostling movement under the robe, the majestic thrusting movement of the masked figure and the contorted face of the girl gave public testimony to her deflowering.

The girl's cries became continuous and she raised her head off the dais, as if in pain. Her hands clenched and unclenched and her nails scraped the rough wood. The folds of the robe flounced and swayed and now the girl arched her back in a hollow. Her thighs swung and jerked like a puppet's and she appeared to be attempting to writhe away from her tormentor. Her buttocks were partially and momentarily revealed and then with an imperious gesture the masked man leaned forward on her, grasping the backs of her upper arms and pressing her helplessly down while his loins beat out their rhythm against the convexities of her rump.

'Ayeeeee . . . Ayeeeee!'

The cry seemed almost unearthly against the vast background of the bush. It caught at Angela's entrails, bringing her further back to reality.

The girl was straining against the imprisoning hands. Her eyes rolled and closed, mouth opened. The mask was impersonal above her, the hips thrust in concealment and the drums maintained their throbbing, genital beat.

The girl's cries changed subtly, evolved into a scream. The watching villagers began to chant in rhythm with the drums and the pistoning movement of the hips. An air of excitement began to rise. Fresh fuel was flung on the fires so that they blazed up in a symbolic flare of passion. Muscles rippled and quivered in the legs of tormentor and victim and in the girl's straining back.

Angela was suddenly hit with panic. Her thought blazed on to the significance of her nude captivity.

And suddenly a roar issued from the mouthpiece of the ferocious mask, a roar amplified by the mouthpiece. The pistoning stroke simultaneously ground to a hard slowness, tensed in a deep and long-held thrust and then relaxed.

The witchdoctor figure straightened, towering over the girl again while she remained prostrate and broken on the dais.

The villagers chanted on and the masked figure drew back from the girl, leaving her revealed once more. She didn't move, but when two members of the tribe touched her arms, she came slowly alive and allowed herself to be led away into the darkness.

Almost immediately the girl was replaced by another, a second masked man appeared and the whole enactment was repeated.

Angela began to get numbed into a sense of unreality once more. She felt she understood the friends who had told her blue films were devastatingly boring after the first couple of reels. Her mind wandered off again into the safety of title-hunting.

Maybe 'Ravishing Rites in Rhinoland' or 'Ritual Rape in the Rift'. How about 'Cock Kinetics in Kenya'. Pity to discard any of them really.

She was still working on it when leathery hands began to untie her bonds and skeletal fingers gripped her arms to lead her to the dais.

Reality was suddenly there again with devastating force She went hot, then icy cold. She felt faint – and then she began to scream and struggle, lashing out with feet and knees, tearing her arms from the clutching hands. For a wild moment she was free and making a short, jiggling run for the darkness. Then hands were on her again and dark muscular bodies all around and everything was a reeling phantasmagoria of flames and thatch and sky and earth and the dais looming large and rough with obscene statuettes waiting like demons and a tall, grotesquely masked figure like death . . .

She felt a waft of heat from a torch and the drums seemed to be beating inside her head. She saw the bowl of liquid, the bevelled edge across which she was being forced. Around her, muttered oaths and the crackling of flames and the distant murmur of the crowd. And then the fearsomely masked figure towering over her . . . a ghastly diabolical creature . . . everything began to whirl and fade.

The noise of the drums and the sense of hands on her dragged Angela back to consciousness. Her nostrils were assailed with a musky fragrance and around her, darkness and flickering light and movement gradually separated into meaning.

She was face down across the dais, her breasts, belly and cheek flattened against the cold wood whose bevelled edge was uncomfortably pressed against the tops of her thighs. Her legs were widely spread, leaving her totally vulnerable. She tried to move, but, unlike the other women, she had been tied by wrists and ankles to projections on the platform. She was helpless. Her famous bottom soared nakedly like a cleft fruit. The coolness of the air touched her where she was to be impaled as the others had been. There was absolutely nothing she could do. Tears came to her eyes.

The fragrance was from the liquid which was being massaged into her body by the strong hands of the masked African who was to partner her in the ritual. She felt the firm, fluid movement over her back and buttocks, down her thighs and calves and up again to her loins. She gave an involuntary start as he touched her, but his anointing probe was relentless.

Angela lay with her cheek hot against the cold wood, steeling herself to submit as his hands flowed over her belly and breasts. She became aware of people out there on the edge of the darkness, faces and movement partially seen in the flickering flames. She could see Albert, pale and hopeless, unable to move. And then the scene misted from the tears which welled over and ran down her cheeks.

She could feel the weight of the man as he leaned over her. Through the folds of his robe his rigidity pressed against her. In a few moments he would raise the robe, drop it over her and the hard flesh would tear and bruise her in an evil, impersonal rape. The tears were salty on her lips.

A voice with a superb Oxbridge accent suddenly began to address her, very low and urgent.

'You really must forgive these indignities, Miss Carter, but my hands, like yours, so to speak, are tied. Listen very carefully. In a matter of seconds, I shall cover your hips and go through the motions of intercourse. If we are successful to carry out this deception, I'm afraid it will be incumbent upon you to act your part to the full. Do you understand?'

The voice went silent behind the grotesque mask. The hands massaged her shoulders, sending fresh wafts of fragrance to her nostrils. Angela's astonishment was paralysing.

'Miss Carter – are you all right?' the voice asked urgently.

'I – I don't understand . . . ' Angela said faintly.

'Well, it's rather delicate and I had hoped you might,' the voice resumed. 'You have witnessed the previous copulations. I suggest you do your best to emulate the – er – reactions of the ladies. Not slavishly, of course. I mean you probably have your own – er . . . The essential thing is that we must, absolutely *must*, put on a convincing performance or we'll both be up the creek, so to speak.'

The hands moved on to her neck. Angela tried to deal with this new threat to her sense of reality.

'Who are you? What's happening?' she asked weakly.

'Allow me to introduce myself, Miss Carter,' the voice murmured politely above her spreadeagled nudity. 'Humphrey Jonah of the Kenya Foreign Service – Security, actually. Sort of Secret Service and all that nonsense. I'm a colleague of Lavinia Mungai, whom I believe you've already met.'

The hands massaged her upper arms.

'But how . . . how . . . ?'

'If you're wondering how I come to be here, Miss Carter, the answer is by sheer skulduggery, I'm afraid. We infiltrated the sect some time ago, of course, but tonight I've forcibly replaced the gentleman who was to . . . to have partnered you, so to speak.'

'What's going to happen?' Angela asked.

'The idea was that you and your – er – Mr Divine were to be sacrificed before the fertility gods in the morning, following this symbolic fertilising of the sect's good fortunes. However, I am happy to say that will not, now, be the procedure. It will be touch and go, so to speak, but I do have every confidence we can get you out of here.'

Angela lay silent, aware of the drums and the hostile world all around. She was stunned. And yet she felt like laughing. The hands moved down her back and briefly massaged her buttocks.

'Miss Carter,' Humphrey Jonah said, 'I can't tell you how very embarrassing this is for me. I would ask you to realise that it is in the line of duty and that the enemy must be given no grounds for suspicion. Perhaps it may be some consolation to you to compare this apparent disrespect with the alternative loss of your life. But, in any case, please accept my most profound apologies.'

'Oh please don't apologise,' Angela said. 'I'm so terribly relieved . . . Mr Jonah, I'm afraid I'm going to laugh.'

'Miss Carter, you must try to simulate a more appropriate reaction, but if laughter is unavoidable, then please God, make it hysterical.'

The hands moved off her behind and Angela controlled herself with a great effort.

'Good show, Miss Carter.'

She forced herself not to picture the barbaric and frightening mask with the civilised, polite voice issuing from it.

'How can we possibly get away?' she said.

'When you speak, Miss Carter, try not to use your lips so much,' Humphrey Jonah said. 'I suggest you leave your mouth open and try to form the words with your tongue.'

Angela opened her mouth.

'Is this better?' she said in a muffled voice, like a man with no roof to his mouth.

'Jolly good,' Humphrey Jonah said encouragingly. 'A little later you and Mr Divine will be put under guard in a hut or huts. A colleague and I will get you out and into the bush where we'll be picked up. We'll be exchanging our cover for your safety. Now, Miss Carter, I'm going to throw my robe over your . . . over you and then I shall thrust into you – I mean, I shall pretend to. You must forgive my . . . the fact that . . . the thing is, Miss Carter that I have to lift my garment and give evidence of my readiness to fulfil all the expectations of fertility, so to speak. You must understand that my . . . my turgidity means no disrespect to you.'

'Please don't give it a thought,' Angela said, in her roofless mouth voice. 'Your turgidity is my salvation.'

'Quite. Very well phrased.'

A few moments later Angela felt the folds of cloth flap down over her bottom and then Humphrey Jonah's thighs touched hers as he thrust forward. She felt his erection glance the inside of her right thigh.

'Miss Carter,' he whispered urgently. 'Reaction, *please*! They have all seen that it is eight inches long.'

Angela reacted, pulling on her tethered arms, opening her mouth wide and arching her back.

'Damn good show!' Humphrey Jonah muttered. 'Synchronisation wasn't perfect, but they won't notice. Keep it up!'

Angela felt the rough movement of the cloth and the warmth of Humphrey Jonah's thighs. His loins began a continuous battering oscillation against her rump, but his eight inches jerked harmlessly somewhere in the space between her spreadeagled thighs.

'I think a little moan occasionally, Miss Carter,' he suggested. 'I mean, I don't know how you usually . . . The phonetic reaction is very much regarded by the African.'

Angela started to utter a loud moan every thirty seconds.

'How did you get your Oxbridge accent, Mr Jonah,' she asked, mouth-rooflessly.

'Well, at Oxford, actually,' he replied. 'Trinity College.'

His rigidity grazed Angela's thigh, gouging its softness.

'I am *so* sorry, Miss Carter,' he whispered. 'I am doing my best to . . . to avoid contact. But the margin for error, so to speak, is small.'

'That's quite all right,' Angela said, phonily rolling her head and contorting her face. 'You can't be held responsible for accidents.'

'It really is most generous of you to take such a view. I think a little more straining of the shoulders.'

'Do you think there's any risk they'll see through us –' Angela asked, complying.

'No, no, Miss Carter. My family motto is "Defeat is Alien" '

'All right. I guess we can make it.'

'Which means, so to speak, that we cannot. Truly the English language is a flexible tool.'

Which is more than I can say for yours, Angela thought, as the ramrod battered the inside of her thigh again. Suddenly she thought of Albert. She'd forgotten all about him. Forgotten everything, in fact, in her utter astonishment at the turnabout in the situation. She glanced in his direction. He appeared to have his eyes closed. Of course, he assumed . . . oh God! He thought it was really happening. If only she could wink at him. But instead she stuck to her duty, uttering a variety of groans and swirling her hips madly.

'That's the idea, Miss Carter,' Humphrey Jonah said. 'A very good performance.'

'Thank you very much,' Angela said.

'Oh please don't misconstrue my praise,' Humphrey Jonah said quickly. 'Miming talent is rare. And simulation without stimulation, so to speak, is difficult indeed.'

'You seem to have quite a bit of talent yourself,' Angela said.

There was an embarrassed silence and she added: 'I'm only joking, Mr Jonah.'

After a few moments he answered rather stifly, his hips maintaining their vigorous rhythm.

'You must not forget, Miss Carter, that the male nervous system can be tangibly stimulated by the sight of the female body. I mean, I would be hardly human if . . . There is no disrespect to you, Miss Carter . . . '

His sex suddenly brushed the lips of her vagina. She arched her bottom involuntarily and Humphrey Jonah exclaimed in horror: 'Oh my sainted aunt! Do forgive me Miss Carter. I . . . I lost concentration – and I think you sank a little.'

Angela felt laughter welling up in her again.

'You did it on purpose, Mr Jonah,' she said, rooflessly.

'On my honour, Miss Carter, it was the purest accident. I assure you it will not happen again.'

'Five to one,' Angela said.

'I beg your pardon?'

'I'll lay you odds of five to one.'

'You're on, Miss Carter. Indeed. I shall now bring our ... bring this ordeal to a conclusion. I think you had better cry out dolorously.'

'Just a minute!' Angela cried. 'That's not fair! You're not giving me a chance.'

'You have touched on my weakness, Miss Carter. I'm afraid I'm a betting man. I shall count five and then ... and then I advise your strongest reaction. One ... two ... '

'It's not gentlemanly!'

'Three ... '

'You're taking advantage ...

'Four ...'.

'Of a defenceless girl!'

'Five!'

Humphrey Jonah let out a muffled but impressive roar and his thighs tensed against Angela's, with his wager-winning weapon carefully extended below the danger zone. Angela had no choice but to utter a simultaneous sobbing scream.

'Magnificent, Miss Carter!' Humphrey Jonah applauded. 'As recompense for your very fine efforts I shall not hold you to the bet.'

Chapter Fourteen

ANGELA SAT quite still in the rather chilly darkness of the hut. Through the small doorway she could see the glow over the centre of the village and the silhouettes of the two squatting guards. The drums were silent now, and the village itself was quiet.

They has not returned her clothes and she pulled one of the rather smelly animal hides around her shoulders, telling herself that the cold at least helped her to stay awake. She had no idea how long she'd been in the hut and she had no idea how they could possibly escape through the miles of dark bush with all its dangers. The confidence an Oxford upbringing imparted!

For a while she listened to the meaningless murmur of her guards chatting. They were solid men, after all, and no doubt armed. Escape from the hut seemed unlikely, let alone the bush. She found she was trembling.

Outside, a third man softly greeted the guards and squatted down with them. Angela could make out his humped figure. Things were getting worse!

She heard the odd plonking sound and saw the two shapes sort of waft backwards and keel over before she understood what was happening. The third shape filled the hut door and the Oxford voice called to her very softly: 'Miss Carter – hurry, please!'

Angela slipped from the hut as Humphrey Jonah carefully arranged the dead guards in a squatting position against the walls of the hut. He took her hand.

They went quickly but without haste through the labyrinth of huts and beyond to the edge of the bush. Albert and another African appeared.

'Albert!' Angela gasped, only to be immediately hushed by the Africans.

Humphrey Jonah pointed and silently they ran for a clump of trees, Albert and Angela between the two Africans.

A shadow came out of the trees and confronted them, saying something in Swahili. Again Angela heard the curious plonk and the shadow fell backwards without a cry. They plunged into the trees, Angela awkwardly holding the hide around her, cutting her feet on twigs and small stones, the thorny scrub tearing at her bare legs. Her heart was pounding like a pneumatic drill. Albert was breathing painfully beside her.

They passed through the trees and headed for another copse some distance off. Now Humphrey Jonah led and the second African followed in their wake. Their feet swished in the grass and the clump of trees loomed in dark silhouette under the sliver of moon.

At first, Angela's thoughts centred on the prospect of pursuit. Would it be audible, or would it be completely silent, stalking them down like some great cat at home in the bush? But after a while, she could think of nothing but clutching Albert's hand and forcing herself forward. Once she stumbled and twisted her foot and an ache grew in it, more pronounced with every step.

They went right through the second copse and Humphey Jonah didn't pause. Angela staggered to a halt and raised her injured foot, gasping. Albert stopped beside her and the African behind closed in, exhorting them to continue.

'Mr Jonah,' Angela called, 'I've hurt my foot and I must get my wind.'

'Sit down a minute,' Albert said.

Humphrey Jonah appeared beside them.

'I am truly sorry for your ordeal, Miss Carter,' he said. 'As an athletics blue, I myself will confess this is most difficult terrain.'

'Will somebody tell me what's going on,' Albert said.

'We have approximately another half mile to go,' Humphrey Jonah said. 'We shall then come to a stretch of land where a helicopter will pick us up. With any luck we shall be in the air within fifteen minutes. But those minutes are precious. Miss Carter, if you can endure a little longer . . . Perhaps if you lean on Mr Divine and me we shall manage to breast the tape together, so to speak.'

They stumbled on, with Angela linked to Albert and the African. The glow of the village was no longer visible against the vast night sky.

Suddenly a burst of machinegun fire exploded far behind them. Humphrey Jonah turned and called in Swahili to his colleague.

'They have discovered our departure,' he said. 'But they are shooting at shadows.'

'Just so long as there are plenty of shadows,' Albert said,

'Ah, I hear the helicopter,' Humphrey Jonah cried. 'Hurry – one last effort, Miss Carter.'

'I can't hear a bloody thing,' Albert said.

'You were not born in the bush, Mr Divine,' the African said. 'The big city, with all its advantages, has a deleterious effect on many of our senses, you know.'

The hum of the helicopter gradually became evident and way out ahead, a searchlight suddenly beamed down to the ground, brightly illuminating an area of grass.

'There we are,' Humphrey Jonah said. 'Superbly timed.'

They ran towards the light and the fuselage of the aircraft grew clear, glinting dark metal and glass. A nylon ladder snaked down from the open hatch to within a foot of the ground.

'Surely we don't have to climb that thing?' Angela gasped.

'It will save minutes,' Humphrey Jonah said.

Angela tried to frame a protest, but in seconds they were close to the beam with the roar of the helicopter above them, its rotary blades whirling and the rush of air flattening the grass around them.

'Up you go, Miss Carter – hurry.'

Albert pulled off his jacket and Angela put it on in place of the hide. Then, with both hands now free she began the swaying ascent. The men below watched the beginning of her erratic climb, as the underside of her rump was revealed beneath the jacket, Humphrey Jonah looked tactfully away.

He muttered something to the other African, who also, a trifle reluctantly, lowered his eyes.

'Right, Mr Divine – up you go.'

Albert followed Angela up the beam of light, with the wind flinging his hair in all directions. As he was hauled through the hatch, both security agents were already swarming up the tough ladder. As they in turn were manhandled into the helicopter, the engine exploded with power and the craft seemed almost to spring away from the earth. The beam snapped out as the ladder was wound in and dropping away below, the bush was a great, shadowed expanse with dark patches, which were clumps of trees and toadstool mounds, which were single ones.

There was a small cheer inside the plane, congratulations flowed all around, clothes were produced for Angela, sandwiches, flasked coffee and brandy were passed around, Angela's foot was bandaged, disinfectant rubbed on cuts.

Angela peered curiously at Humphrey Jonah.

'Unmasked at last,' she said.

'I trust you prefer my face, Miss Carter.'

'What do you mean – unmasked? Albert broke in.

'Oh darling, Mr Jonah was the man in the mask who . . . '

Humphrey Jonah in turn cut in sharply.

'The man in the mask who went through the pretence of performing the fertility rites with your . . . with Miss Carter, Mr Divine.'

'Pretence?'

'Oh yes, Albert. Nothing really happened. It was hysterically funny . . . '

'But I saw with my own eyes. He was . . . '

'Mr Divine, you have a fine actress for a . . . in Miss Carter. If you could be deceived, small wonder the whole tribe was taken in. A real coup de théâtre, so to speak.'

'And a fine actor in Humphrey Jonah, too,' Angela said.

'When you two have finished congratulating each other,' Albert said with heavy sarcasm, 'I don't want to sound ungrateful, but as far as I could see you two were having a ball.'

'Mr Divine – please!' Humphrey Jonah was shocked. 'How could you think . . . ?'

'Albert,' Angela said very firmly, 'we were acting. Mr Jonah is a fine gentleman and he just pretended.'

'Pretended! I don't see how the most gentlemanly will in the world would enable one to avoid the target.'

'Well I did have a half blue in swordsmanship,' Humphrey Jonah said diffidently. 'Epee. I understand the cut and thrust, so to speak.'

'Look Albert,' Angela said. 'It's really quite simple. If I bend over like this and then Mr Jonah . . .'

'Children,' Lavinia Mungai cut in, 'Do you mind if we postpone these sex demonstrations. You're rocking the plane.'

Chapter Fifteen

LAVINIA MUNGAI whisked the hot chocolate in the elegant, Portuguese-tiled kitchen of the Mayfair flat which had been placed at her disposal as a refuge.

'No, Albert,' she said, 'from my personal knowledge of Humphrey Jonah, I would say he definitely was not lying. He is just too terribly gentlemanly. I think it comes of reading all that Conan Doyle and Arthurian legend. Gallantry is his way of life. Of course, I can't speak for your girlfriend.'

'No,' Albert said. 'Neither can I.'

'Are you sure you won't have some of this chocolate? Much better for you than that Scotch.'

'No thanks,' Albert said. 'Don't you ever drink?'

'Not usually on duty.'

'Duty? I was trying to think of us as a young honeymoon couple.'

She smiled and poured the chocolate into a mug.

'Well since we've gone to all the trouble of putting you and Angela in separate hideaways while we lure the opposition, it wouldn't do for me to get blind drunk, would it? I am supposed to be protecting you.'

She turned away and glanced slantingly down between the lace curtains to the street four floors below, where a stream of one-way traffic made a fast flow. Albert glanced sidelong at her. He had to admit he was very impressed. All that toughness and savoir faire and with it that African beauty and a sort of lazy femininity. It really was a ridiculous situation. Here he was in his black silk dressing gown with the olive paisley design. And there she was in that long green bathrobe that hugged her hips. And around them was this luxury flat full of goodies. Yet it was all in the cause of duty. In a short while she would go off to her bedroom to nurse the pistol under her pillow; he would go off to his to dream about lost amours.

She turned toward him, the bathrobe moulding the lithe lines of her body. She sipped her nutritious chocolate, looking at him with those intelligent dark eyes and the slightly flaring nostrils.

'It looks cold out there,' she said.

'You don't really think Mau Mau is stalking through the winter streets of Mayfair, do you?'

'Not yet. But they will. That's why not even the porter knows we're here. This flat is rented to a Mr Eustace Pickles, who's very English.'

The telephone rang in the lounge and they both walked through the flat to the padded luxury of the room with its log fire adding visual cosiness to the central heating.

Lavinia Mungai picked up the receiver and said hello.

'Okay,' she said a moment later. 'But I wouldn't ring again if I were you until it's over. We can't be too careful.'

She passed the instrument to Albert.

'It's for you.'

'Hello?' Albert said.

'Albert, do you really think this is necessary?' Angela's voice demanded.

'Well it is a very useful way of communicating,' Albert said. 'Before the telephone, they had to send messages by hansom cab, or something.'

'Albert, don't be stupid, you know perfectly well what I mean. You're alone with that girl, aren't you?'

'It's all right,' Albert said. 'She's promised not to hurt me. She's on our side.'

'Albert, there are times when I could cheerfully throttle you. You're sleeping in that flat alone with Lavinia Mungai, aren't you?'

'Well it is in the interest of the nation of Kenya.'

'It's also in the interests of Albert Divine, I'll bet. What are you doing at this moment?'

'Well, we were just getting ready for bed.'

'I thought so. It's just ten-thirty and you never go to bed

before one a.m. You're going to get into her bed, aren't you?'

'Well for someone who was discovered in the act with a white hunter and witnessed by a whole tribe copulating with a witch doctor you're taking a pretty mean line.'

'Albert, I was not in the act with either of them, ever. Anyway, why have we been separated like this? It doesn't make sense to me?'

'To confuse the enemy, I gather. If you want more explanation, you'll just have to send a diplomatic note to the High Commissioner. Anyway, who are you alone with right now?'

'Well, Humphrey Jonah's here to protect me, but he's gone to his room to do some study.'

'You mean to say he has to learn to improve on his previous performance?'

'You're a rotten bastard, Albert Divine.'

'Well at least I'm not a rotten lover.'

'There's no need to tell that girl. Is she listening?'

'She doesn't have time. She's practising the martial arts in preparation for the enemy.'

Angela made a disbelieving noise. He could picture her pouting.

'I'm sure it's all very unnecessary, Albert. There's room for a regiment to take refuge in these High Commission quarters.'

'That's funny – there's only room for two in this flat.'

'Albert, I hate you!'

Albert grinned.

'So why all the fuss?'

'Do you like her Albert? Do you think she's beautiful?

'Good lord no,' Albert said.

'Oh you liar! She is beautiful.. You fancy her Albert, don't you. Admit it.'

'What's the trouble?' Albert said. 'Has Humphrey turned chicken? Perhaps he left his regimental mask in Africa. You might get him one in Woolworth's. And he probably needs an audience. Better issue an appeal to the High Commission staff. Tell them rats' tails are de rigueur.'

'You rotten, rotten bastard! If that girl comes on with you, you tell her not tonight Lavinia. Albert – will you tell her that?'

'You forget I am a gentleman – I couldn't be so rude,' Albert said, imitating Humphrey Jonah's accent. 'Besides I have a blue in films to live up to.'

The phone rasped in his ear and went dead. He stood looking at the receiver. Lavinia Mungai took it from him and hung up.

'That was Angela,' he said. 'Checking up.'

'Checking up? Did she expect to hear orgasmic noises.'

'Possibly. She's very jealous.'

'How appropriate. So are you. Aren't you?'

She smiled at him ironically.

Albert stared at her broad lips as they smiled. They were dark and firm and very well defined. Her whole, dark, firm face and above all those eyes with the startlingly clear whites. *Did* he think she was beautiful! He threw back his Scotch.

'Yes and no,' he said.

He poured himself another Scotch while Lavinia Mungai moved over and probed the fire. Sparks flew in vivid patterns and the logs flared up.

'Look,' Albert said, gazing around with satisfaction, 'why don't we just hibernate here and emerge on March twenty-first all refreshed for the spring?'

'At your rate of alcohol consumption, you'd be carried out on March twentyfirst all depressed for spring, summer and autumn.'

'A white hunter led me astray,' Albert said.

'Okay, maybe I'll have a small brandy to keep you company,' Lavinia Mungai said.

Albert sorted the brandy enthusiastically out of a cabinet.

'Marvellous,' he said. 'I'm the only person I know whose character defects are contagious.'

She took a sip of the brandy and gave an appreciative shudder.

'It's very nice,' she said. 'Every time I have a drink I realize just what I'm missing.'

'Yes,' Albert said. 'Fatuous, giggling conversations,

followed by maudlin, depressive ones, succeeded by fates worse than death and culminating in terrible hangovers and dreadful embarrassment. A drinker's life is indeed a full one.'

'You sound like a very militant member of the temperance society.'

'Unfortunately no. I am a very passive member of the suicidal society of sots – SSOS for short. Even more desperate than SOS.'

Lavinia Mungai stared at him wide-eyed. Her lips formed a circle of surprise.

'Did you just think that up?' she asked.

'Once the devilish liquor gets me,' Albert said, 'there's no stemming the inspiration short of hurling a heavy object accurately at my temple.'

'Why is your girlfriend so jealous?' Lavinia Mungai asked.

'I really have no idea,' Albert said innocently.

'You've lost your inspiration already. I think that's what I have against liquor – its effects are so erratic.'

She took another sip of her brandy and suddenly finished the glassful.

'Bravo!' Albert cried. 'I do trust the effects will be erratic.'

'Surely you don't want me to have a fatuous, giggling conversation with you.'

'We can skip that bit if you like.'

'Well I'll have another small brandy – and I mean small.'

'How about your duty?'

'Oh I perform even better on a small quantity of alcohol.'

Albert made an involuntary break in the act of pouring.

'Perform?'

'Yes, the relaxing effect of the alcohol seems to make me more limber – gets rid of my inhibitions.'

Albert finished pouring and handed her the glass, looking at the swell of her breasts under the bathrobe. His mind was boggling at this unexpected turn.

'What happens is that I'm prepared to take chances with my body,' Lavinia Mungai said. 'I'm ready to extend myself a little more than when I haven't had a drink.'

Albert's eyes gleamed. An image of that lithe body taking

chances, extending itself, began pulsating furiously in his head.

'Do you perform often after drinking?' he asked.

'No, it's only happened a few times, sort of accidentally. Normally I'm dead cold sober, but you can't always pick and choose the place and circumstances.'

'No,' Albert said. 'I suppose not.'

'Very often, I perform absolutely at my best when someone jumps on me unexpectedly,' Lavinia Mungai said. 'They get quite a surprise.'

'I bet they do,' Albert said. He gazed around the room, vaguely figuring he might try an unexpected jump.

'Most men simply don't imagine you can lift your legs as high as their neck and they don't expect such thrust from the hips,' she said.

'Oh I don't know,' Albert said. 'It depends on their previous experience.'

'That's true, of course, but very few of them have experienced a girl like me.'

Albert felt a small hammer begin to tap in his chest as an accompaniment to the pictures in his head.

'Do they survive?' he quipped breathlessly.

'Oh yes, they're just knocked out. Takes them a while to recover.'

Albert felt knocked out already.

'It really depends which position they adopt,' Lavinia Mungai pursued. 'I like them to come at me from behind. There are special kicks for that.'

Albert broke out in a light sweat. There was no keeping one's cool in this situation.

'I also like to use my fingers and elbows,' she went on. 'Lot's of effective things you can do with them to a man's sensitive parts.'

'Well I can see fingers,' Albert said. 'I don't quite see elbows.'

He couldn't remember when a woman had so turned him on just with an advance pep talk.

'Oh, you'd be surprised – when you're in really close together,' Lavinia Mungai explained. 'That normally happens when there's more than one of them, of course.'

'More than one of them!'

'Oh I've often had two or three together.'

'What! All at the same time?'

'Simultaneously.'

'It's not possible!'

'One in front, one behind, one from the side. They come from all directions.'

'Even so . . . ' Albert was slightly put out by this revelation. It either indicated a kinkiness beyond his imagining, or that she was making the whole thing up.

'There's nothing so surprising in that,' Lavinia Mungai said. 'Theoretically I could take on eight men at once, though I must confess I wouldn't care to try. One at a time's okay, but preferably not eight together. It would be rather exhausting.'

'I should think it would!' Albert said. 'I'm beginning to see that the liquor's inspiring you.'

'Are you implying that I'm exaggerating?'

'Of course not.'

Lavinia Mungai smiled and gave a little shrug. She sipped her brandy.

'Well I don't have eight men here,' she said, 'but I could give you an individual demonstration.'

Albert gulped. Women's lib had nothing to teach Africa! None of your sophisticated put-offs and come-ons. He managed an off-beam smile.

'All right,' he said. 'You may learn a bit from me, too. I'm not exactly a tyro.'

Lavinia Mungai gazed at him.

'You're not!'

Albert's face clouded.

'Well, what the hell!' he said. 'I am well over twenty-one. And you only have to be eleven in today's world to know what it's all about.'

'In Japan, perhaps,' she said. 'But not elsewhere.'

'What's Japan got to do with it?'

'The eight-year-olds learn all about it there.'

'Oh come on,' Albert said. 'You don't really believe that?

'Believe it? I know it. I was there and I can tell you some of those eight-year-olds are remarkable.'

'They are?'

Albert was beginning to feel a little confused. Japan? True they'd always had geisha girls and hara kiri, but . . .

'The younger the better, you know,' Lavinia Mungai said. 'It gets your body supple. When did you start?'

Albert was taken aback.

'Well . . . er . . . when I was thirteen actually. A cousin of mine . . .'

'Well that's pretty young. You must be very good.'

Albert grinned diffidently.

'Oh well, I get by, you know.'

'Have you kept it up ever since?'

'Very much so,' Albert said.

Lavinia Mungai looked impressed.

'Well you must be *very* good,' she said. 'Why didn't you tell me?'

'Well, one doesn't usually introduce oneself with a description of one's prowess, does one?' Albert said. 'Unless one's terribly insecure, of course.'

'True, but you let me go on a bit. You're probably better than I am.'

'Oh I doubt that,' Albert said modestly. 'I couldn't take on three together, let alone eight. It would ruin me.'

'What's your style?' she asked suddenly.

'My style? Albert was at a loss. 'Well, sort of casual style, I suppose, until I get worked up.'

Lavinia Mungai smiled quizzically.

'I'm not sure that I believe you,' she said.

Albert made a movement towards her.

'Well, we can put it to the test,' he said.

He choked over the words as her bare foot lashed out and caught him in the solar plexus.

'I must say, your reactions are not too fast,' she said.

'For Christ's sake!' Albert protested.

Her leg flicked out again at lightning speed and the instep of her left foot stung his right ear. At the same instant she lunged at him and her closed fist shot at his jaw, to the accompaniment of a terrifying yell, stopping short just at the point of contact.

Albert recoiled, cowering, bent from the waist, clutching his ear.

'In fact, you're slow,' Lavinia Mungai said. 'And you don't have any spirit.'

'Just stop that!' Albert cried. 'I thought you were here to protect me. What's got into you?'

'Well, for someone who allegedly took up karate at thirteen, you haven't got much idea of how to look after yourself.'

Albert was pervaded with a depressing mixture of sheepishness and disappointment. Images of making it with Lavinia from behind, sideways or upside down were shattered to smithereens.

'Are you all right?' she asked. 'You look a little sick.'

She approached him maternally and Albert drew back in alarm. She crossed her fingers smiling.

'Okay – truce,' she said. 'You shouldn't make such false claims. I mean, I am a third dan. You couldn't expect to get away with it.'

Albert drew himself up with wary dignity.

'I was not making false claims,' he said. 'I had quite simply misunderstood your allusion. I was referring to prowess of a quite different sort.'

She looked at him blankly.

'In my innocence,' he said stiffly, 'I mistakenly interpreted your comments on your performance as relating to your worthiness in bed.'

He picked up his Scotch, removed the ice and held it to his flushed ear. Lavinia Mungai stared at him. Her top row of beautiful white teeth appeared and covered her bottom lip. The whites of her eyes got larger. She smiled. The smooth skin around her eyes crinkled. She collapsed with sudden laughter.

'Well it may be funny to you,' Albert said magisterially. 'But my stomach isn't laughing. Nor is my ear. I thought you were bound by etiquette to pull those kicks, except in combat.'

'Oh but I did.'

She came towards him solicitously, ignored his involuntary cringing and held the ice to his ear for him.

'I'm trying to remember what I said.'

Albert's ear smarted under the ice.

'Well,' he said tartly. 'For a start there were references to eight men at once and what you could do with your elbows.'

Lavinia Mungai collapsed with laughter again.

'Hey, take it easy – that's my ear!'

'I'm sorry. So you don't know karate at all, poor man?'

'That must be painfully clear.'

She removed the ice and put her cool fingers tentatively against the lobe of Albert's ear. He was suddenly overwhelmingly aware of her body almost touching his and her face smiling at him.

'Perhaps I should teach you the rudiments,' she said. 'In compensation.'

Her fingers slid from his ear and rested momentarily on his shoulder. Albert, with astonishing lucidity for an injured man, saw that if it was a choice between going to his lonely bed and having her tend his inevitable wounds, then karate it was. He regretted judo was not her speciality.

'It might be interesting,' he said. 'I quite fancy those long black belts.'

'Well, if you're prepared to train very hard for a few years.'

'There's always a catch.'

'I'll just show you a few basic techniques,' she said.

'Don't hit me.'

'Don't worry.'

She moved back from him a few feet and raised her right hand.

'First we have the film-famed *shuto* or chop,' she said. 'Hand flat and rigid, fingers pressed tightly together, thumb in to the palm. Then with either hand you make sharp, swinging strikes to certain parts of the body, for instance the neck . . .'

She advanced on him with a lithe movement and swung her hand with blurring speed at his neck, stopping it short and then allowing it to touch his skin and remain there.

'You try,' she said.

Albert raised his hand, palm upwards and stared at it. His mind seemed to go blank. She took the hand gently and arranged it. She was wearing some sort of flowerlike perfume. Albert glanced at the swelling coffee-coloured flesh in the v of the bath robe.

'Now draw it back behind your head and swing it in an arc, giving the wrist a final flick on contact,' she said.

Albert did as he was told in slow motion. His hand made contact with her neck and brushed the skin.

'You've got the idea,' she said. 'Now we have the *tsuki* or punch. It's a very special technique. You pull your hand back in a fist, level with the breast, fingers uppermost, while the other arm's extended. You shoot out the withdrawn arm in a punch, keeping the shoulders completely square and turning the fist over at the last moment to make contact with the first two knuckles. As you punch you pull the other arm back hard to add impetus. The punch comes up from the floor through a straight back leg, aided by a twist of the hips – so . . .'

She shot out a punch, at the same time lunging forward with her body so suddenly that Albert had no time to react. The fist stopped on his chin and rested there, knuckles caressing his jaw.

'Normally, of course, you withdraw the arm fast once you've punched,' she explained. 'But this is slow for demonstration.'

Albert tried the punch, lunging forward like a carthorse – with the cart in tow. The skin of her jaw was taut and delicate.

'Shoulders back, hips thrust forward,' she said.

Her hands eased his shoulders into the correct position and then arranged his hips. She tapped his buttocks. 'Tight!' she said. 'They should be tight. You're pushing against the floor so the body's all one from foot to fist.'

Albert's body was suddenly all one from foot to foreskin. The rest of him was a separate amorphous mass of desire.

'Look,' Lavinia Mungai said. 'You really have to push on

that back foot. Feel my buttocks and you'll see what I mean.'

She adopted the punching stance. Albert's amorphous mass twisted itself in knots. She must be joking!

But she was all brisk and businesslike. He could see her buttocks separately outlined, jutting against the bath robe. He stepped forward and ran his fingers over them. She was right, of course. They were tight and tense, moulded like marble. His hands trembled.

'Okay,' she said. 'Got it?'

Albert nodded. He certainly had! Like nobody's business.

'Right,' she said. 'The punch we just did was *jodan tsuki* – *jodan* means upper. Now we have *chudan*, or middle – to the solar plexus. Like this . . . '

Her fist was suddenly on his belly. Albert followed her example, unprompted.

'A little high,' she said.

Albert could feel the firm bulge of her underbreasts against the back of his hand. How could she expect him to be accurate in circumstances like this! He slid his fist down over her belly. Its contour was firm and slightly pliable.

'That's right,' she said. 'That's the spot.'

Albert could only grunt. It wasn't quite the spot, but it would do for a start.

'And then we get *gedan tsuki*,' she instructed. '*Gedan* means lower. It's a punch to the groin . . . '

Her fist flashed for his genitals and grazed gently down his all too obvious erection. Albert thrust out his hips ecstatically.

'Now you,' she said.

Albert executed the movement with the speed and agility of a brontosaurus, his fist ending against her pubis. Even through the bathrobe he could feel the bush of hair on the bulging Mount of Venus.

'A little lower,' she said.

He moved his fist until he could feel the bulge of her thighs.

'Buttocks tight, don't forget,' she commanded. She put

her arms around him, hands on his rump and pushed his hips forward.

'Better,' she said. 'But *still* not tight enough. Feel mine.'

Albert moved closer in, putting his arms around her in turn and grasping the firm cheeks of her bottom. His erection thrust against her robe, which fell open slightly. His flesh touched her thighs, which she opened, and slipped between them. She clamped her thighs back on his sex.

'This is the anti-rapist technique,' she said. 'Done hard with strong thighs it can be excruciating.

Albert's breath had left him. For some seconds they stood eyes half closed, loins sliding gently against each other.

'What's my reply to that one?' Albert asked faintly.

She took his hand and drew it between her thighs. Albert followed her instruction and found himself titillating the hard little clitoris. Lavinia Mungai gasped.

'That's your best effort yet,' she murmured.

She drew his head down and took a gentle bite at his neck.

'That can be . . . fatal,' she murmured.

Albert followed her example, sliding his lips along her neck, across her cheek until their mouths met and crushed violently together. Their tongues fought a surprisingly equal duel while their hands ruthlessly inflamed their martial spirits.

Lavinia Mungai suddenly slithered down Albert's body, pulling his gown apart as she went. She knelt against him, making soft animal noises which were dutifully emulated by Albert as her lips closed on his member. He placed his hand on her dark, curly head, felt convulsively for the lips that devoured him. He tensed his buttocks and she slipped her hands around them.

'That's perfect,' she muttered in a muffled tone.

'I'll take it up,' Albert muttered back. 'I'll do all the years of training.'

He reached down and pulled her robe off her slim shoulders. He uncovered her firm, coffee-coloured breasts with their huge, dark nipples. He held them in his hands and fondled them as they bobbed against him.

Her mouth sucked tormentingly away from him and she

rolled back on to the thick carpet, slapping her arms down on it, keeping her chin into her neck.

'What's that?' Albert asked breathlessly.

'How to fall . . . ' she murmured.

She undid the belt of her disarranged robe and peeled off the garment, revealing the entire well-developed leanness of her body.

'You . . . you slap your arms down on . . . on either side of me . . . as you fall,' she whispered.

Albert was out of his dressing gown with a speed which made his earlier sluggishness seem like a con trick. He fell inexpertly, but quite adequately. Her body was hard and hot, except for the softness of the cushioning breasts. Her thighs grasped him in a grip only a karate woman could have managed. Her fingers reached him.

'This is the payoff . . . ' she said softly. 'Guaranteed to overpower . . . '

The fingers guided him and Albert applied the coup de grace.

They both uttered a cry whose vehemence would have done any karate expert proud.

Albert thrust hotly into her, tightening his buttocks to the ultimate, as she had instructed. Lavinia Mungai thrust back at him and did all sorts of tricky writhing things with her hips and thighs just to show him she was master and he was student. Of course. Albert was not concerned to argue rank. He was not concerned to do anything but to plunge headlong into this surf-ride of sensuality. He was ready to drown in her loins. His whole being was just an inflamed extension inside her. He was expanding . . .

The telephone rang.

For several seconds they both pretended they were going to ignore it and then Lavinia Mungai gradually slowed down.

'I'll have to answer it,' she sighed. 'It might be important.'

She wriggled off his impalement, catching her breath. Albert rolled over, his frustration threatening the ceiling.

'Hello. Yes, Lavinia Mungai . . . '

Albert listened impatiently. He was nothing but a suspended genital rapture.

'Well I was doing my exercises. Oh yes, I always get a little breathless – they're very strenuous. Yes, he's here. Hold on.'

She held out the receiver to Albert with a smile in her dark eyes. Her lips were sultry. Albert gazed at the instrument uncomprehendingly and then stumbled to his feet. Angela again!

'Hello?' he said.

'Albert, say "the quick brown fox jumped over the lazy dog",' Angela said.

'What on earth do you mean?'

Albert gazed at Lavinia Mungai's swinging breasts.

'Why are you out of breath, Albert?'

'I am not out of breath,' Albert said, forcing his eyes away from the lithe waiting body and simultaneously slowing and steadying his breathing.

'You were in bed with that girl, weren't you?'

'No,' Albert said, with the ring of truth. 'I wasn't.'

'Do you swear that, Albert?'

'I swear it.'

'What were you doing then?'

Albert's attention was distracted by Lavinia Mungai walking away from him towards the liquor cabinet: slim shoulders and back and the slim legs accentuated the oval hips with their firm buttocks. She had dark dimples above her rump and the slim ridge of her backbone was visible.

'Albert, are you afraid to tell me what you were doing?' Angela's tone was sharp.

'I was practising karate.'

There was a long silence during which Lavinia Mungai turned back to Albert, presenting him with a full frontal view of her finely-moulded body. She came towards him.

'You were doing *what*.' Angela demanded.

'Karate,' Albert repeated. 'You know – that unarmed combat thing.'

'But you don't know the first thing about karate?' Angela sounded strangely disapproving.

Lavinia Mungai, smiling slightly, pressed close to Albert and rubbed her breasts against his chest. She began to play with his most responsive part.

'Oh!' Albert cried.

'What?' Angela said.

'Oh yes I do!' Albert said quickly.

'Since when?'

Albert made a frantic effort to keep his voice steady.

'Since Lavinia Mungai taught me a few moves a little while ago,' he said.

Lavinia Mungai right now seemed to be going quietly out of her mind. Her body was all over him. Suddenly she forced him, by main strength, to sit down on the carpeted floor. Then she pushed him flat. Albert unexpectedly found himself speaking into the telephone while gazing up at the ceiling.

'I see,' Angela said tautly. 'What kind of moves?'

Albert tried to remember.

'Oh – skis and dans and things,' he said.

Albert, stop pretending.'

He let out a lustful yell, desperately covering the mouthpiece as Lavinia Mungai, who had straddled him, sank quiveringly down, impaled.

'What's the matter, Albert?'

Albert removed his hand and coughed noisily into the mouthpiece.

'Dry throat,' he said. 'Been coughing all evening.'

He covered the mouthpiece feverishly as Lavinia Mungai sank down on him again, tearing an ecstatic gasp from his lips.

'What's the idea of her teaching you karate?' Angela demanded suspiciously.

Albert groaned. He kept his hand clasped over the mouthpiece. This was unbearable. He made a supreme and rapid effort as Lavinia Mungai rose up, removed his hand and barked: 'So I can protect us better in future!'

He slapped his hand back on the mouthpiece with the last syllable as Lavinia Mungai descended, splaying out her thighs on either side of him, straining her torso back so that her breasts stuck out. Albert gasped and panted, like an orchestral audience trying to rid itself of coughs during the interval.

'Whose idea was it?' Angela snapped.

Albert waited until Lavinia Mungai was rising up again, revealing his full length and her own moist excitement. He took his hand from the mouthpiece.

'Mine!' he barked – and slapped his hand back to utter a tortured cry at the new descent.

'There's no need to snap at me like that, Albert,' Angela said, stiffly. 'It sounds a very intimate thing to be learning from a girl. I knew of a woman who was raped by her judo instructor while he had a headlock on her.'

Albert's entrails seemed to be in the process of being sucked from his body. His stomach heaved wildly. Groans and gasps streamed unchecked and uncheckable from his contorted mouth.

'I suppose you're implying that's not worth comment,' Angela said. 'Well I'm not sure how different judo and karate are, but I'm sure that girl could take liberties with you if she wanted to. Albert?'

Albert made another herculean effort. He took his hand from the telephone.

'Definitely not,' he said – and simultaneously Lavinia Mungai gave an agonised moan.

Phrenetically Albert clamped his hand over the instrument.

'Albert – what on earth was that!'

Albert raised one side of his hand an inch.

'What?' he barked into the space.

'Sounded like an awful moan. Albert, what's the matter? What's going on there?'

Albert waited his moment. He now had the further difficulty of synchronising the telephone unveilings with less vocal moments from Lavinia Mungai as well as from himself. He slid his hand away and held it tremulously on the edge of the mouthpiece, ready for a lightning return.

'Must be a crossed line,' he cried. 'I heard it too.'

'Why are you talking so fast, Albert? Are you trying to get rid of me?'

'Course not!' Albert snapped. He flashed his hand over

the mouthpiece as Lavinia Mungai uttered a howl. Her head rolling. Muscles stood out around her ribs and hips as she rose and fell.

'Well it sounds like it. You're not only talking fast, you're not really saying anything. Albert – you're not in trouble, are you?'

Albert's agonised eyes followed Lavinia Mungai's slightly moist breasts as they bounced above him. How could he be expected to make speeches at a time like this!

'Albert, if you're in trouble but can't say so,' Angela articulated very slowly and deliberately, 'you can simply say, "I'm tired and I'm going to bed", then I'll understand and get these security people in action immediately.'

Albert gritted his teeth, narrowly missed biting his tongue and then gasped afresh as Lavinia Mungai crushed down and ground her bottom against his thighs. He hung on for the ascent, tore his hand from the mouthpiece and blurted: 'There's nothing wrong!'

'Well!' Angela was indignant. 'I don't know about that! Anyway, there's no need to get sharp with me!'

Albert was growing to bursting point; Lavinia Mungai was howling. He kept his hand hard down on the telephone. There was no question of speaking, let alone attempting to reassure Angela. He met the African girl's plunges with a battering upward thrust. Veins stood out dark in her brown neck. Her stomach shook like a belly dancer's.

Albert tensed his thighs and pushed. It was too much! Get it over!

'Albert?' Angela said.

Albert's breathing was like a steam train climbing a mountain. Lavinia Mungai flopped forward a little and gripped his shoulders while her hips continued to dance. Her smouldering eyes told him it was all about to happen.

'Albert?' Angela repeated. 'Albert!'

Albert arched his body. Lavinia Mungai's mouth opened wide, her eyes dilated.

'Albert!' Angela snapped. 'If you think this is a joke, you're wrong! Will you kindly tell me what's going on there – I mean it!'

Albert tensed his hand preparatory to snapping a desperate word into the telephone, thought better of it as he felt the familiar cell-shattering suction in his loins.

'Albert – will you answer me!' Angela insisted.

But Albert's anxiety had given way to uncontrollable passion. He could not keep any part of him still – including the extension of his body which was the wildly contorting African girl. He wanted to grab her body, but couldn't release the telephone. He suddenly gripped it with great force, afraid he might drop it or simply let it go.

Lavinia Mungai ran her hands over his chest. Her eyes were frenzied. She nodded frantically and he thrust up to meet her as her fingers scratched and she came down on him with an animal cry. At the same time Albert tensed and all his insides seemed to shoot out in a powerful torrent to an accompaniment of Lavinia Mungai repeatedly crying his name and Angela crying it, too, in a tiny, distant echo.

The girl sagged forward on him with a long, shuddering groan. She clung to him, penetrated still, with her head against his chest. Albert gradually subsided to normal. He got his breath. There was silence from the telephone. He waited a while and then said languidly: 'Hello?'

Angela's voice exploded at the other end of the line.

'Hello!' she yelled. 'What do you mean, "hello?" This is your special way of telling me to shut up, isn't it?'

'I'm sorry,' Albert said drowsily. 'The telephone seemed to go blank. I couldn't hear you.'

'That's because I'd stopped wasting my breath speaking,' Angela said with heavy sarcasm.

'No I mean the blankness after the electrical interference.'

'What *are* you talking about? I didn't hear any interference.'

'I realised that when you didn't answer my questions.'

'Your questions?'

'Yes, I was asking you what you were up to.'

'Listen Albert, I'm not up to anything – that's what I was asking you.'

'Well I'm not up to anything either.'

'Albert I don't know what you're talking about – and

what's happened to your voice, anyway.'

Lavinia Mungai's face moved against his chest. Her lips softly implanted a kiss on his shoulder.

'My voice?'

'Before, it was terribly fast and snappy aud now it's all slow and sleepy. They haven't given you drugs, have they?'

'They?'

'*Are you drugged, Albert.*'

'Don't be ridiculous,' Albert said. 'Just a bit tired.'

'Albert, will you promise you won't do any more karate with that girl? I don't want her taking liberties.'

'Okay.'

'What's she doing?'

'I think she's gone to sleep.'

'Well I don't like it at all,' Angela said peevishly. 'They could have protected us both at the High Commission.'

'That's the Secret Service for you,' Albert said. 'Very complicated lot. Anyway, it's only for a few hours.'

'It'd better be,' Angela said, 'or they'll have an insurrection on their hands. Do you miss me?'

'If it wasn't for the training while you were in the States, I couldn't bear it.'

'Liar. All right. Good night.'

'Sweet dreams.'

Albert replaced the receiver and squinted down at Lavinia Mungai. She lifted her head and smiled lazily at him.

'You devil,' she said. 'Such bare-faced fabrication.'

'I know,' Albert said. 'I shouldn't do these things, but I just can't resist temptation.'

'Let's go to bed, then, and you can give in all night.'

Albert traced the line of her spine.

'Actually,' he said, '*I* don't see why we weren't both given refuge in the High Commission, any more than she does.'

'It's really very simple.'

'It is?'

'It's simply that I arranged it this way.'

'Why?'

'Really! I should have thought that was rather obvious.'

'You mean to say . . . ?'

'Just that I fancied you.'

She knelt and placed her hands on his loins.

'I still do,' she said. 'How soon do you think you can fail to resist again?'

Chapter Sixteen

ALBERT, WRAPPED in a huge Mexican towel and still steaming from the bath, stretched out on the sofa and waited for Lavinia Mungai to finish her shower so she could prepare their breakfast. Well, lunch, in fact. He smiled to himself and wriggled his toes contentedly. Truly a vintage night. How fortunate he was not to be a high-principled, right-minded paragon. Three cheers for frail sinners.

The telephone rang.

Albert walked into the bedroom and listened to the shower running in the adjoining bathroom. Oh well, he'd answer it himself in a disguised voice. He glanced at the rumpled sheets. They looked as if a colony of ghosts had been using them to frighten people. He smiled happily and returned to the lounge.

He picked up the telephone.

'Allo,' he said. 'Zees ees Armand de Tallyrand oo spiks.'

'Albert – that took you long enough,' Angela said.

'Oh hi, Angela,' he cried. 'Have a good night? Sleep well?'

'You sound terribly cheerful,' she said primly.

Albert tried to tone down his blithe spirits.

'It's just that I had a long, restful night,' he said.

There was a doubtful silence and then Angela said: 'I have just learned that it's that woman's intention to keep you cooped up there for at least another night.'

'Really?'

'Well you don't sound very concerned.'

'I most certainly am,' Albert snapped. 'Another night? That's insufferable! How do you know?'

'Humphrey told me. And what's more he couldn't give me a good reason for it.'

'Well, that's the Secret Service for you,' Albert said. 'Their ways are inscrutable.'

'Personally, I think it's *her* ways that are inscrutable. It seems she's in charge. She obviously has an ulterior motive for keeping you there.'

'Hardly,' Albert remonstrated. 'A dedicated agent like that? Her sole motive for anything is to destroy the enemies of the State.'

'Albert, you are an innocent. That woman has designs on you. She might keep you there for a week.'

'God forbid,' Albert said, with a break in his voice. 'Angela you're not being lucid. She's simply doing her duty in difficult and possibly dangerous circumstances.'

'Albert, you don't know anything about women if you think that. And Humphrey's very embarrassed when I try to get any sense out of him.'

'From what you tell me he embarrasses easily anyway.'

'Albert, there's no doubt in my mind that woman wants to get you into bed. These women agents are very unscrupulous.'

'Do you come across them often?'

'It's no joking matter. I'm not putting up with it.'

'Well, since I'm the one who has to put up with it . . . '

'Where is she now?'

'Having a shower.'

'Exactly. Getting all prepared for the seduction scene. She'll probably appear in nothing but a towel and ask you to rub her back, the bitch.'

'Oh come on,' Albert said. 'Everyone takes a shower in the mornings.'

'Albert, I begin to doubt if we're in any danger at all. It was different in Africa. But this is England. I think they're just playing games. And that's precisely what she wants to do with you.'

'Angela, be reasonable. Would she . . . ?'

'I'm coming round there, Albert.'

'Coming *here!*'

'Why, what's wrong? Are you afraid to see me?'

'Of course not,' Albert said. 'But this place is supposed to be a hideaway. You're not supposed to come here because you feel like it. Anyway, you don't know where it is.'

'You can tell me.'

'I can't do that, Angela. It wouldn't be right.'

'You mean to say you won't tell me where you're shacked up with another woman?'

'But I'd be letting down the Kenya Intelligence Service, giving away state secrets. There might even be a penalty.'

'You miserable coward! Well don't worry, I've got it from Humphrey already.'

'I don't believe it.'

'Please yourself.'

'Angela, if you've got the address, *how* did you get it from him?'

'Never you mind. You're in no position to question me.'

'Angela, I demand an answer.'

'What would you imagine?'

'Are you implying . . . ?'

'I taught him to dance.'

'You taught him to *dance!*'

'Just like that woman taught you karate.'

'There's a lot of difference.'

'I dare say there is. Albert, it wouldn't astonish me if she'd already seduced you.'

'Doubtless you showed Humphrey what he'd missed in Kenya – if he really did miss it.'

'You spent the night with her, didn't you?'

'Don't accuse me. This is all a blind to hide your own carrying-on with that phony gentleman.'

'He is not a phony. He's very solid.'

'Yes and I bet you made him more solid.'

'I don't see that you have a leg to stand on.'

'I'm so tired, I almost don't.'

'Albert, you made it with her all night, didn't you. And now when she comes out of the shower in her towel, you'll make it with her again.'

'As I said, I'm pretty tired. But these karate women are very strong, you know.'

'I'm coming straight round, Albert!'

'Angela, don't be . . . '

There was a decisive click. Albert stared at the phone in

consternation. Did she really intend . . . ?

Lavinia Mungai appeared in the doorway inadequately draped in a white towel, which contrasted superbly with her dark skin. She came over to him, exposed legs and breasts glistening from the shower. Albert replaced the phone.

'That was Angela,' he said.

'Mmmm. Persistent, isn't she? Will you rub my back please?'

Albert began mechanically drying her shoulders.

'She said she was coming round here.'

'What nonsense.'

'She said Humphrey'd given her the address.'

'I see,' Lavinia Mungai said inscrutably.

'Do you think he has? And if so – why?'

'She might have embarrassed him into it. Who knows? I think we'd better get dressed and clear the place up. I can't stand scenes.'

A little later Albert stood beside the lace curtains gazing down into the street while the aroma of bacon and eggs wafted to him from the kitchen.

'How do you like your eggs, Albert honey?' she called.

That could get into a dangerously careless habit, for a start.

'Turned over,' he called back.

He saw the taxi turn into the road and nose along the street, halt for a moment outside the house and then pull off into a parking space.

'Here comes Angela!' he yelled.

Lavinia Mungai was beside him in a couple of seconds.

'She's in that taxi,' Albert said.

'Did you see her?'

'I just know it.'

'How can you . . . ?'

Angela flounced on to the pavement in a swirl of black fur and auburn hair. She fumbled in her purse, chatting to the driver, studying their building all at the same time.

Lavinia Mungai grabbed Albert's hand.

'Come on,' she snapped. 'We've got to get out of here.'

'You don't really think . . . ?'

'They'll have been watching the High Commission like hawks. Come *on!*'

Albert allowed himself to be dragged across the room.

'But where shall we . . . ?'

'Only safe place now is the High Commission. Hurry.'

'They pulled on coats, Albert almost throttling himself with his scarf. They emerged quickly on to the landing outside the flat.

'The stairs,' Lavinia Mungai ordered.

Albert obeyed implicitly. They went down the stairs two at a time around the lift well. They reached the top of the last flight just as Angela was being directed to the lift by the porter.

'Number six, Miss. But I think he's away.'

Lavinia Mungai jerked Albert back out of sight as Angela strode for the lift. Three black men were coming in off the street beyond the double doors leading into the foyer.

'Angela!' Lavinia Mungai called softly.

Angela saw them at once and tripped primly up the stairs.

Lavinia Mungai yanked her out of sight, utterly ruining her starchy composure.

'You've been followed,' she whispered to Angela.

Angela put her hand to her mouth.

'We'll have to try and slip out as they come up in the lift,'

Lavinia Mungai said. 'They may send one up via the stairs, so keep on your toes.'

'Oh dear,' Angela said. 'What have I done?'

'Keep quiet!'

The three Africans approached the porter's desk. They were tall and lean and one was dressed in a dark lounge suit, the other two in student's sweaters and leather jackets.

'Where do you lot think you're going?' the porter demanded, belligerently.

'We've come to see a friend of ours,' the one in the suit said.

'And who might that be?'

'We believe he's changed his name. Which flat do the black people live in?'

'Now what's all this about, then?' The porter raised his

chin, pompously. 'There ain't no blacks in this block, I can tell you.'

They stared at him, momentarily put out and he added, for good measure: 'This is an 'igh class residence. I'll 'ave to ask you to leave – rules of the management.'

'Don't be stupid,' one of the student types snapped. 'The young lady who came in just now was also going to see our friend. Will you please tell me which flat she's gone to.'

'Now look 'ere,' the porter said. 'I just told you it's a management rule. No blacks. Out you go now.'

Albert bristled, listening.

'That's outrageous!' he whispered. 'And against the law.'

'Shut up and keep back!' Lavinia Mungai whispered back.

'My dear chap,' the man in the suit said. 'You can't be serious.'

The porter stood up disdainfully and came out from behind his desk.

'I'm very serious,' he said. 'There's property values to be considered in an area like this.'

'It's out-and-out racialism!'

'Quite right. You darkies come over 'ere and think you can treat the place like your own. Lowerin' all the standards.'

'You will please tell me the number of the flat I want,' the man in the suit snapped. 'And I shall then report you and your management to the Race Relations Board!'

'Bloody barrack room lawyer, eh?' the porter said loftily. 'You do what you bloody well like, mate!'

The second student type suddenly produced a wallet and flashed a five-pound note at the porter.

'We quite understand – you have your job to do,' he said. 'May I offer you this token of our gratitude for bending the rules. If anyone complains we'll say we forced our way past you.'

The porter gazed at the note. His face darkened.

'You bloody ape!' he said. 'You think you can buy ex-Regimental Sergeant Major Parkinson! Get back to your war canoes, the lot of you. Leave the 'igh class property to civilised people.'

The first student type, smiling nastily, said: 'If a moron

like you represents civilised values, then we'll be glad to. But first we have to see our friend – and we intend to.'

'Now don't you take that line with me!' the porter barked, raising an admonitory finger, 'or you'll find yourself in trouble, mate. Deported chop, chop.'

The African, still smiling nastily, put a hand in his pocket, but his colleague in the suit laid a restraining hand on his arm.

'You realise we are people of standing,' he said. 'We can make a holy stink about this.'

'You make an 'oly stink at the best of times,' the porter said. 'Now if you don't buzz off . . . Officer! OFFICER!'

The police constable wandering past the doors halted, gazed with deliberation through the glass doors and came sedately into the foyer. He gazed severely at the Africans and then at the porter.

'Afternoon, Jim,' he said. 'What's the trouble?'

'These blokes are being very difficult, George,' the porter said. 'Insulting me – and threatening.'

'Are they now.'

'Officer,' the man in the suit said, 'we are looking for a friend of ours and this man is breaking the law by discriminating against us.'

'Is he now?'

'They called me a moron,' the porter said. 'I told them no friend of theirs lives 'ere. They don't even know 'is name.'

'So what are you gentlemen after?' the constable asked.

'Bloody black trash!' the porter muttered.

'You are trash – and your mother's trash!' the first student type spat.

''Ere. You mind your bloody language and don't you dare insult my deceased mother, or you'll get a thick ear.'

'And I'll break you neck,' the African said.

The man in the suit again put out a restraining hand. Things were going all awry.

'He doesn't mean that, officer,' he said. 'He's just defending himself.'

'Defendin' 'imself?' the porter sneered. ''E's not capable. Women do all the work where 'e comes from.'

The black hand swung and slapped the porter resoundingly across the face. The ex-RSM's eyes bulged. He quivered, managed just to control himself.

'Did you see that, Jim?' he cried.

The constable moved between them, facing the African.

'You can't do that sort of thing, you know,' he said.

'I'll get 'im!' the porter cried. 'I'm bringing charges for assault and battery.'

'I think you'd better all come along to the station,' the constable said.

'You realise this was provoked, officer,' the man in the suit said sharply.

'We can't have violence, sir. But I daresay we can straighten this out with a little chat at the station.'

The man in the suit motioned to his two colleagues, cooling them down. Clearly he didn't want trouble.

'Can't we possibly settle this now, officer?' he said. 'It's very important that we see our friend.'

'I'm sorry, sir. I think the station is the best place to sort this out. We don't want any more violence, do we.'

'All right, officer, we'll be very happy to cooperate with you,' the man in the suit said, diplomatically.

Lavinia Mungai, Albert and Angela, hidden around the top of the first flight of stairs, listened to them go. Lavinia Mungai chuckled.

'Even killers don't want an open clash with the law,' she said.

'That porter was disgusting,' Angela said. 'He deserved to be killed.'

'If they don't make a complaint to the Race Relations Board then *I* shall!' Albert snapped.

'Don't be silly,' Lavinia Mungai scolded. 'He saved our bacon. I could have written his script.'

Chapter Seventeen

For the first time in his life, Julius Jack Freedman was very much on the defensive. Apology was not something that came easily to him and right now, in his penthouse office with the drizzle spattering against the great windows overlooking the Thames, he towered like some abashed bear that might turn nasty at any moment. But Albert refused to be deflected from his flaying of injustice.

'The fact is, Mr Freedman, that you wittingly put my life in danger under false pretences. I'm having my lawyer look into this and you'll be hearing from him.'

'Now look, Mr Divine . . . '

'Had I kicked the bucket, which at one time seemed almost certain, my descendants would have lost the benefits of my income to the current tune of, shall we say, £40,000 a year, with every prospect of its rising. Taking a period of 50 years remaining work life, that gives us a figure of £2 million. This, at the very lowest estimate, is what we shall be suing you for.'

Julius Jack Freedman's eyes looked wildly pained.

'Mr Divine,' he said, 'you're still alive and kicking and you haven't got any descendants. I sure as hell wish . . . '

'I have suffered such mental shock and anguish from the events of the recent past that I may never successfully be able to work again,' Albert said. 'As for my descendants, I shall not need fertility statues to help me remedy the lack as soon as is necessary.'

'Now look, Mr Divine, I've said I'm sorry. I'll make an adjustment in the remuneration. You want a few oil shares, you can have 'em. You prefer fish finger shares, they're yours.'

'You really expect to fob me off with fish fingers after

conning me into risking my life on a nefarious mission!' Albert scoffed. 'You underestimate me, Mr Freedman.'

'No I don't,' Julius Jack Freedman cried. 'Those shares could be a gold mine. Everybody's eating fish.'

He went to the cocktail cabinet and agitatedly poured himself a large Bourbon and Albert an even larger vodka.

'Here, Mr Divine,' he said. 'Let's have a drink and figure this out. You want to throw the glass at the wall, then go ahead.'

He knocked back a good half of his Bourbon in one go. He looked at Albert apprehensively, awaiting the smashing ceremony. Albert sipped his drink impassively.

'Fact is,' Julius Jack Freedman said unconvincingly, 'I never thought there was any real danger. Figured George would get hold of those cocky statues discreetly and nobody'd figure an international art dealer would be interested in such crap.'

'That's another point,' Albert snapped. 'The lowering of my reputation. Both as a selector of inferior items and a receiver of stolen goods. I think £3 million may well be the level of our claim for damages.'

Julius Jack Freedman furiously threw back the remainder of his Bourbon. He gazed fiercely at the series of fertility gods squatting sexily on his desk where Albert had delivered them. He quickly poured himself another drink.

'And you realise that due to your desire to acquire sacred property, three anti-communist government agents died,' Albert said, twisting the knife.

Julius Jack Freedman's nostrils twitched, he shook his pugnacious head.

'My God! Those Commie bastards!'

He began to pace the room, muttering to himself.

Albert sipped his vodka. He needed it. Julius Jack was not the only disturbance around here, right now. Unknown to the tycoon, the place was surrounded by Kenyan intelligence agents – possibly with background support from British intelligence. On their insistence, Albert had baited the trap for the Mau Mau subversives by openly carrying the fertility figurines from the High Commission to this penthouse suite.

It was reckoned the revolutionaries would be unable to resist this first opportunity to recover their property and wreak vengeance. Albert was reminded that this final move, too, was the result of the American ensnaring him in this crazy operation in the first place. He finished his vodka.

'I'll have another of those!' he ordered.

Maybe the alcohol would insulate him from dread things to come.

Julius Jack Freedman distractedly poured him another drink. 'Mr Divine,' he said. 'There's something I oughta tell you. Your journey was a mistake . . . '

'You bet it was!' Albert snapped. 'Biggest mistake of my life!'

'What I mean is . . . '

'What you mean is you'll never find another sucker like me to be lured into a death trap for a paltry £2,000.'

Julius Jack Freedman pointed an admonishing finger at him.

'Now just a minute Mr Divine. It's three thousand. I insisted, remember? Plus all expenses for two. And I'm gonna double it. And fish finger shares . . . '

'I hate fish fingers!'

'Oh yeah, I forgot you got these Commie tastes. Well, I'll let you into a secret, Mr Divine. I got shares in Polish pickles. Really catching on in this country. I'll give you shares in Polish . . . '

The door from the outer office suddenly burst open.

A couple of Africans in leather jackets stood in the doorway smiling nastily and pointing automatic pistols. Beyond them was a glimpse of more Africans herding the distraught secretaries into a corner. Albert's heart missed a beat. This was the count down.

Julius Jack Freedman glared at the gatecrashers. His massive shoulders squared.

'What the hell is this?' he demanded.

A third African – Albert thought he recognised the man in the suit who had tracked Angela to the Mayfair flat – appeared between the other two and said mildly: 'You have every reason to be alarmed, Mr Freedman. We have come for our property.'

Julius Jack Freedman advanced on them, chin thrust out, eyes glaring.

'You just get the hell outa my office!' he snapped. 'You get out and knock before you come in and introduce yourselves to my secretary and she'll tell you whether I'm free. Okay? You get your goddam Commie crudeness outa here!'

The African smiled indulgently.

'Mr Freedman, you purloin sacred tribal emblems and then object when we come to claim them. I can think of many words to describe that capitalist behaviour.'

Julius Jack Freedman glowered at him.

'I paid good money for those goddam bits of wood,' he said. 'Keep a whole tribe for a month on what I paid for them.'

'Those "bits of wood" are priceless to us, Mr Freedman, the African said. 'And the money did not go to the tribe, but to a thief.'

Julius Jack Freedman simmered down a little.

'I don't know the details,' he said. 'Left that to my cousin. But you oughta be more practical. Cash'd do you streets more good than those idols.'

'Your opinion is of no interest to us.'

The African and his colleagues stood aside to make way for a newcomer. Another black man came into the office, flanked by bodyguards. He was dressed in a big black overcoat and a Russian fur hat. His dark spectacles swept the room, alighted on the statuettes. He gave a grim smile under his little black beard and moustache. Albert gazed at him incredulously.

'Joseph Mbula!' he exclaimed.

Joseph Mbula looked at him sardonically.

'You know this guy?' Julius Jack Freedman demanded.

'Met him in Kenya – he's a painter,' Albert said.

'Creative guy, huh?'

Joseph Mbula called to the outer office.

'Lock the doors. Bring girls in here.'

More Africans appeared, ushering the secretaries before

them. Cornelia O. Bottom filling out her tweeds; Patsy, Emma, Gwendoline and Genevieve all very attractive in their slit midis, satin trousers, sweaters.

Joseph Mbula studied them menacingly. Apart from the man in the suit, his fellow Africans had an air of dissident student about them. Albert found this all difficult to believe.

'What on earth are you doing here, Mr Mbula?' he asked rather fatuously.

Joseph Mbula dragged his eyes from Cornelia Bottom's bottom. He looked at Albert and Julius Jack Freedman for a long sinister moment.

'Killing you,' he said, 'recovering statues, selling paintings, buying arms, seeing swinging London.'

'What do you mean – killing!' Julius Jack Freedman demanded, advancing on the African.

Joseph Mbula's lenses confronted him; half a dozen pistols swung at him. He stopped short, glaring around as if the significance of the intrusion had finally got to him.

'Killing,' Joseph Mbula repeated. He ran an explanatory hand across his throat, made two fingers into a gun. The Africans laughed. Two of the secretaries gave a faint shriek.

'Aw come on now,' Julius Jack Freedman said, abruptly changing tactics. 'Be serious. Here, here's your statues – and you can keep the money. Oh, that's right, you didn't get the money, huh? Well you can have some more. Live and let live. That's my philosophy.'

Albert glanced at the tycoon. Capitalist opportunism at its most pure.

'You give us more money?' Joseph Mbula said.

The other Africans watched and listened. Clearly Joseph was in charge.

'Sure why not, since you didn't get the first lot. I'm a fairminded guy. I told my cousin to buy those statues, thought you'd be glad to sell. Tell you what. We'll all have a drink on it. Miss Bottom, drinks for everyone.'

The African in the suit started to protest.

'We're not interested in . . . '

But Joseph Mbula cut him short with an imperious hand.

'Who is Miss Bottom?' he asked.

'There she is – the little doll who's gonna pour us doubles in double quick time,' Julius Jack Freedman said, urgently motioning his personal assistant towards the liquor cabinet. All eyes turned on her, checking the aptness of her appellation.

'Bottom,' Joseph Mbula said with relish.

All the Africans laughed.

'Swinging bottom,' Joseph Mbula said.

The Africans laughed some more. Julius Jack Freedman beamed encouragingly, allowing only a flicker of apprehension to show as his eyes met Albert's.

Cornelia Bottom walked with selfconscious dignity to the cocktail cabinet, her buttocks undulating through the tweed skirt.

'What'll you have gentlemen?' Julius Jack Freedman cried. 'You name it, we got it.'

'Scotch,' Joseph Mbula said.

There was a blanket demand for Scotch.

'Any of you gentlemen ever try Bourbon?' Julius Jack Freedman asked. 'I'm not saying it's better than Scotch – just different. We got plenty of both. You like to try both? See what you think? Okay Miss Bottom, double Scotches and Bourbons for everyone. We got enough glasses. Mr Divine's not being ceremonious today.'

The Africans spread around the room, studying it: the conventional landscapes on the walls, the graphs, the intercom, the furniture, the view over the river and the Embankment beyond. Cornelia Bottom, sensing the underlying urgency of the social veneer which had fallen on her, rushed out enormous drinks for everyone, nervously smiling and making herself pleasant. Her fellow secretaries also did their best to be accommodating.

'Vodka for Mr Divine . . . that excellent drink from Russia,' Julius Jack Freedman cried. 'And ladies, what'll you have?'

Joseph Mbula approached Julius Jack Freedman, sipping both his drinks alternately. He raised the Scotch.

'Better,' he said. 'Much better.'

The American's face cracked into a painful smile.

'You think so, Mr Mbula? Well I guess some people would agree with you.'

Joseph Mbula sipped again. He gazed menacingly at Albert and the tycoon. He's about to order our execution, Albert thought, and glugged his liquor like a condemned man savouring his last.

'Where is swinging London?' Joseph Mbula demanded. 'See-throughs, pot, pussy, gang bangs, acid, groupies . . .?'

Albert's mind groped seriously with this question.

'Well,' he said, 'There's no one single place where . . . '

'Swinging London!' Julius Jack Freedman roared. He laughed wildly. 'Swinging London! You're in it fellah!' He encompassed the room with his gesture, the Thames, the city beyond.

Joseph Mbula's lenses roved around the penthouse suite. He sipped steadily.

'This is swinging London?'

'Sure as hell it is. You see those beautiful girls. Real swingers. Oh yeah!'

Joseph Mbula fell silent. He gazed thoughtfully at the secretaries, who were beginning to recover confidence and spirit under the influence of the alcohol.

'More drinks, Miss Bottom!' Julius Jack Freedman roared. 'Scotch versus Bourbon. The all-time heavyweight contest. Fill 'em up!'

Cornelia Bottom, aided by Patsy, Emma, Gwendoline and Genevieve, filled every glass in sight. Albert began to feel almost cheerful. This was getting to be just like any other party – if you ignored all those pistols.

'So you're a creative guy?' Julius Jack Freedman said to Joseph. 'Really admire creative guys myself. They got something the rest of us lack.'

'What?' Joseph Mbula asked.

The American stared at him.

'Well,' he said. 'Well . . . '

'You lie!' Joseph Mbula said. 'You are business. You shit on creation.'

'I shit on *creation!*' Julius Jack Freedman roared. 'I spend all my time trying to create. Christ, that's why I wanted . . .

never mind. What do you create, Mr Mbula?'

'He creates cunt,' Albert said.

He heard himself with surprise. Success, success. He was getting plastered.

'Creates *what*.' the American cried.

'You heard right the first time,' Albert said.

Joseph Mbula's facial lines indicated a slight smile.

'Cunt,' he said with great deliberation. 'C-U-N-T. You know . . . ' He motioned to the secretaries.

Julius Jack Freedman stared at him, cleft jaw jutting, craggy head bristling, eyes wild. He suddenly snapped into laughter, slapped his thigh.

'You don't *say!*' he murmured. 'You mean you literally...'

'Cunt,' Joseph Mbula repeated, nodding his head.

'That really is something,' the American said, shaking his head. 'I guess that makes you pretty much of a specialist.'

'Unique,' Joseph Mbula said.

'Yeah, I guess so. Say, tell me, do you get . . . I mean, these models, do they . . . it must be pretty tricky, huh?'

'Angela nearly modelled for him,' Albert said.

'She did?'

'No good,' Joseph Mbula said emphatically. 'No good.'

'How was that?' Albert said, falsely casual.

'Prejudice. Racism.'

'I don't believe it,' Albert goaded.

Joseph Mbula shrugged.

'There is a sign on her cunt,' he said. 'Whites only. I have many witnesses.

'You have witnesses!' Albert exclaimed.

'You got any of those paintings with you?' Julius Jack Freedman cut in.

'What witnesses?' Albert demanded.

'Yes – here to sell,' Joseph Mbula said to the American.

'I sure would like to see them. Like to buy a few.'

'What did the witnesses witness?' Albert cried.

'Okay,' Joseph Mbula said to Julius Jack Freedman. 'I show them to you.'

'And I have quite a few friends I'd think would be interested,' the tycoon added enthusiastically.

'Mostly black cunt,' Joseph Mbula said. 'But some white.'

'Whose is the white?' Albert demanded sharply.

'I could probably sell the lot for you,' Julius Jack Freedman said. 'How much you asking?'

The African became canny.

'I think about it,' he said. 'Work of genius – unique.'

'Yeah, yeah – that's okay. Hey Bottie – Miss Bottom – more drinks. Fill 'em all up!'

'Did you or did you not paint Angela's cunt?' Albert demanded loudly.

Joseph Mbula turned his lenses on him.

'No good,' he said. 'Closed – okay. Open – racist.'

'Closed! Open!'

Joseph dismissed the startled Albert, turned his attention back to the American. He waved a hand around the room where Cornelia Bottom was filling up glasses yet again and hostility and distance had dissolved with a vengeance.

'Swinging London?' he asked.

'Sure.'

'These girls are screwing?'

'Well – huh – not right now as we see them – huh. But, you're interested, well . . . they're swinging chicks all right.'

Joseph Mbula carefully removed his dark glasses to see the girls better. He appeared completely to have forgotten the reason for his presence in the office.

Albert placed his hand firmly on the African's arm.

'Listen,' he said. 'What went on with Angela at your studio?'

Joseph Mbula didn't even glance at him.

'We have orgy,' he said abstractedly.

He turned back to Julius Jack Freedman. He pointed to Cornelia Bottom with a wavering finger.

'I want that one,' he said.

The American slapped him on the back with such powerful abandon that the African staggered, turned aggressively, and then smiled as he recognised his host was merely complying with his request.

'You want her – you shall have her!' Julius Jack Freedman bellowed. 'We'll have a swinging London scene. Really show you gentlemen what's happening in this great, sexy metropolis. Hey everyone . . . !'

He raised his arms.

'We're gonna have an orgy – okay? Bottie, get some music on that hi-fi!'

There was an enthusiastic reception to this suggestion. Cornelia Bottom moved fast to a hidden hi-fi set, whisking off the cloth that covered it, fiddling with knobs, glasses chinked, conversation hummed, black hands strayed on to white flesh.

Albert glanced around in an astonishment only slightly offset by his being three sheets in the wind. The African in the suit was still slightly aloof, standing near the door, pistol in one hand Scotch in the other. His fellow revolutionaries, however, seemed to have forgotten about their guns and intent. Many had replaced them in their pockets. Albert concentrated his attention again on Joseph Mbula. The important thing was to discover what had happened with Angela. How many had seen . . ? And what else had they . . . ? In his mind's eyes Angela danced naked before a million African sex maniacs. Danced on her hands . . .

Julius Jack Freedman beamed around the room.

'You babies gonna show these gentlemen just what's swinging in permissive old London, eh?' His tone was forceful. 'Just so we can all be good friends and they can see they got everything to gain from our friendship, eh?'

The strident tones of the Star-Spangled Banner played by some brassy marine band suddenly blasted through the room. Julius Jack Freedman sprang momentarily to attention and then yelled: 'Turn that thing off, Miss Bottom! What the hell! Something else for Jesus Christ's sake!'

He gazed apologetically around the room, but the nature of the music had not penetrated the barrier of noise, drink and lust.

'We have very little else, Mr Freedman,' Cornelia Bottom called, primly.

'Whatever it is it'll do? You trying to commit suicide, Miss Bottom?'

He beamed around the room again like a crazy radar device.

'Yeah,' he cried. 'We're gonna show these visitors to Britain just what goes on in this city when the lid's off. We're gonna make their hair stand on end.'

The rollicking strains of a hillbilly square dance suddenly erupted in the room. Julius Jack Freedman glanced over to where Cornelia Bottom was eyeing him reproachfully.

'Is that the best you can do, Miss Bottom?' he yelled.

'I didn't choose the records, Mr Freedman,' she said tartly.

One of the Africans suddenly started jumping around the room in time to the music. Another joined him, laughing, letting out whoops. Soon they were all leapfrogging over one another, vaulting the furniture. Joseph Mbula began to clap in time with the music.

'*Turkey in the straw, turkey in the hay . . .*'

Julius Jack Freedman's beam returned.

'Well done, Bottie – a fine choice!' he boomed. 'Okay girls – more drinks for everyone. And how about showing how beautiful and swingin' you are? It's hot in here, heh, heh!'

Cornelia Bottom trotted over to him and said in a low, intense voice: 'Are you suggesting, Julius, that we . . . that we *entertain* these gangsters!'

'Shut up you goddam fool!' the American whispered back. 'It's our only chance of survival. Pass the message on for Chrissake!'

Joseph Mbula nosed in and placed his hand on Cornelia Bottom's bottom. He seemed quite fascinated. She smiled sourly at him and moved off.

'Have another drink, Miss Bottom!' Julius Jack Freedman roared threateningly.

A moment later, Patsy in her tight blue sweater and tight satin trousers weaved through the crowd to Julius Jack Freedman, who was now tapping his big foot in time with the music.

'Mr Freedman,' she said softly. 'We can't go through with this.'

The American patted her plump bottom reassuringly.

'No need to worry Miss Pritchett,' he said. 'It'll never get beyond these four walls.'

'It's not that I'm embarrassed, Mr Freedman. It's just that it's time – maximum fertility time. I could get pregnant.'

'Jesus – it slipped my mind!'

'And it's the same for Patsy and Emma . . . '

'Okay, okay. Well, you got other orifices. Use your imagination!'

'I don't think that would work,' Patsy said. 'Those Africans keep saying they're interested in one thing.'

'Cunt,' Albert intoned.

'Okay, okay,' Julius Jack Freedman repeated angrily. 'Well we got no alternative. If that's what they want, that's what they gotta get.'

'But Mr Freedman . . . '

'You wanna see me dead?'

'Oh no, Mr Freedman.'

'Then get back there and let 'em have your . . . give 'em what they want!'

Patsy Pritchett drifted uncertainly back into the throng. Albert glanced at the American. He chuckled suddenly.

'You're going to have some little black heirs,' he said.

Julius Jack Freedman glanced down at him furiously. He spoke from the corner of his mouth.

'Shut your dirty mouth, Mr Divine!' he snapped.

'There's nothing dirty about black heirs,' Albert said indignantly. 'They're beautiful.' He chuckled again convulsively.

The tycoon looked away.

'You're a pretty subversive guy, Mr Divine,' he said. 'I guess I just don't really know which side you're on.'

Albert grinned. The atmosphere was now riotous. Bottles of spirits were being passed from hand to hand, someone turned the music up to a deafening roar.

TURKEY IN THE HAY, TURKEY IN THE STRAW . . .

Joseph Mbula flipped up Cornelia Bottom's skirt to reveal the strong lobes of her bottom in her white-lace edged black pants. An African began to undress. Another grabbed

Emma and tore up her sweater, rolling his eyes at the big breasts in their half-cup brassiere.

By now, the girls were too plastered to care too much. There was a lot of giggling and cavorting to the music. Garments began to fly like streamers. Julius Jack Freedman knocked back Bourbon, beaming continuously and occasionally emitting a hillbilly '*Yow*' or '*Yippee*'. Albert watched, wondering how the hell the girls were going to face the consequences of this particular bit of swinging.

Very shortly everyone was naked, apart from the African in the suit, who reluctantly maintained his role of sentinel. Albert reflected that the scene was definitely subversive. An African was prancing around in Gwendoline's brassiere. Another had hung all five pairs of women's pants from his erection and was daring the girls to get back into them without using their hands.

And then Joseph Mbula caught hold of Cornelia Bottom, thrust her face down over a divan so that her named attraction rose deliciously before him, cleaved it with his hands and brutally thrust at its centre. Cornelia Bottom uttered a scream at this rough penetration, but the African placed hands on the small of her back, held her in a vice and gave full exercise to his long-standing fascination.

This was the signal for the swinging to begin. In a matter of seconds bodies were writhing all over the floor and the furniture in flailing patterns of black and white.

To the fairground roar of music, the scraping of furniture and the bellowed encouragement of Julius Jack Freedman the secretaries were passed from man to man, penis to penis, no orifices barred in a wild pageant of anatomy, screams, giggles, groans and moans, slaps and motion that was almost surrealist. Every so often an orgasmic yell pierced the general noise and a girl's protests against an unnacustomed intercourse rose and died to a whimper.

Turkey in the Straw, turkey in the hay . . .

'Swinging London, swinging London . . . ' Julius Jack Freedman grated in time with the music, generously handing over his harem to the perpetration of penetrations he'd never even thought of.

And over all, the fertility gods paraded their swinging genitalia, ensuring full fruition from the current rites enacted before them.

Such was the bedlam that nobody heard the silenced shots that smashed the lock to the outer door, nor yet the entry of Lavinia Mungai, supported by Humphrey Jonah and three more Kenya Government agents. And by the time their presence was observed there was no resistance to offer since the pile of revolutionary clothing had been isolated in the next room.

Lavinia Mungai turned the music off. Julius Jack Freedman's singing slowly faded. The Mau Mau members gazed in drunken incredulity, as if unaware what was happening or which country they were in. Those secretaries who were capable, covered themselves with any object that came to hand. A slow, cooling partial awareness crept into the atmosphere.

Lavinia Mungai smiled broadly. She glanced at Albert and Julius Jack Freedman.

'This is the work of genius,' she said. 'I can hardly believe it.'

'Behold a genius,' Albert said, pointing to Julius Jack Freedman.

'Who the hell are these people?' the American roared.

'They're on our side, Mr Freedman,' Albert said. 'They've come to rescue us.'

'All right,' Lavinia Mungai said to the Africans, 'get over in that corner and don't make things difficult for yourselves.' She smiled. 'You've had your fun.'

Joseph Mbula rigidly withdrew from his second incursion into Cornelia's bottom.

'Dirty capitalists!' he spat.

'Come on now, Mr Mbula,' Julius Jack Freedman said. 'We were only showing you swinging London – at your own request.'

'Dirty, corrupt city! Filthy capitalists!' Joseph Mbula spat. 'White whores!'

The secretaries, who had been hurriedly pulling on their clothes, seemed to awaken at this reference.

'Mr Freedman, we're going to be pregnant!' Patsy

Pritchett cried. 'What're we going to do? What're we going to do with the black babies?'

Julius Jack Freedman grinned crazily.

'I'll tell you,' he said. 'Mr Divine here gave me an idea. What I'll do is see you through the best private hospital, give you a whole lotta dough and in return you sign over your babies to me, okay?'

'You mean you want us to have them? And then you want to adopt them?' Genevieve asked incredulously.

'You catch on fast, sweetheart.'

'Just a minute,' Albert said. 'You don't have to do that. I mean, abortion's no trouble these days. And now you've got the fertility statues you can try again. Can't you?'

The American looked at him abstractedly.

'Oh yeah,' he said, 'that was the ironic thing I was trying to tell you early on, Mr Divine. That your journey was a mistake. You see I finally went to a doctor – coupla doctors, best in the country. They laid it on the line . . . well, I gotta face facts . . . I just can't have an heir – not me. So I gotta adopt one – or more.'

'You're going to have a black heir?' Albert said, askance.

'You bet. That way I got an heir *and* I've converted one potential Commie into a good, patriotic American capitalist. It's God's will, I tell you.'

'Ha!' Joseph Mbula snarled. 'Your heirs will be born communists, born revolutionaries. You will never convert them!'

Julius Jack Freedman's jaw jutted, his brow darkened.

'I'm gonna make them into fine, upstanding Bourbon-drinking capitalists!' he cried.

'Never,' Joseph Mbula shouted. 'They will grow up and annihilate you!'

'Not on your life!' Julius Jack Freedman roared. 'I'll show them a better way of life. I'll show them what Black Power can mean!'

'You are stupid, stinking capitalist. They will be Trojan Horse!'

'You Commie bastard, you'd better . . . !'

'All right, let's get moving,' Lavinia Mungai cut in. 'You

can get your clothes on now.'

She began herding the Africans into the outer office.

Albert and Julius Jack Freedman were left staring at each other.

'Mr Freedman,' Albert said. 'I take my hat off to you. You managed that whole scene brilliantly. And now you're going to have black heirs! I'm not going to sue you after all.'

'You haven't gotta hat, Mr Divine. Let's have a drink on it instead. Jump to it Miss Bottom. Vodka for Mr Divine.'

Albert raised a restraining hand.

'Mr Freedman,' he said, 'you've set a shining example. We all have to break out occasionally, face the unknown.'

He turned to Cornelia Bottom.

'Make mine a Bourbon,' he said.

Where's Poppa?

Robert Klane

Some people have all the luck. Money and jobs and girls. Especially girls. Gordon Hocheiser had the job, and the money, but whenever he thought he was getting anywhere near a girl, there was Momma. Momma – sitting in the apartment, waiting for Poppa to come home, and seeing to it that no one but herself laid hands on her son. Momma was quite a woman!

25p

Also by Robert Klane

The Horse Is Dead **25p**

The Love Clinic

Hugh Marner

'Sex is dirty and women don't enjoy it' – those were Toby Dainty's reasons for spending so little time in bed with his beautiful wife Beatrice.

But Beatrice, not so frigid as her husband believed, longed for a real lover who could arouse and keep alight the flames of her passion. So Toby found himself in the Kensington Love Clinic – fees by arrangement – where, under (and over) the expert guidance of the gorgeous Suzanne Beaumarchais his primitive drives were unleashed and subtle seductions practised.

25p